T0308000

EXPLORING
Wild ALABAMA

THE UNIVERSITY OF ALABAMA PRESS TUSCALOOSA

Published in cooperation with the Alabama Bicentennial Commission

EXPLORING *Wild* ALABAMA

A GUIDE

TO THE STATE'S PUBLICLY ACCESSIBLE NATURAL AREAS

KENNETH M. WILLS & L. J. DAVENPORT

WITH A FOREWORD BY CHRIS OBERHOLSTER

The University of Alabama Press
Tuscaloosa, Alabama 35487-0380
uapress.ua.edu

Copyright © 2016 by the University of Alabama Press
All rights reserved.

Inquiries about reproducing material from this work should be addressed to the University of Alabama Press.

Typeface: Scala Pro

Manufactured in Korea

Cover image: Pulpit Rock, Cheaha State Park;
courtesy of Alan Cressler
Cover and interior design: Michele Myatt Quinn

200 ALABAMA BICENTENNIAL

Published in cooperation with the
Alabama Bicentennial Commission

Cataloging-in-Publication data is available
from the Library of Congress.
ISBN: 978-0-8173-5830-3
E-ISBN: 978-0-8173-8877-5

For our children and grandchildren

CONTENTS

Lower Sequatchie Valley / Lake Guntersville Area

Lookout Mountain Area

Little Mountain Area

Bankhead National Forest / Sipsey Wilderness Area

RIDGE AND VALLEY

Coosa River Area

Birmingham Area

BLUE RIDGE OUTLIERS

Talladega Uplands Area

PIEDMONT

Anniston Area

FALL LINE HILLS

Florence Area

Tuscaloosa Area

Montgomery Area

Auburn Area

BLACK BELT

Limestone Prairie Area

CHUNNENUGGEE RIDGE

Sandy Ridge Area

RED HILLS

Forks of the Alabama and Tombigbee Rivers Area

COASTAL ZONE

FOREWORD

When I first arrived in Alabama as a graduate student at Auburn University in 1987, I found it difficult to explore the natural habitats of our state. Such information was scattered in a wide array of unpublished sources, much of it only in the field notes or heads of scientists, birdwatchers, and other enthusiasts. I also recall the disappointment I felt when I learned how few nature preserves or other permanently conserved wild places there were in Alabama compared to South Africa, where I grew up, or many of the other fifty states.

Thankfully—due to the efforts of the Alabama Forever Wild Program, the Nature Conservancy and other land trusts, local governments, and federal agencies—the situation is vastly improved today. In the intervening years, literally dozens of permanently conserved and publicly accessible natural areas have been established, totaling several hundred thousand acres scattered widely across Alabama.

And the information needed to explore these wild reaches of our state is now available, right here in your hand. In *Exploring Wild Alabama*, Ken Wills and Larry Davenport have done an outstanding job of pulling together—in one place for the first time—everything you need to know about these natural areas, from how to get there to what you can expect to see and do, and why it's so vitally important to protect them.

Both authors are well-qualified to bring us this essential guide.

Ken has been actively involved in many conservation organizations, including the Alabama Environmental Council and Friends of Moss Rock Preserve. Larry is a biology professor at Samford University with an abiding interest in writing about nature. He has served on the Board of Trustees of the Forever Wild Land Trust and other organizations.

The authors note throughout the book that Alabama is one of the most biologically diverse of our United States. Through a combination of diverse geological settings, moderate climate, and other factors, Alabama is not only among the top five states in the nation in sheer number of plant and animal species but also harbors entire habitats and hundreds of species found nowhere else on Earth.

As a long-time employee of the Nature Conservancy in Alabama, I have witnessed the rapidly growing interest in our state's natural heritage. It is particularly gratifying to see that leaders in business, economic development, and industrial recruitment increasingly value and support the critical roles that public parks, preserves, and greenways play in enhancing our communities. Healthy, functioning, natural systems contribute directly to our quality of life, provide essential services like filtering water and managing floodwaters, and form the basis of some of the most important sectors of our economy, including tourism, fisheries, forestry, and agriculture.

Many of these unique Alabama places are now preserved and readily accessible. Over the years, my family and I have spent hundreds of hours enjoying the places depicted in *Exploring Wild Alabama*. I am grateful to see that some of our favorites, like Ebenezer Swamp Ecological Preserve with its long stretches of boardwalk, now provide ideal access for our daughter's wheelchair. I am also excited to learn about places we have never visited before, and I look forward to future adventures in these secluded corners of our state.

I encourage you to do the same. Use this book to learn about Alabama—its natural history and its natural riches. Hike a mountain trail to a hidden waterfall. Explore an urban forest and marvel at its wildflowers. Or lay a canoe into a blackwater river and lazily paddle down to the next landing.

Exploring Wild Alabama will take you there.

Chris Oberholster
Executive Director, Alabama Chapter of the Nature Conservancy
August 2014

ACKNOWLEDGMENTS

This book has a long history, dating back to the authors' fathers, who taught them to love the woods and waters. Actual writing began in the 1990s, when the senior author embarked on a series of exploring trips accompanied (and encouraged) by John Robinson; the detailed notes from these trips became the book's basic text. Ken's wife, Mary Ellen, and children later joined in the adventures.

The raw manuscript for this book was delivered to Beth Motherwell at the University of Alabama Press in 2010. That's when the junior author—not "junior" in age, by any means—came on board to edit and "ground truth" the text. Larry thanks his wife, Rebecca, for sharing much of the latter happy task.

Final editing, design, and production then fell into the capable hands of our friends at the Press. Beth Motherwell is singled out for pushing and prodding this project through its many hoops and hurdles. And the unwavering support of Curtis Clark *must* be mentioned.

We also thank the photographers, who added so much to the beauty of our book. Special thanks go to Craig Remington and the University of Alabama Cartography Lab for the production of the exquisite maps, which truly get people out *Exploring Wild Alabama.*

One final note: The Press secured our website (www.exploringwildalabama.info) when this book was just a rough, hardly publishable idea! We will always be grateful for such confidence in our abilities.

ABBREVIATIONS AND SYMBOLS

ALDOT	Alabama Department of Transportation
CCC	Civilian Conservation Corps
Corps	US Army Corps of Engineers
NWR	National Wildlife Refuge
SWA	Small Wild Area
TVA	Tennessee Valley Authority
WMA	Wildlife Management Area
USFWS	US Fish and Wildlife Service
	Hiking
	Handicapped Accessible Trail
	Nature Observation
	Camping
	Fishing
	Hunting
	Horseback Riding
	Canoeing

Caving

Mountain Biking

Bicycling

Cabins

Picnic Tables

Playground

Supply Store / Gift Shop

Lodge

Restaurant

Boat Launch

Swimming Area

Rock Climbing

Boat Rentals

Museum / Nature Center

Historic Features

Beaches

EXPLORING
Wild ALABAMA

INTRODUCTION

Alabama contains a great variety of natural areas—from cool, secluded canyons in the north to sparkling white beaches on the Gulf of Mexico. While most Alabamians have visited the major state parks and national forests, only a few lucky ones have experienced the full diversity of landforms, plants, and animals that make up our state. In this guide, we provide the details—*where, when, how,* and even *what time of year*—to visit Alabama's publicly accessible natural areas. We also tell you the *why* of what makes these sites ecologically special. We hope that, by helping you find and enjoy these places, you'll then get involved in promoting their continued preservation and future expansion.

Alabama's Biological and Physiographical Diversity

Alabama contributes far more than its share, sizewise, to the biodiversity of the United States. Its location in the transition zone between humid-temperate and humid-subtropical climates is one major factor, with deciduous hardwood forests of the relatively cool Tennessee Valley transitioning to broadleaf evergreen forests on the warm Gulf Coast. In addition, no other state offers so much physiographic- or landform-related diversity in such a small space. (Of the United States, Alabama is second only to California in its landform diversity, with ten physiographic provinces and subprovinces.) Our state's diverse physiography is due to its unique position at the southern end of the Appalachian provinces and its central location among the various Coastal Plain subprovinces. Alabama is also blessed with an extensive river system that contains one of the world's greatest aquatic biodiversities, including a great number of fishes, crayfishes, aquatic insects, mussels, and snails. This rare combination of diverse physiography plus north-south climate variation plus abundant freshwater resources has produced the fifth richest biodiversity in the nation.

If planned properly, a one-day car ride across Alabama could pass through the eleven physiographic regions mapped on page 3. Such a ride would take you past Ice Age remnant beech-hemlock forest in the canyons of the Appalachian Plateau; the habitat of unique albino aquatic animals in the water-carved limestone caverns of the Interior Low Plateau; pools of rare plant life on granite outcrops in the Piedmont; pygmy Virginia pine clinging to windswept quartzite outcroppings of the Blue Ridge Outliers; rivers with an unbelievable diversity of fishes, snails, and other species in the Ridge and Valley; seasonally flooded cypress swamps in the Fall Line Hills; chalk cliffs of the Black Belt; open pine forests of the Chunnenuggee Ridge; beech-magnolia forests of the Red Hills; rich carnivorous plant bogs in the nutrient-poor Lower Coastal Plain; and ocean beaches in the Coastal Zone. We suggest, however, that you *slow down* in order to best enjoy Alabama's natural wonders! Pick one location at a time and get to know it well.

How to Use This Book

The natural areas listed in this book are arranged by physiographic provinces and subprovinces, so that similar landforms and habitats are grouped together. To find a natural area near your place of interest, consult the state map on page 4. Here you'll find the locations of all of the 150 publicly accessible natural areas covered in this book. A table of contents tells you the name of each numbered area as well as the pages that describe it. The table of contents also shows how we divided Alabama into 25

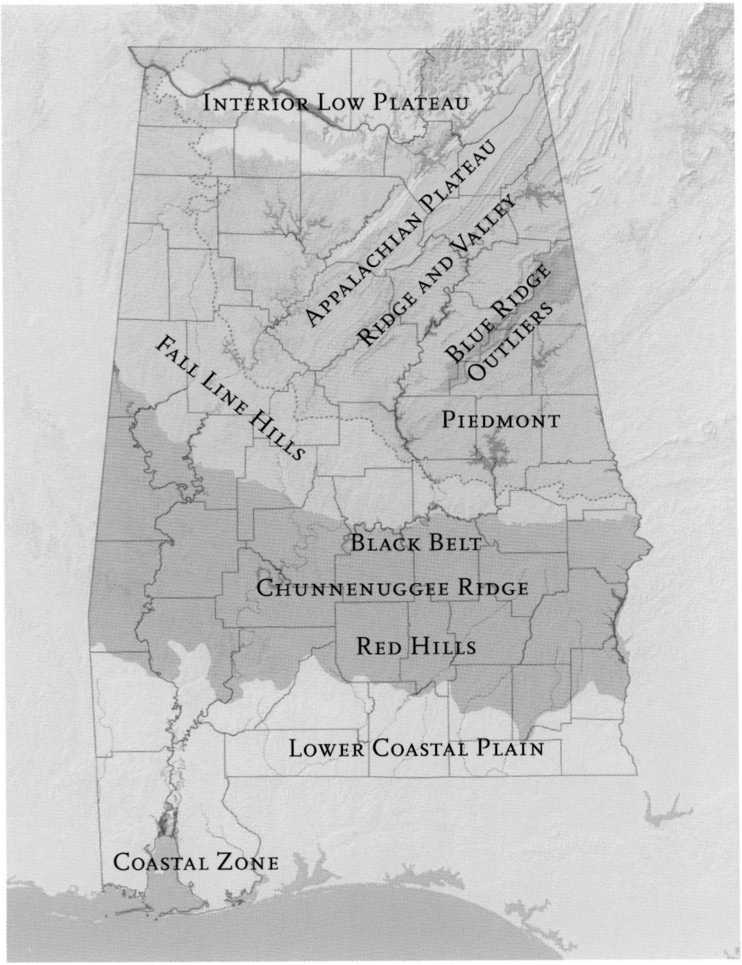

Major physiographic regions of Alabama; courtesy of Mark A. Bailey

geographical areas, mostly based around major cities, each with its own enlarged map.

This book is meant to be *more* of a travel guide to natural areas and *less* of a hiking-canoe guide. Therefore, we focus on

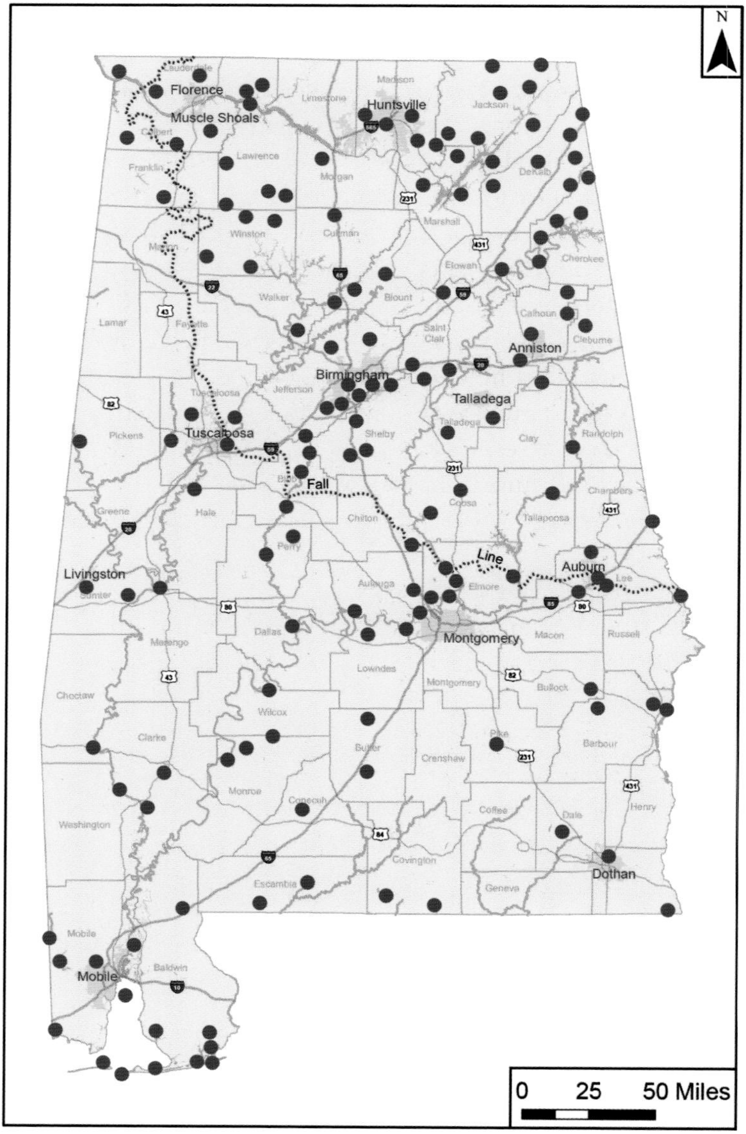

● The 150 natural areas covered in this book.
See detailed area maps before each section.

what makes the various areas ecologically special. While we summarize the recreational resources of a given area, such as trails and boat launches, we don't give detailed information unless a particular trail or float segment is important to seeing specific natural habitats and species. While most of these areas are publicly owned and easily accessible, a few are in private hands. We include a privately owned area only if it is possible to view its significant features from public roads. Of course, we hope that such a unique property will someday reside within the public domain.

While this book is meant to be a nature guide, it also contains a good bit of human history related to the sites. Some of our state's best natural areas, in fact, are located within historical parks. In these cases, we have tried to tell both stories—the natural history and human history—of a site, plus the interactions between the two.

What's Included and What's Not

We tried our best to include a similar number of sites in each geographical area presented. And at least one site is located in every county!

There is one set of seminatural areas purposely left out of this book: Alabama's 23 state fishing lakes. We decided to leave out these areas because it is easy to obtain information on them at the State Lands Division website (see References and Websites toward the back of this book). And while such lakes usually have natural uplands surrounding them, their management is focused, quite understandably, on fishing, which is not a major emphasis of this book.

Also, you might wonder why some of the state's wildlife management areas (WMAs) are covered here while many are not. Some of Alabama's WMAs are on public land, and the state is actively purchasing more such land; however, many of these areas involve only short-term leases on private land for the purposes of game management and public hunting access. Again, you can find the information that you need at the State Lands Division website. But pay close attention to hunting seasons!

Finally—and in keeping with the above hunting motif—we realize that printing information about Alabama natural areas is like shooting a moving target. Publicly accessible natural areas are often (happily) added and (sadly) taken away. To stay abreast of such changes and updates to this book, please consult our website, www.exploringwildalabama.info.

APPALACHIAN PLATEAU

Our state's largest upland province, the Appalachian Plateau, angles southwest from New York to Alabama. Its southernmost section (found in central Tennessee and northern Alabama) is called the Cumberland Plateau.

The Appalachian Plateau is home to many spectacular cliffs, boulders, canyons, natural bridges, and waterfalls. The plateau originated as a sandy river delta that built up, one layer on top of another, like a stack of pancakes. The sediments hardened into rock layers, which were then uplifted to form a flat-topped mountain or plateau. Over millions of years, creeks, streams, and rivers eroded larger and deeper crevices in this surface, forming magnificent canyons and valleys. While the tops of the plateau are made of erosion-resistant sandstone, the slopes and valleys contain rock outcrops and soils derived from limestone and other more erodible rocks. The sequence of layers can be easily seen today in road cuts and on cliff faces.

Natural History

Underneath the sandstone cap of the Appalachian Plateau, the limestone layers have been slowly etched away by carbonic acid. This weak acid, formed by the combination of water and carbon dioxide, flows into cracks in the limestone and dissolves it away, creating an extensive cave system. Sometimes the roofs of these caves collapse, forming sinkholes. Areas of extensive caves and sinkholes are known as *karst* landscapes, and surface streams in such places often run dry because much of the water flows down to the underground cave systems. And water from the cave systems sometimes returns to the surface, bubbling up as springs. The Appalachian Plateau is full of such springs, many with unique flora and fauna.

The varied landforms of the Appalachian Plateau, plus its temperate climate, produce a wide variety of vegetation. The poor soils of the sandstone caps are dominated by oak-hickory and oak-pine forests, while the richer soils of north-facing limestone slopes contain a diverse mixed hardwood forest known as *mixed mesophytic* or *cove hardwood*. Cove hardwood forest is well represented in the northeast corner of Alabama, where it contains yellow buckeye (at its southern range limit), sugar maple, basswood, white ash, cucumber magnolia, and many other hardwood species. This type of forest fosters a rich humus layer that supports a great variety of woodland wildflowers. This forest also produces brilliant fall colors that are well worth the effort to see them.

The northwest Alabama portion of the Appalachian Plateau and adjacent areas reveal a "relict environment" left over from the ice ages. Because this area has an unusually high amount of rainfall and cloud cover throughout the year, the deep canyons form a cooler-than-expected microclimate that supports remnant pockets of cold-temperate plant species. (Most of these species migrated north as the climate warmed following the ice ages.) These canyons are cool enough to allow eastern hemlock to thrive and form beech-hemlock forests similar to those found in New England and at higher elevations in the southern Appalachians. As you walk though one of these hemlock forests, you can almost imagine a mastodon running through the trees pursued by nomadic hunters with Clovis point spears.

Some sandstone and limestone outcrop environments of the Appalachian Plateau support relatively treeless environments called *glades*. Here, the lack of trees results from a combination of poor, shallow soils with (to a lesser degree) periodic fires. In addition, some poorly drained mountain areas contain bogs—damp, relatively treeless lands maintained (to a great degree) by periodic fires. In northeast Alabama, some of these bogs are dominated by the threatened green pitcher plant.

The Tennessee Divide

The Appalachian Plateau drains into the two great deltas of the Gulf of Mexico—the Mississippi Delta in Louisiana and the Mobile-Tensaw Delta in Alabama. What separates the two drainages is the Tennessee Divide of northern Alabama and Mississippi. Rainwater north of the divide flows into the Tennessee River to the Ohio River and, finally, south to the Mississippi Delta. Rainwater south of the divide flows south (either through the Alabama or Tombigbee River systems) to Mobile. Most importantly, the two sides of the divide form two distinct biological worlds, especially in terms of their aquatic animals—fishes, mollusks, gastropods, macroinvertebrates, and more. Sampling the two sides of the divide is a great take-home lesson in Alabama's biodiversity.

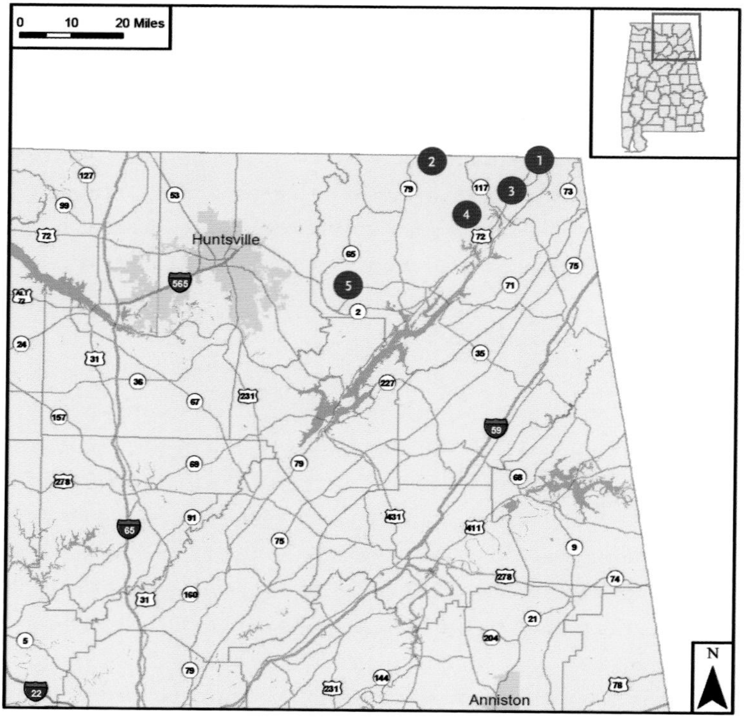

SKYLINE MOUNTAIN AREA

The Skyline Mountains are composed of the southern fingers of the main portion of the Appalachian or Cumberland Plateau, poking into Alabama's portion of the Tennessee Valley from the north. You'll find them north of the Tennessee River primarily in Jackson County, Alabama, with some of their range extending into Madison County near Huntsville (Monte Sano State Park). The Skyline Mountains host extensive cave systems and spring-fed streams; Jackson County, in fact, contains 18 of America's 100 deepest caves. Pine trees are rare in the Skylines; the climate is wetter and cooler than in most of Alabama and fires, which pines require in order to compete with hardwoods, are infrequent. The calcium-rich soils, derived from limestone (calcium carbonate), support large numbers of calcium-loving trees, like red cedars. Springs in the Tennessee Valley feed bottomland hardwood wetlands, including extensive water tupelo swamps.

The Skyline Mountains include critical land and water habitats for numerous species, including rare birds. For example, the unfragmented forests of this area provide one of Alabama's last strongholds for the rare and declining cerulean warbler.

1 Russell Cave National Monument

34°58'42.98"N
85°48'35.63"W

This small, 310-acre national monument was established in 1961 thanks to land donated by the National Geographic Society to the American people. The monument protects one of the oldest known human habitations in the eastern United States. A rock overhang near the mouth of Russell Cave was used for shelter

Inside looking out, Russell Cave

Mouth of Russell Cave

(starting about 10,000 years ago) by Native Americans during the Archaic Period as the climate warmed following the last Ice Age. A museum tells the story of these early people, who used spear throwers (*atlatls*) instead of later-developed bows and arrows.

The most impressive aspect of the park is the huge mouth of Russell Cave. Fog often condenses at this mouth, where the constantly cool and moist "inside" air meets the warmer air outside. The park has a short paved nature trail that goes up the slope of Mount Carmel, passing by a sinkhole and an ancient burial mound. Going up this trail, you'll also see how the forest transitions from rich cove hardwood forest (including yellow buckeye, sugar maple, and basswood) to upland oak-hickory forest, with fine examples of black locust.

Directions: Russell Cave is located in Jackson County, Alabama, just south of the Tennessee state line, five miles west of US 72. From US 72 follow Co. Rd. 75 north one mile to Co. Rd. 98, then north four miles to the park entrance.

2 The Walls of Jericho and James D. Martin–Skyline WMA

34°58'35.89"N
86°04'49.31"W

The 26,000-acre James D. Martin–Skyline WMA was partially renamed to recognize the work of former Alabama Department of Conservation commissioner James D. Martin, who contributed to the establishment of this WMA and also played an important role in the establishment of Alabama's land trust program, Forever Wild. The Skyline WMA is recognized as a significant wildlife habitat and is thus being managed for its wildlife resources.

Skyline's lands lie in several units. The Mill Creek portion is largely upland oak-hickory forest with some pine plantations. In contrast, the Little Coon Creek drainage contains limestone

The strenuous White Trail leads through hardwood forest to and from the Walls of Jericho

Above: The amphitheatre at the Walls of Jericho

Opposite: Limestone sink at the Walls of Jericho

formations that support red cedar stands, upland forests dominated by chinquapin oak, and pockets of cove hardwood forest containing yellow buckeye, sugar maple, and basswood.

This large, publicly accessible area includes state-owned as well as private land that is leased by the state. For example, the Little Coon Creek drainage area—with its important cove hardwood forest—is owned by Alabama Power Company, and the state has a lease on that land until near the end of the 21st century. The state-owned portions consist of donated and purchased land. The Mill Creek portion was donated to the state by the Nature Conservancy, while the Walls of Jericho area was purchased by the Forever Wild program with matching funds from the federal Pittman-Robertson Fund.

Until its purchase by Forever Wild, the Walls of Jericho was a famous place that few had seen. This huge area, once hunted by

the equally famous frontiersman and congressman, Davy Crockett, was private land closed to the public during the mid-1970s. After years of effort by many, the Nature Conservancy succeeded in buying a 12,510-acre Alabama tract surrounding the walls, which connects to other Skyline WMA units and lands in Tennessee, altogether creating a 50,000-acre conservation complex. The Alabama land was subsequently sold to Forever Wild for inclusion in Skyline WMA.

The Walls of Jericho proper consists of a bowl-shaped limestone formation along Hurricane Creek surrounded by impressive cliffs. The creek cascades, waterfalls, and even disappears in the limestone as it drops out of the bowl to progressively lower levels. And during heavy rains, the walls reach their most impressive state, with water pouring out of holes in the raw rock walls.

The state of Alabama has developed a six-mile hiking trail that descends from AL 79 down through the canyon to the Walls of Jericho. *Be forewarned*: This trail descends 1,000 vertical feet from the top of the highway to the valley floor below and then requires an additional lengthy hike up a side canyon to the walls themselves. Hikers should be in fairly good shape because the climb back out is especially strenuous.

If you have not been scared off by our description, then enjoy a hike down the slope through an upland hardwood forest with some limestone outcrops and sinkholes. Once you reach the valley floor, cross a clear stream that is formed by this protected subwatershed of the Paint Rock River. You will soon reach a large grassy area maintained for wildlife, which provides great views of the mountain you just descended and the climb you will have to make going back out. The trail continues past an old graveyard and up a scenic side canyon to the walls themselves.

Directions: The Little Coon Creek portion of Skyline WMA is reached by taking AL 117 north from Stevenson and turning left on Co. Rd. 53. From Co. Rd. 53 take a right onto Co. Rd. 54 and follow it up the cove; the road becomes very rough at stream crossings just inside the WMA. You can park here and walk the road up to the mountain top.

The Lower Big Coon Creek Unit lies to the south of the Little Coon Creek Unit. It can be accessed by following Co. Rd. 53 past the Little Coon Creek Unit turnoff and taking a right onto Co. Rd. 55, which runs through the edge of the Lower Big Coon Creek Unit near its namesake stream.

The Mill Creek Unit can be accessed by taking AL 79 north of Skyline. A left turn puts you on AL 146, which passes through the area.

To reach the Walls of Jericho, take AL 79 north from Scottsboro to the Skyline/Hytop community. The Walls of Jericho tract is just north of Hytop, with AL 79 cutting through it. The first parking lot that you encounter is for the horseback riding trails; the second parking lot is for the hiking trails.

3 Crow Creek and Other nearby WMAs

34°51'01.44"N
85°51'30.74"W

The 2,161-acre Crow Creek WMA consists of bottomlands in the Tennessee River Valley. The land is owned by the Tennessee Valley Authority (TVA) but is managed by the state. Southern red oaks and pines occupy the higher ground, while the lower and wetter soils support a true bottomland hardwood forest.

The state of Alabama manages other TVA-owned lands adjacent to the Crow Creek WMA. These state-managed lands are the 2,496-acre Crow Creek Refuge, the 8,193-acre Mud Creek WMA, and the 7,080-acre Raccoon Creek WMA. The habitats of these areas are similar to the Crow Creek WMA, offering backwater sloughs and fields managed for waterfowl. In addition, Mud Creek WMA served as Alabama's first bald eagle hacking site, where young eagles are raised at a potential nesting area and then subsequently released.

In 2004, Forever Wild purchased the 182-acre Jacob Farm, thereby connecting the Lower Big Coon Creek Unit of Skyline WMA and the Crow Creek and neighboring WMAs along Big Coon Creek. Wildlife enthusiasts and recreationalists now have a continuous, protected natural area with habitats ranging from mountain tops to bottomlands along the Tennessee River.

Directions: The Crow Creek WMA can be accessed by taking Co. Rd. 45 west out of Stevenson.

The Crow Creek Refuge lies immediately south of the Crow Creek WMA and can be accessed from the WMA or from US 72, which passes through it.

Mud Creek WMA lies to the west of Crow Creek Refuge and can be accessed off US 72.

Raccoon Creek WMA lies across the Tennessee River from Crow Creek Refuge and can be accessed from AL 117.

4 Southeastern Cave Conservancy Properties (access is restricted)

The Southeastern Cave Conservancy was formed in order to acquire and manage caves for research and conservation. The conservancy owns and leases caves and their overlying above-ground habitats in Kentucky, Tennessee, Georgia, Alabama, and Florida. In Alabama, the conservancy owns or leases properties in Madison and Jackson Counties, including some with very unusual names: Glove Pit, Neversink, Gourdneck, Horseskull, and Valhalla.

If you want to explore these caves, then check the website listed in our References and Websites. Also, be aware that, due to the fear of spreading white nose syndrome (a catastrophic bat disease), many caves may be currently closed.

5 Paint Rock River

34°39'11.55"N
86°17'54.22"W

The Paint Rock River is a relatively short river with its headwaters in the Walls of Jericho area. It is one of the most pristine examples of a free-flowing river in the Tennessee River drainage of Alabama. The Paint Rock River is home to over 100 species of fishes and about 45 species of mussels. Two of the mussels (pale lilliput and Alabama lampmussel) are found nowhere else in the

Paint Rock River near Hollytree

Natural spring at Fern Cave, Paint Rock River Valley

world. The Paint Rock is home to the only known population of the endangered snail darter in Alabama, and another fish (palezone shiner) is confined to this stream and one in Kentucky. The Nature Conservancy is working with landowners to ensure that the watershed retains its high water quality, which is necessary to support the rare and endangered aquatic species.

The headwaters of the Paint Rock River can be explored by visiting the Walls of Jericho. If you want to see habitats along the main stem of the river, you can visit Fern Cave National Wildlife Refuge (NWR). The 199-acre Fern Cave NWR contains a large cave along the Paint Rock River that houses the world's largest wintering colony of the endangered gray bat, with over one million hibernating bats each winter. (Large numbers of the

American hart's-tongue fern at Fern Cave

endangered Indiana Bat use the cave as well.) The inside of the cave is closed to the public in order to protect the bats from disturbance. The cave was named after the endangered American hart's tongue fern, which is also found on the property. Sadly, plant thieves have decimated this fern population, although the US Fish and Wildlife Service (USFWS) hopes to restore the plant's numbers.

Visitors to Fern Cave NWR have to park outside the refuge gate on Co. Rd. 500 and walk along the road through the property. This route follows the Paint Rock River. The beautiful blue color of the river is due to its high lime content, which is leached from surrounding limestone caves and formations. Across the river from Fern Cave NWR is the Nature Conservancy's 323-acre Roy B. Whitaker Preserve, which is preserving and restoring bottomland hardwood habitats along the river to help protect adjacent river habitats and water quality. If you would like to visit the Whitaker Preserve, consult the Nature Conservancy of Alabama website.

Directions: From Huntsville, take US 72 east to Gurley. North of Gurley, turn left on Co. Rd. 500 (just past where US 72 crosses the Paint Rock River). Co. Rd. 500 is now closed by a gate but foot traffic is still allowed. Hike along the old road as it winds along the Paint Rock River and look for the NWR signs.

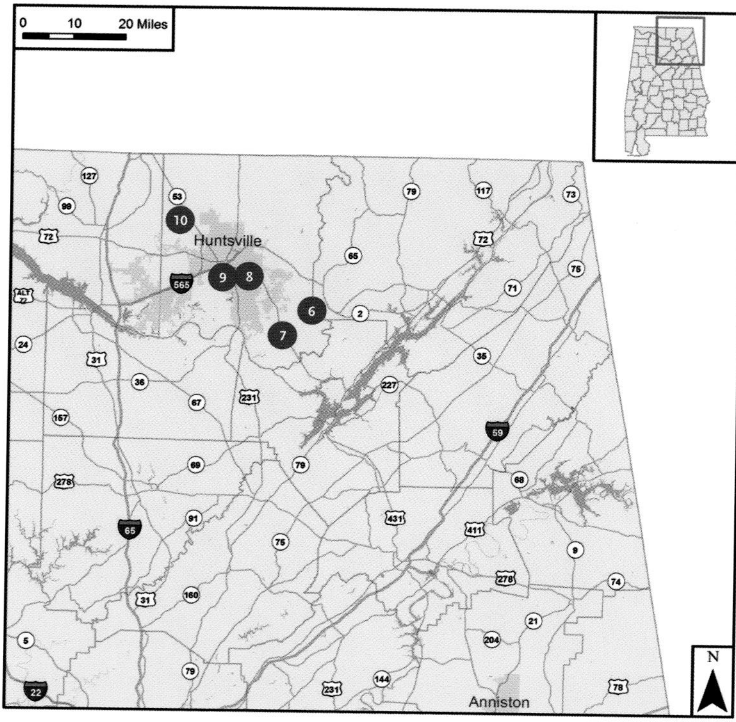

HUNTSVILLE AREA

The area immediately surrounding Huntsville is famous for its hiking, biking and spelunking adventures, plus the more pedestrian pursuits at the Huntsville Botanical Gardens.

6 Keel Mountain

86°17'54.22"W

86°20'41.99"W

Morefield's Leather Flower at Keel Mountain Preserve

The 310-acre Keel Mountain Preserve is owned and maintained by the Nature Conservancy. It was established to protect a key population of the endangered Morefield's leather flower, which is known from only six populations, all within the mountains around Huntsville. The preserve also protects other rare plants including Cumberland rosinweed and limerock arrowwood.

The preserve is part of the limestone karst slopes of Keel Mountain. Most of its streams run only during times of high water, with that water disappearing down sinkholes. A small waterfall enters one such sinkhole, the Lost Sink. The Lost Sink Nature Trail leads visitors to the mountain's karst slopes, passing through forests of red cedar, shagbark hickory, and chinquapin oak. Some of the moist slopes along the mostly dry stream bed are transitioning to a cove hardwood forest with sugar maple, yellow buckeye, and black walnut. Higher up on drier slopes, the rare smoke tree grows in the understory. The trail passes lots of large limestone outcrops as well.

Directions: From Huntsville, take US 72 east to Gurley. In Gurley, take a right onto Little Cove Rd. and travel about two miles to McMullen Rd. Take a left on McMullen Rd. and follow it for four or five miles. (Stay to the left when the road forks.) There is a small parking area and sign for the preserve on the left-hand side of the road, just past a sharp turn.

Ephemeral pond at Keel Mountain Preserve

7 Flint River

34°38'45.36"W
86°27'28.55"W

The Flint River flows out of central Tennessee toward the Tennessee River near Huntsville, separating the Monte Sano Mountain area from the similar and much larger Skyline Mountain range to the east. This free-flowing river is an excellent canoeing stream, and Madison County, Alabama, has developed canoe launches and take-out areas along many of the roads that cross it.

One of the best places to experience the river and its surrounding corridor is the Hays Nature Preserve and Goldsmith-Schiffman Wildlife Sanctuary. The late Ann Hays donated 538 acres of land along the Flint River to the city of Huntsville for the purpose of establishing a nature preserve. Unlike many of the protected natural areas around Huntsville, this area protects lowland habitats. The preserve features significant river frontage, bottomland hardwood and tupelo swamps, at least seven miles of foot trails, a rail-to-trail bike path, and a large borrow pit lake.

Start your visit at the picnic area along the river. This area showcases beautiful frontage on both sides of the river, plus several trails (including a handicapped accessible one) that lead out into the bottomland forest. The dominant tree of this bottomland forest is water oak, with sycamore and American hornbeam present as well. The preserve and sanctuary are still under development, so check its website for future recreational opportunities.

Directions: From Huntsville, take US 431 southeast to Hays Preserve Rd. This will be a left turn a short distance before crossing the Flint River.

8 Monte Sano Mountain

34°44'42.42"N
86°30'41.93"W

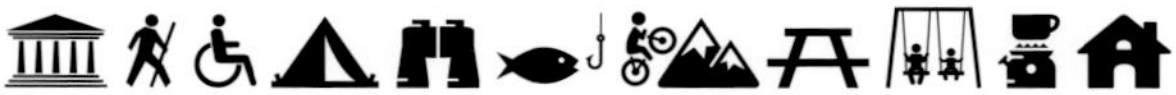

Monte Sano Mountain is a western outlier of the Skyline Mountains, separated from the main plateau area by the Flint River Valley. Monte Sano Mountain lies within the city limits of Huntsville and has seen much residential development.

The 2,400-acre Monte Sano State Park was established in the 1930s with help from the Civilian Conservation Corps (CCC). The park was intended to protect remaining portions of the mountain's sandstone top and limestone slopes from further development. Unfortunately, the park was divided into several units, and during the 1980s urban sprawl encroached upon and threatened

Above: Cabins available for rent, Monte Sano State Park

Opposite: View from the lodge, Monte Sano State Park

the habitat and recreational quality of those units. Local conservationists formed a land trust, now called the Huntsville and North Alabama Land Trust, which worked with the city of Huntsville to purchase and protect the land between and adjacent to the state park units. A large portion of this recently acquired property is found in the land trust's 1,020-acre Monte Sano Mountain Preserve, which includes year-round access to trails and periodic access to the property's man-made caves, formed by unusual limestone quarry methods. Together, the land trust, the city of Huntsville, Burritt Museum, and the Forever Wild program have protected a 3,400-acre block of land.

Although the mountain lies within the city, it contains some great natural wonders. The mountaintop portion of the state park is dominated by upland oak-hickory forest, with spectacular views across the Flint River Valley to the Skyline Mountains. The park also has some exceptional trails through limestone karst landscapes. Dry limestone outcrops, including those along trails on the land trust's property, are dominated by red cedar, shagbark hickory, and chinquapin oak. North-facing slopes and protected coves feature cove hardwood forest, including the biologically significant Cold Springs Natural Area.

The Cold Springs Natural Area has one of the few permanent freshwater sources in this karst landscape, and the spring run is surrounded by some of the best old-growth cove hardwood in the state. The trail through this area passes our state champion yellow buckeye, basswood, and cucumber magnolia trees. Although slope slippage (and possibly air pollution) is causing the death and decline of some individuals, it remains a forest of giants. The forest floor reveals a high diversity of spring woodland wildflowers, such as bent trillium and shooting star; some of the higher ridges include old-growth northern red oak. There are no special land animals here, but as you pass the namesake spring, be sure to flip over some rocks. You just might find a bright orange cave salamander.

Other areas of the Monte Sano Mountain ridge are worth seeing. The Burritt Museum has an assortment of technology and frontier buildings, plus a handicapped-accessible interpretive nature trail. Further south, the ridge is called Green Mountain, and the 72-acre Madison County Nature Trail Park sits along a pretty lake on top of this portion of the mountain. (Fishing is allowed at the lake on weekdays.) In the lowlands to the west of Green Mountain lies Huntsville's Aldridge Creek Greenway, which provides a trail with views of streamside habitats and wildlife, such as yellow-crowned night herons.

Directions: Most of the protected natural areas on Monte Sano Mountain can be accessed by taking US 431 east from downtown Huntsville, which will climb the mountain. Pass a picnic area (containing smoke trees) on your left, then make a left onto Panorama Dr. SE, which is marked by signs pointing to Monte Sano State Park and the Burritt Museum. The Burritt Museum will appear on your left. Soon after that, make a right turn into the main portion of the state park. If you continue going straight on the main road and start going down the north face of the mountain, you will see a small parking area for the Cold Springs Natural Area on your right.

If you continue going down the slope on the road that curves to your left, you will see the parking area for the Huntsville and North Alabama Land Trust Monte Sano Mountain property on your left.

The Green Mountain Nature Trail can be reached from Huntsville by taking South Memorial Pkwy., then Weatherly Rd. to the east; turn right on Bailey Cove Rd., left on Green Mountain Rd., and right on Shawdee Rd. to the park, situated on your right. To reach the Aldridge Creek Greenway, enter it at McGucken Park on the above mentioned Bailey Cove Rd.

9 Shelta Cave and Huntsville Botanical Garden

34°42'38.55"N
86°37'55.13"W

The headquarters of the National Speleological Society (NSS) is at the entrance to Shelta Cave in the middle of Huntsville. The NSS is dedicated to promoting spelunking (cave exploration) safety and cave conservation. The headquarters hosts an extensive library that is available to NSS members; you can also purchase a variety of books at the gift shop.

A very short trail leads from the parking lot through a small patch of forest behind the NSS building to the mouth of Shelta Cave. Like most protected caves in Alabama, the cave entrance is gated to guard its unique resources from vandalism and other disturbances. Not surprisingly, the surface vegetation is limestone-loving, including hackberry trees. Headquarters staff members are available to show you maps of Shelta Cave and describe the impressive array of life within it, like an albino blind fish and three cave-dwelling species of crayfish. (Having three species of crayfish in a single cave is most unusual; normally, one eliminates the rest.)

Other natural habitats and exhibits can be found at the nearby Huntsville Botanical Garden, including a nature center, butterfly house, and a wildflower garden featuring trilliums.

DIRECTIONS: To reach Shelta Cave from the US 231 area, go west on Oakwood Ave. NW, then take a right onto Pulaski Pike NW. The NSS headquarters building is located on the southwest side of the junction of Pulaski Pike NW and Cave Ave. NW. Parking is in the rear of the building, and the trail to the cave entrance is to rear of the parking lot. The headquarters building is open only on weekdays.

To reach the Huntsville Botanical Garden, take I-565 exit 15 and proceed east on Bob Wallace Ave. The garden is on the right.

10 Rainbow Mountain

34°44'05.48"N
86°43'45.96"W

Rainbow Mountain is a 65-acre property protected by the combined efforts of the Huntsville and North Alabama Land Trust and the Sierra Club. The property is one of the western-most outliers of the Appalachian Plateau as it merges into the Highland Rim on the north side of the Tennessee River. The forest soils on the slopes of Rainbow Mountain, like other mountains north of the Tennessee River, are derived from the area's limestone and are thus covered by limestone-loving species like shagbark hickory. In addition, Rainbow Mountain has a significant amount of natural pine, possibly because—unlike most Cumberland Plateau formations north of the Tennessee River—it also has a great number of sandstone outcrops. And these outcrops are its greatest attraction. The most unique formation is called Balance Rock; it looks like a toy top balanced upon its point, and you expect it to topple over at any moment.

As you enter the parking lot next to the water tower on the mountain top, take the unmarked service road/trail to the right of the narrow unmarked hiking trail. The service road quickly turns into a looping trail system, with the right fork passing by Balance Rock.

Besides Rainbow Mountain and the previously mentioned Monte Sano Mountain Preserve, the Huntsville and North Alabama Land Trust has several other properties in the area. More information, including amenities and directions, can be obtained at the land trust's website.

DIRECTIONS: From Huntsville, head west on US 72 into the suburb of Rainbow Mountain Heights. Turn left onto Hughes Rd., left onto Thomas Rd., left onto Concord Rd., right onto Stoneway Trail, then right at a T-intersection to the water tower on the mountain top. An information kiosk is located in the parking lot.

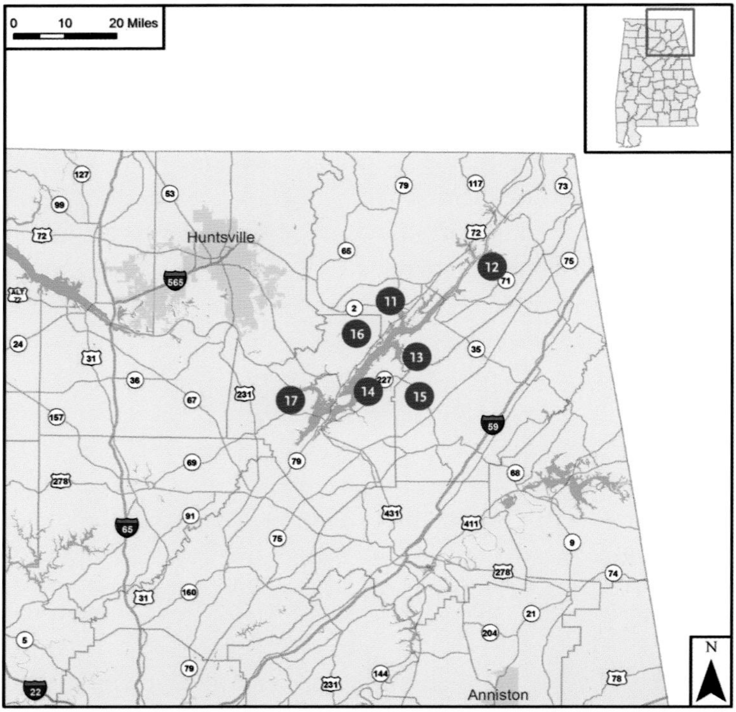

LOWER SEQUATCHIE VALLEY / LAKE GUNTERSVILLE AREA

Guntersville Lake was formed when the TVA dammed the Tennessee River in the 1930s. (The Crow Creek area and adjacent WMAs of the upper lake were mentioned earlier.) The lake lies in the Sequatchie valley, which splits the Appalachian Plateau, starting up in Tennessee. In Tennessee, the mountains surrounding the narrow valley are quite tall, with very impressive cliffs; by the time the Tennessee River (now in the form of Guntersville Lake) reaches Alabama, the valley has broadened greatly and the mountains and cliffs are shorter and farther apart. The Sequatchie valley and its associated formations continue southwest of Guntersville Lake to Blount County and Rickwood Caverns, where it fades into the general Appalachian Plateau.

Even with the extreme modifications to the river itself, the Sequatchie valley area surrounding Guntersville Lake still contains several natural treasures.

11 Sauta Cave NWR

34°36'53.46"N
86°07'48.18"W

The 264-acre Sauta Cave NWR (formerly known as Blowing Wind Cave NWR) is located near Guntersville Lake. The cave is home to the world's largest colony of the endangered gray bat. At Sauta Cave, from spring through fall, visitors can stand on an observation deck by the cave entrance at dusk to watch more than 200,000 bats emerge. The bats feed on flying insects (including mosquitoes) along Guntersville Lake; they hibernate during the winter months when the number of such insects declines.

An iron grate at the cave entrance protects the bats from human disturbance. The cave was mined for the gunpowder ingredient, saltpeter, by the Cherokees during the 1790s as well as by Anglo-Americans during the War of 1812 and the Civil War. Like many other caves, it was used as a hidden dance hall during the Prohibition era. These and later disturbances led to the bat's numbers plummeting by the 1970s. Although gray bats are now rebuilding close to sustaining levels, the previously mentioned white nose syndrome disease complicates that recovery. For now, it is best to restrict access inside this and other key bat caves.

The adjacent TVA Blowing Wind Cave Gray Bat Sanctuary and

Crab spider on white-flower leafcup, Sauta Cave NWR

state-managed North Sauty Refuge (5,200 acres) protects additional habitat for this species. Waterfowl are abundant in this area during the winter, and the nearby Goose Pond Colony Park in Scottsboro offers a few miles of walking trails along Guntersville Lake as well as other amenities.

Directions: The Sauta Cave NWR area is reached by traveling seven miles west of Scottsboro, Alabama, on US 72 and turning left after you cross the North Sauty Creek embayment bridge. Park in the large cleared area to the side of the gate into North Sauty Refuge and walk down that road; you will see signs when you enter the refuge. The cave observation platform will be on your right.

Goose Pond Colony Park can be reached by taking AL 279 southwest from its junction with US 72 in Scottsboro; simply follow the signs from AL 279.

12 Pisgah Gorge

34°40'08.37"N
85°51'47.85"W

Pisgah Gorge is one of several canyons carved by streams dropping off Sand Mountain to the Tennessee River valley below. The gorge is one of the few places between northwest Alabama and Chattanooga where eastern hemlock can be found. And it may be the only place in Alabama where hemlock grows with a shrub layer of rhododendron. (The association of hemlock and rhododendron—although a different species—is common farther north in the Appalachians.)

Pisgah Gorge is largely private property. However, a park in the town of Pisgah provides a trail along the gorge's rim where two large waterfalls plunge into the water below. Hemlock trees and rhododendrons can be seen above the upper waterfall. The area is particularly scenic in May when the rhododendrons are blooming.

Directions: To reach Pisgah Gorge, take AL 35 south from its junction with US 72 in Scottsboro. Follow AL 35 across the river and up Sand Mountain and turn left on AL 40. Turn left on AL 71, and then left again on Co. Rd. 58 toward the town of Pisgah. Finally, turn left on Co. Rd. 374 and park at the Pisgah town park.

13 Buck's Pocket State Park

34°28'25.27"N
86°03'10.77"W

The 2,000-acre Buck's Pocket State Park includes a small but deep canyon where South Sauty Creek drops off Sand Mountain into the Tennessee River valley. This scenic rocky stream runs the length of the park and, due to the karst landscape, is sometimes great for white-water boating—and sometimes sand dry. The creek becomes impounded by Guntersville Lake before it leaves the park.

Buck's Pocket contains some short hiking trails, and a roadside overlook at the top of the canyon has rhododendron growing next to it. In some places, the trails are bordered by other spring blooms, including the large and beautiful red wake robin trillium, which is not common in Alabama.

The 12-mile-long Lickskillet Trail links this park with nearby Lake Guntersville State Park.

Directions: Follow AL 227 north from Guntersville past Lake Guntersville State Park and follow the signs to Buck's Pocket State Park.

14 Lake Guntersville State Park

34°23'38.29"N
86°11'40.28"W

The 6,000-acre Lake Guntersville State Park is located where Sand Mountain meets the lake. Impounded creeks, such as Town and Short, offer scenic boating and canoeing opportunities where their canyons cut into the river valley.

Since its creation in the 1930s, the lake has attracted a large number of waterfowl and wintering bald eagles. Once threatened with extinction, bald eagles have recovered due to the banning of certain pesticides (which weakened eagles' eggshells to the point of breaking) and hacking/reintroduction programs. Alabama's initial hacking efforts at Mud Creek WMA, upstream from Lake Guntersville State Park, resulted in mature birds returning to the place of their raising to nest.

Lake Guntersville State Park sponsors eagle awareness weekends during January, including "packages" for the park's lodge. Visitors can obtain information on the best places to see eagles and waterfowl in winter at any park facility. You can see them in some detail with binoculars, but a spotting scope is needed to bring them in close. (Often there is a birdwatcher with a scope at these locations, just in case you don't have one.) Most of the

Left: Pileated woodpecker, Lake Guntersville State Park

Below: White-tailed buck, Lake Guntersville State Park

wintering waterfowl are coots and gadwall. However, portions of the lake, such as the shore around the state park campground and the nearby city of Guntersville Municipal Park, can be good places to see eagles, loons, grebes, and diving ducks such as goldeneye, scaup, and ruddy ducks.

There are plenty of trails to explore year-round at the state park. The scenic Sand Mountain terrain includes some limestone formations with caves. The lakeside forest has good pockets of sugar maple and a few yellow buckeyes on the cliffs, which during the fall drop their fruit into the lake with a loud splash.

Directions: To reach Lake Guntersville State Park, follow AL 227 east from Guntersville until it passes through the park. Stop at the park office to learn where to best see eagles and waterfowl and to obtain other information. Signs will also direct you to some park amenities.

To reach Guntersville Municipal Park, follow US 431 north or east through the city until it reaches the tall bridges over the main river. Pull into the parking lot on your right before you cross the river and scan the old municipal boat harbor pilings for mergansers and gulls. The site offers a great view of Lake Guntersville State Park and its cliff-top lodge. Subsequently, cross US 431 and follow the drive along the lakeside city park, stopping at the various parking lots whenever you see waterfowl of interest. Some of the best waterfowl viewing is at the park's boat launch (just before you reach AL 69) and along the park drive after it crosses AL 69.

15 High Falls County Park

34°24'04.03"N
86°03'58.94"W

View from on top, High Falls County Park

High Falls County Park is located on Sand Mountain's freeflowing Town Creek before it becomes impounded at Lake Guntersville State Park. This little-known park, owned and operated by DeKalb County, features the spectacular High Falls— one of the widest and highest volume falls in Alabama, very reminiscent of Little River Falls. Erosion below High Falls created a small natural bridge through which the stream flows, making it one of the most beautiful waterfall areas in the state. The park offers picnicking, swimming, and a bridge over the creek. Visitors walk from a parking lot down a short sloping road to reach the falls and main picnic area. This walk gives you an opportunity to enjoy the surrounding forest and its wildflowers, such as coreopsis. The park currently contains a few short trail segments; the county hopes to acquire additional lands from willing landowners to

View from the side, High Falls County Park

enlarge the park and its trail system. One unique aspect of this park is that a county sheriff blares his siren 20 minutes before closing time to encourage people to leave. *And he means it!*

DIRECTIONS: High Falls County Park can be reached by following AL 227 north from Geraldine in DeKalb County. You will soon cross Town Creek, but keep going until you see signs for High Falls Park pointing to your left. Follow the signs from there. (Just before you reach the park you will reach a confusing unmarked Y junction; take the left fork of the Y to get to the park.) After visiting the falls, you can backtrack to AL 227 and go northwest to nearby Buck's Pocket and Lake Guntersville State Parks.

16 Cathedral Caverns State Park

34°34'25.56"N
86°13'38.24"W

This state park contains a world-class cave. The mouth of the cave, surrounded by yellow buckeyes and other uncommon hardwood trees, was once inhabited by Native Americans. The cave tour passes impressive formations of stalactites hanging from the ceiling and stalagmites projecting from the floor. (Some of these natural formations have artificial reflection pools below them; however, they appear natural.) The most impressive and unique thing about the cave is the giant stalagmites, giving you the feeling of being in a petrified forest. The site (or sight) is so spectacular that it was featured in the Disney movie *Tom and Huck.*

DIRECTIONS: From the city of Guntersville, follow US 431 north or east for several miles, then turn right on Word Mountain Rd. Turn right at Cathedral Caverns Hwy./Co. Rd. 5. Turn right at Cathedral Caverns Rd./Cavern Cove Rd. Turn right on Cave Rd. to the park.

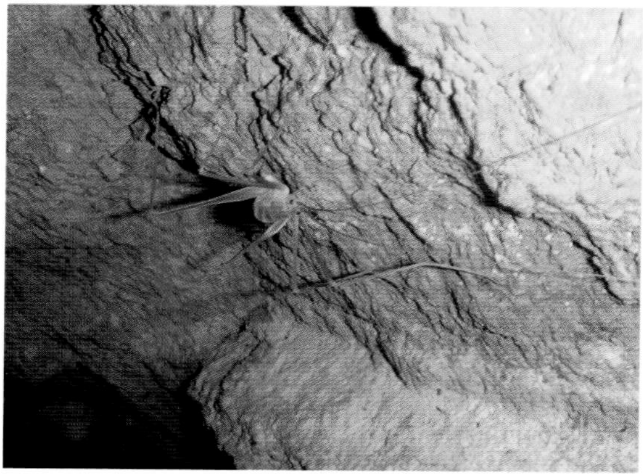

Cave cricket,
Cathedral Caverns

Interior of Cathedral Caverns

17 Cave Mountain SWA and Lake Guntersville Tailrace

34°25'06.88"N
86°24'11.34"W

This TVA Small Wild Area (SWA) is located on the south bank of the Tennessee River just downstream from Guntersville Dam. The area has a great diversity of natural habitats. Limestone ridges contain upland oak-hickory forest with basic (nonacidic) soil-loving species such as chinquapin oak and shagbark hickory. North-facing slopes support cove hardwoods with yellow buckeye, sugar maple, and basswood. Bloodroot, liver leaf, and trout lilies bloom in early spring among the hardwoods. A tupelo swamp occupies the river bottoms directly below the cove slope.

The cave itself is open to exploration on your own. Bring extra lights and prepare to get wet. And make sure you can find your way back out!

Because the area below Guntersville Dam retains a flowing river habitat similar to that "enjoyed" before the damming of the Tennessee River, several rare, threatened, and endangered mussel species can still be found here. Species present below Guntersville Dam include the spectaclecase, spike, longsolid, pink mucket, sheepnose, rough pigtoe, pyramid pigtoe, round pigtoe, kidneyshell, and black sandshell.

The TVA has several other SWAs along Lake Guntersville. Raccoon Gulf SWA has some nice old-growth chestnut oak forest below the cliff lines of Sand Mountain, while Big Spring Creek SWA contains old-growth bottomland timber. Honeycomb Creek SWA has a long trail through mature shortleaf and loblolly pines as well as upland hardwoods, sinkholes, caves, and other karst features; some settler cemeteries occur here, too. South Sauty SWA preserves beauty along the lake, while Mink Creek and Honey Bluff Habitat Protection Areas protect caves for gray bats.

Directions: To reach the Cave Mountain SWA and the south side of Guntersville Dam, take AL 69 north or west from Guntersville. After a few miles take a right onto AL 66 and subsequently a right on Co. Rd. 27, which leads to the dam area. The SWA is to your left upon entering the dam reservation and is marked with a sign.

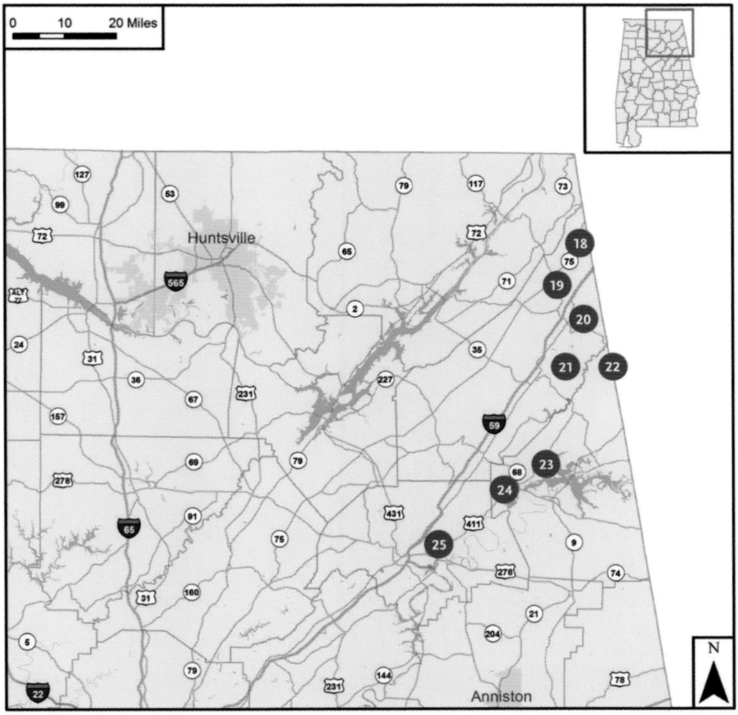

LOOKOUT MOUNTAIN AREA

Lookout Mountain includes the highest Appalachian Plateau land in Alabama. The mountain is separated from the much larger Sand Mountain by the Big Wills Creek Valley, which was named after the mixed-blood Chickamauga/Cherokee chief, Red-Headed Will. During the late 1700s, the Chickamaugas warred against encroaching white settlements in Tennessee until their main towns around Chattanooga were destroyed. Some left for Arkansas long before the chief's namesake, Willstown (later known as Fort Payne), was turned into a roundup stockade for the Trail of Tears. The valley's famous Sequoyah Caverns is named after

Willstown's most famous resident, who invented the Cherokee alphabet while living there.

Lookout Mountain is highest near its northern tip in Chattanooga, Tennessee, and decreases in height as it passes through Georgia down to Gadsden, Alabama. While Lookout Mountain is not the state's largest plateau, it contains some of Alabama's most spectacular scenery in the form of canyons, waterfalls, and views of the Big Wills Valley. Reaching nearly 2,000 feet in elevation near Mentone, Alabama, the plateau is about 10 degrees cooler than the surrounding valleys, turning Mentone into a thriving summer resort town in the days before air conditioning. The coolness also helps spring weather arrive later on the mountain than elsewhere in Alabama.

18 Fox Mountain (access is restricted)

Fox Mountain is a small plateau between Lookout and Sand Mountains that straddles the Alabama–Georgia border. Fox Mountain forms part of the Tennessee Divide, with water to its south flowing into the Big Wills Creek–Coosa-Mobile River System and water to its north flowing into the Tennessee-Ohio-Mississippi River System. Small but tall, its butte (chimney-looking) formation looks like those in the southwestern states. However, unlike the buttes of the desert Southwest, Fox Mountain is covered with trees (like shagbark hickory) on lower limestone slopes, which overlie significant caves.

A good portion of Fox Mountain's Georgia side has been protected by the Southeastern Cave Conservancy. Currently, the Alabama side is all privately owned, with no publicly accessible trails. You can view the mountain (to the northwest) from I-59 around the Georgia border.

19 Sequoyah Caverns

34°40'10.06"N
85°36'25.84"W

This is a commercial cave in Big Wills Valley near Lookout Mountain, with spectacular formations well worth admiring. The formations are reflected in pools, and the cave contains many fossils (including deer prints) on the roof of the cave. "Wild" cave tours (to areas not generally open to the public) and overnight tours are offered in addition to traditional ones. From December to February, the cave is open only on weekends.

DIRECTIONS: Take I-59 north from Fort Payne and follow the directions given by billboards and signs to the cave.

20 DeSoto State Park and DeSoto Falls

34°30'15.85"N
85°37'29.32"W

The 3,502-acre DeSoto State Park is located on the West Fork of Little River and contains most of the area's developed park facilities. It is named after the Spanish conquistador who was the first European to travel through and pillage the Southeast in a vain search for gold. (Although doubtful, his route during the 1500s may have taken him through this general area of Alabama.) The main portion of the park has trails along the West Fork where Catawba rhododendrons bloom during early May. There are great examples of nodding trilliums along the trails as well. The pink lady's slipper orchid grows in other parts of the park. (Due to the orchid's rarity and past problems with overcollecting, we will not

Left: Pink ladies' slipper orchid, DeSoto State Park

Opposite: DeSoto Falls, West Fork of the Little River

reveal its location. Ask a park ranger about them, and you may be told—*if you can be trusted.*)

A separate unit of DeSoto State Park is located upstream at DeSoto Falls. Here the West Fork of Little River flows across the dam of a small lake and then plunges into a deep canyon. Rough trails are found on both sides of the canyon below the falls; some of them go down into the canyon itself on the east side. Below the falls on the west (parking lot) side are some unique geological formations known as the Welsh Caves. The bluff above the caves shows the remains of a defensive wall that protected cave occupants from invaders. Early settlers attributed the wall to the legendary Modoc, who supposedly brought a band of Welshmen to Alabama before Columbus's 1492 voyage. But the wall was probably built by Native Americans instead. Access to the caves may change due to current development on adjacent private land, so ask a park ranger before you attempt it.

DIRECTIONS: Take AL 35 east from Fort Payne. Climb to the top of Lookout Mountain and take a left onto Co. Rd. 89. This road passes through the main unit of the state park, with various amenities marked by signs. Continue northeast on the main road toward Mentone and you will see the turnoff for the DeSoto Falls area on your right.

21 Little River Canyon National Preserve

34°23'42.75"N
85°37'31.94"W

The 14,000-acre Little River Canyon National Preserve is Alabama's largest national park unit. The East and West Forks of Little River join to form the main stem of Little River in the upstream end of the preserve. The upper area is a plateau top that was heavily timbered prior to being purchased for the preserve—an oak-pine forest in recovery. This area is part of Little River WMA and is open to many forms of recreation, including hunting.

The endangered green pitcher plant can be found in the upstream end and other portions of the preserve where drainage is poor. This insectivorous plant depends on periodic fires to keep its bog habitat relatively free of competing shrubs and trees. In the preserve, controlled burns are used to mimic natural fires and keep habitat available for pitcher plants and other fire-dependent species. Green pitcher plants are so rare and have been so overharvested by unscrupulous collectors that we will not disclose their exact locations. However, if you explore the upstream end of the preserve you will likely see them.

Left: Little River Canyon onion, Little River Canyon National Preserve

Below: Little River Falls, Little River Canyon National Preserve

Canyon Mouth Park, Little River Canyon National Preserve

During the wetter times of the year, the upper end of the main stem of the Little River provides an opportunity for a slow, scenic canoe trip. However, this gentle stretch ends abruptly (and dangerously) as the river plummets over Little River Falls at the head of Little River Canyon. These are among the widest and highest volume waterfalls in Alabama. During the wet early spring, the falls are particularly spectacular, sending up spray that forms small rainbows.

Below the falls, Little River Canyon offers some of the most challenging (and treacherous) white-water kayaking and canoeing opportunities in the state. Many people have been killed paddling this canyon. You should only attempt it if you are highly skilled and willing to risk your life.

Non-risk-takers content themselves with standing on the canyon rim, looking across at its towering sandstone cliffs and down at the white-water rapids hundreds of feet below. During the wetter times of the year the state's highest waterfall, Grace High Falls, makes a 100-foot drop into Little River Canyon. Multiple views of the canyon can be obtained at the various overlooks along Canyon Rim Parkway.

The downstream end of Little River Canyon National Preserve is made up of the old Cherokee County Canyon Mouth Park. Here visitors can see where the high canyon walls blend into the Coosa River portion of the Ridge and Valley Province. The river seems much slower, with fewer shoals, as it ends its free run before merging with the impounded Coosa River (Weiss Lake). Little River has been noted as the only river in the nation that runs its entire length on top of a mountain. That is true except here, where the river leaves the old Mouth Park.

The Little River Canyon Field School is a project of Jacksonville State University's Environmental Policy and Information Center. This school offers classes to college students, educators, and the general public on the ecology of the canyon and other areas of northeast Alabama. The school, located on AL 35 just west of Canyon Rim Parkway and Little River Falls, also provides a visitor center for the preserve.

Directions: Take AL 35 east from Fort Payne. Climb to the top of Lookout Mountain and continue until you reach the bridge over Little River. Roads into the northern end of the preserve lie to the left side of the road, but you will need a park map to navigate them. You can cross the AL 35 bridge and take an immediate right into the Little River Falls parking lot and observation area. Or, you can take a right just before the bridge onto the Canyon Rim Parkway. The parkway winds down the mountain to Canyon Mouth Park; along the way are several overlooks that provide excellent views of the canyon. To save on your brake pads, you can also approach Canyon Mouth Park by following AL 273 northeast from Leesburg.

22 Jamestown Cliff (access is restricted)

The beautiful Jamestown Cliff is located to the east of the Little River Canyon National Preserve. The cliff includes a 3.14-acre tract (1,500 linear feet) that was recently purchased and protected by the Southeastern Climbers Coalition (SCC). The SCC works on acquisition projects throughout the Southeast in order to keep rock climbing spots accessible; it also provides some maintenance work at those sites. Currently, due to access issues, you have to be a member of SCC to visit Jamestown Cliff, but the SCC is working for more general access.

View from boulders, Cherokee Rock Village

23 Yellow Creek Falls

34°13'23.47"N
85°43'24.82"W

Yellow Creek plunges off Lookout Mountain into the Weiss Lake impoundment in the form of very impressive waterfalls. Because there is no public access to the privately owned land around the falls, they must be viewed from the parking lot of a private fishing camp on the road below.

> DIRECTIONS: The fishing camp (referred to above) is found on AL 273 northeast of Leesburg, just before you cross the first large embayment of Weiss Lake. The falls can be seen to the north on the side of Lookout Mountain.

24 Cherokee Rock Village

34°10'50.28"N
85°49'01.35"W

This 200-acre park was purchased by the Nature Conservancy and deeded to Cherokee County for public recreation. The park sits on the western brow of Lookout Mountain and offers superb views of the Weiss Lake impoundment in the Coosa River Valley. However, the park's main attraction is the largest concentration of giant boulders in the state. The park has many towering free-standing boulders, which form a maze of passages to be explored. True, the boulders have suffered more than their fair share of graffiti. But the park remains a paradise for those who enjoy photography or climbing big rocks.

DIRECTIONS: Take AL 68 northwest out of Leesburg and follow it to the top of the mountain, then take a left onto Co. Rd. 36. Take another left on Co. Rd. 70; a wooden sign marks this turn. Co. Rd. 70 snakes around to the right and uphill to the park. You will know that you have arrived by the unmistakable sight of large boulders.

25 Noccalula Falls / James D. Martin Wildlife Park

34°02'40.31"N
86°01'14.06"W

Noccalula Falls Park lies at the southern end of Lookout Mountain in Gadsden. The park contains some wonderful natural beauty, plus a neat collection of pioneer cabins, a botanical garden, and a campground. However, the main attractions are the impressive falls formed by Black Creek plunging high off Lookout Mountain and the trails within the natural gorge below.

Noccalula Falls takes its name from a legendary Cherokee woman who jumped to her death rather than forsake her true love and submit to an arranged marriage. A statue at the top of the falls commemorates this story. However, the wardrobe of the statue resembles the classic dress of Plains Indians rather than the local Native Americans.

Nearby, at the impounded mouth of Black Creek, is the James D. Martin Wildlife Park, named for the long-time Alabama conservation commissioner. The park includes land and backwaters along Neely Henry hydroelectric reservoir on the Coosa River.

The lands of the park are covered by marshes and streamside forest species, including eastern cottonwood. A boardwalk passes over shallows that are nearly dry when the lake is at winter levels. Coots, gadwalls, shovelers, and snipes reside in the shallows during the winter months, while the marshes are full of swamp

Winter scene at Noccalula Falls of Black Creek

sparrows. Hooded mergansers, cormorants, and various gulls and terns hang out in deeper portions of the embayment; even white pelicans have been spotted here.

Directions: Noccalula Falls Park is located on US 211 between I-59 exit 188 and US 278/431 in Gadsden.

The James D. Martin Wildlife Park is located on US 431 just north of I-759, behind the Gadsden Mall. If you want to get closer to the boardwalk portion of the park, take the Black Creek Pkwy. exit off I-759, follow the parkway north and then turn right onto south 11th St. You will soon see a parking lot and entrance to your right.

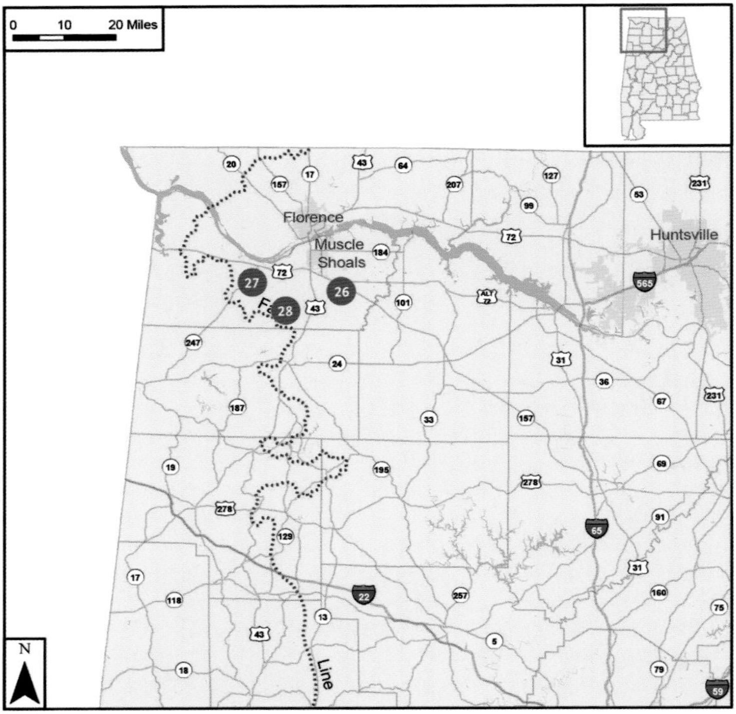

LITTLE MOUNTAIN AREA

The physiographic status of Little Mountain is up for debate. We consider Little Mountain to be a portion of the Appalachian Plateau because it shares many characteristics with the greater physiographic region.

Little Mountain lies between the northern Sand Mountain escarpment and the Tennessee River; its long, narrow mass stretches west from Morgan County to Colbert County. In contrast to the rest of Alabama's Appalachian Plateau, Little Mountain was once a series of barrier islands along an ancient coastline, similar to Dauphin Island today. (The rest of Alabama's Appalachian

Plateau was ancient river deltas.) That coastline was none other than ancient South America, when it was coming together with all of the other continents to form the supercontinent, Pangaea, over 300 million years ago. While most of the Appalachian Plateau is dominated by Pottsville sandstone, those former barrier islands compacted into a different, highly erosion-resistant type known as Hartselle. In fact, the sand patterns produced by ancient hurricanes can still be seen!

Public access to Little Mountain is limited to just a few spots, including the following.

26 LaGrange College Site Park

34°40'26.08"N
87°33'48.68'W

The grounds of the Civil War–era LaGrange College (south of AL 157 near Leighton) offer pioneer buildings and a picnic area with magnificent views of the main Tennessee River valley near Muscle Shoals.

Directions: LaGrange College Site Park can be reached from Muscle Shoals by going south on AL 157 for eight miles and then turning right at the sign.

27 Freedom Hills and Riverton WMAs

34°38'07.77"N
87°57'58.25"W

You can stand upon Little Mountain's sandstone crest at the Freedom Hills Overlook on the Natchez Trace Pkwy. in Colbert County. This overlook is surrounded by the lands of the

31,000-acre Freedom Hills WMA. The colorful Coon Dog Memorial Cemetery lies inside the WMA; only champion raccoon hunting dogs can be buried here. To the north of the Freedom Hills WMA lies the 6,700-acre Riverton WMA, a recent Forever Wild purchase of two large parcels of former paper company lands that are being replanted and restored. Further east, you can see a cave-fed spring on the mountain's limestone toe at the aptly named Cave Spring on Wheeler NWR. That cave is home to a large colony of gray bats.

Directions: The Coon Dog graveyard section of the Freedom Hills WMA is easily found by heading south from the town of Cherokee in Colbert County on Co. Rd. 21.

The Riverton WMA is reached by heading west on US 72 from Cherokee, then taking a right on Co. Rd. 1. This road follows the edges of the two WMA tracts while passing by a county park providing access to the Bear Creek embayment of the Tennessee River's Pickwick Reservoir.

28 Cane Creek Canyon Nature Preserve

34°37'23.28"N
87°47'35.55"W

Cane Creek Canyon Nature Preserve was created by and is open to the public due to the generosity of Jim and Faye Lacefield. They initially bought 40 acres at the head of the canyon and gradually added acreage, so that the preserve now contains over 700 acres. A ten-mile trail system allows visitors to enjoy the property, and a narrow vehicle path provides access for the handicapped and elderly.

The site contains a great diversity of geological formations and natural communities. The brow of the canyon provides views of a

Little River–like canyon and cliffs. Impressive waterfalls plunge over the canyon rim, down past various layers of rock that record the geologic history of the area—ocean bottom covered by various successive layers of sand, mud, and the shells of microorganisms to form sandstone, shale, and limestone respectively. These layers were later covered by the sandy barrier islands that became the Hartselle sandstone cap of Little Mountain.

Visitors to Tree Fern Falls can walk under the waterfall and see the fossil skin of a giant *Lycopodium* (clubmoss) tree on the top of the waterfall's overhang. Other fossils of ancient corals, shellfish and crinoids—from when the area was a tropical sea—appear in the limestone along the Fossil Trail.

The natural communities house many rare species. The sandstone rim of the canyon supports dry forests of pines and oaks with some orchid bogs. Underneath the cliff overhangs is French's shooting star, a wildflower only found in Alabama on Little Mountain; its nearest populations are on similar sandstone in Arkansas and Illinois. The moist slopes formed from calcium-rich shale and limestone support diverse forests containing southern sugar maple, Ohio buckeye, and basswood. This forest contains an abundance of woodland wildflowers including trout lilies, blood root, trilliums, columbo, and Allegheny spurge.

On a narrow band of rubble below the cliffs grows the very rare tree, yellowwood. Unique and diverse wildflower gardens occur on the flat tops of some boulders on the slopes, and these "hanging gardens" have a greater lushness than the ground-level plants subjected to deer grazing. Floodplain forests contain tall stands of cane, making the creek's name most appropriate. The creek's many boulders, shoals, and pools harbor a healthy population of aquatic life.

Directions: From US 72 west of Tuscumbia, turn south on Co. Rd. 65 for seven miles. Turn right on Loop Rd. and proceed due west past chicken houses to the Lacefield home and parking area.

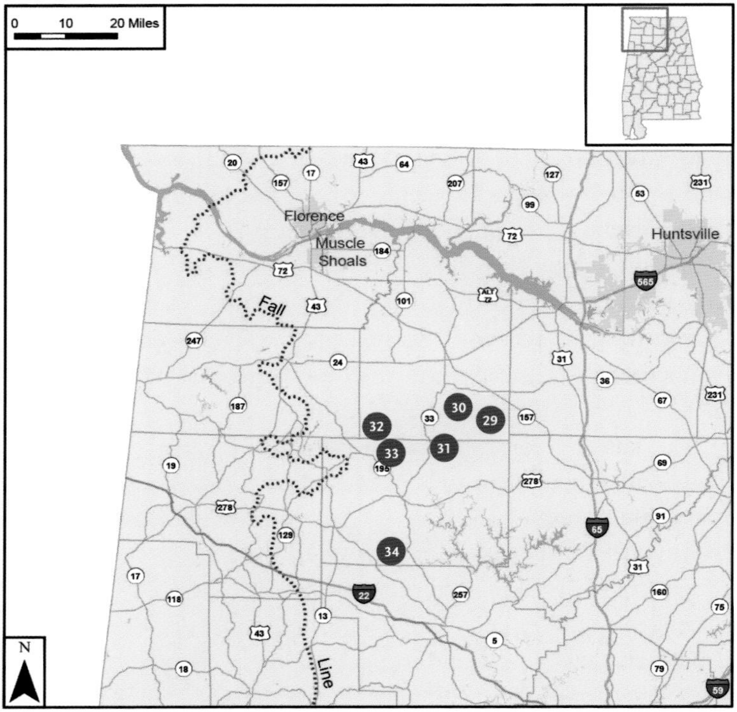

BANKHEAD NATIONAL FOREST AND SIPSEY WILDERNESS AREA

The William B. Bankhead National Forest is one of the most beloved natural areas of our state due to both its spectacular scenery and high biodiversity. The forest has been the site of both environmental abuse and some of the state's largest and most successful conservation efforts.

In the early 1900s, President Theodore Roosevelt set aside a few thousand acres of federal land as Alabama's first national forest. Later renamed in honor of Congressman Bankhead, this original forest contained some virgin or old-growth forest that can still be found in the Bee Branch area of the Sipsey Wilderness. During the Depression, the US Forest Service bought logged-over forests and eroded farmlands, expanding the national forest to 180,000 acres. Much of the old farmland was then planted with loblolly pines, while the logged-over areas naturally regenerated in pines and hardwoods.

Bankhead National Forest was managed using low-impact logging practices until the 1960s, when the Forest Service started clear-cutting the natural pine-hardwood portions and replacing them with loblolly pine plantations. This pine conversion sparked the first efforts to create an officially protected wilderness area in the state and save part of the Bankhead's natural landscape. Environmental and conservation groups banded together to collect scientific data supporting the protection of the Sipsey Wilderness from pine conversion, logging, and road building. These efforts culminated in 1975 with passage of the Eastern Wilderness Areas Act.

The boundary of the Sipsey Wilderness was later expanded, while additional areas of the forest—especially those with unique botanical and cultural values—were preserved. Several of these special areas are described below.

29 Flint Creek Botanical Area

34°21'53.75"N
87°10'41.65"W

This area includes the floodplain and slopes of the Flint Creek valley, which was carved from limestone. The calcium-rich hills and floodplain are covered with cove hardwood forest, including sugar maple and white ash. (A major cove hardwood indicator, the yellow buckeye, does not occur this far southwest in Alabama.) The area contains one of the most diverse and lush displays of springtime woodland wildflowers in the state. During the peak of bloom (normally late March-early April), visitors can see carpets of bent trillium, bluebells, bellworts, dwarf irises, and many other flowers.

DIRECTIONS: From Cullman, take AL 157 northwest toward Moulton. Turn left onto AL 36 at Speake. Take a left on Co. Rd. 81, and follow this road until it crosses Flint Creek. You can park at wide spots on the side of the road. If you cross the bridge you will notice a rough trail on your right that follows the creek bottom downstream. This short trail passes by some of the best wildflowers. Keep on the trail and don't trample the flowers!

30 High Town Path / Indian Tomb Hollow

34°22'59.82"N
87°13'42.68"W

Forest Service Roads 213 and 249 follow the Tennessee Divide, the "break" between the Tennessee and Black Warrior River drainages. The land on the north side grades into the hills and hollows of the north-facing escarpment of Sand Mountain (which meets the Tennessee River valley), while the land to the south drops into canyons of the Black Warrior River drainage. This streamless divide was a logical place for trade paths in prehistoric and early historic times, when bridge construction would have been impractical.

During historic times, a European–Native American trade path ran from the Native American village of High Town (near present-day Rome, Georgia) to Chickasaw villages near present-day Memphis, Tennessee. Even today, signs of Native American

Marker tree, Indian Tomb Hollow

travel camps can be found at springs and cliff overhangs along the way. Administratively protected national forest sites along the High Town Path contain several historic areas, including Indian Tomb Hollow and Native American clay pits in the Flint Creek Botanical Area. Indian Tomb Hollow includes living trees that were bent by Native Americans to mark turns in trails. One such tree, resembling a football goal post, was bent to mark the site of a bloody battle between the Chickasaws and Creeks.

Traveling down the access road from this goal post–like marker tree will take you over a limestone-bedded creek and past a runoff diversion canal; the canal was built by slaves during the antebellum period when a landowner tried to farm this area. You will next reach a place just below the canyon's sandstone walls that displays one of the best stands of old-growth cove hardwood in the state. The stand's rich, sandstone-based soil has never been eroded, giving you the feeling of walking on potting soil. This small patch of forest includes some giant, champion-sized sugar maples, beeches, white ashes, and cucumber magnolias.

Directions: The High Town Path is reached by taking AL 33 south from Moulton. Climb the mountain slope and then either go west on the Path (by taking a right on FS 213) or go east (by staying on AL 33 and taking a left on FS 249.)

Indian Tomb Hollow can be reached by going north on FS 264 from the High Town Path (FS 249). However, the most direct way to get there is to travel west on AL 36 and, after passing the Flint Creek Botanical Area turnoff, take a left on Co. Rd. 86. After entering the national forest, stop and park at a blocked-off road just to the north of Gillespie Creek. Walk down the road to a wide area near its head. The marker tree is in the forest to the right, while the old-growth forest stand is up the slope to the left.

31 Brushy Fork Drainage

34°17'40.15"N
87°16'19.98"W

The Brushy Fork Drainage includes some magnificent canyons along the Brushy Fork of the Sipsey Fork of the Black Warrior River. The old Brushy Fork Roadless Area is still relatively intact, although many of the ridge tops have been converted to pine plantations. Regardless, the canyons around the Brushy Fork are as impressive as those in the better known Sipsey Wilderness, and they are filled with similar beech-hemlock forest. Much like the Sipsey Wilderness drainage, the clean, free-flowing Brushy Fork provides habitat for many endangered mussel species.

A small developed recreation area and trail are found at Brushy Lake. The lake border includes bald cypress, which is a Coastal Plain tree, but no records of them being planted here exist. A visitor can thus stand in one spot and see both rocky hemlock canyons and bald cypress trees—a truly unique view. If you portage around the dam during the wet times of the year, you can canoe down the Brushy Fork to the FS 255 bridge; there are other canoe access points along this stream as well. Although a canoe trip offers the best opportunity to enjoy the area's scenery, there are also rough trails to attractions such as Sougahoagdee Falls.

DIRECTIONS: The Brushy Fork Drainage area can most easily be seen at Brushy Lake, which is reached by taking AL 33 south from Moulton. You will see the Warrior Mountains Trading Post on your left at the junction of AL 33 and AL 36. Keep going south on Hwy. 33 and then turn left onto Co. Rd. 70. This windy route passes by the old log Pine Torch Church before the lake is reached.

The Sougahoagdee Falls area can be reached by taking FS 245 west and southwest from Brushy Lake; take a right on FS 255 and follow it until it crosses the Brushy Fork. Park at one of the wide spots along the road. Walk upstream along the west bank of the creek via the rough trail (and bushwhacking) until you reach a tributary that you can follow upstream to its canyon head and Sougahoagdee Falls.

The northern end of the old Brushy Fork Roadless Area is accessed by traveling south on AL 33 and turning right onto the High Town Path (FS 249) before the Brushy Lake turnoff is reached.

32 Sipsey Headwaters and Kinlock Area

34°18'27.70"N
87°30'11.64"W

The headwaters of the Sipsey Fork are located on Forest Service lands north of the Sipsey Wilderness. One special area within the headwaters is the Montgomery Creek drainage. This area has limestone springs as well as floodplains dominated by stands of bald cypress. Again, these trees may have been planted here, but there is no such record. There are also stands of white pine, which *we know* were planted here. However, some local people claim that white pines grew here naturally prior to these plantings. If true, this would be the only place in Alabama where white pines are native.

The protected Kinlock cultural area is full of historic sites and road corridors, including the home site of legendary Aunt Jenny Brooks. The story goes that, during the Civil War, a band of Home Guard came into the area and killed her husband and eldest son because they were suspected of aiding the Union. The now widowed Mrs. Brooks swore revenge, and over the next 30 years she and her family tracked down the men and killed them, one by one. Jenny Brooks's legend highlights the unique history of the Bankhead area, especially the Winston County portion. After Alabama seceded from the Union, the citizens of Winston County met at Looney's Tavern and decided to, in turn, secede from Alabama. The county became known as the "Free State of Winston" and sent many men to fight for the Union; others tried to remain neutral and were persecuted by the Home Guard. For years, the story of the Free State of Winston has been told in a play at Looney's Tavern Park near Double Springs.

The primary attraction of the Kinlock area is the Kinlock Rock Shelter. Hollows or shallow caves have been carved into many of the Bankhead's sandstone cliffs by the forces of erosion. Such dry cliff shelters were the homes of prehistoric Native Americans during the Archaic Period (see Russell Cave National Monument, previously described). They also served as ceremonial sites for the later Mississippian Period mound builders (see Moundville Archaeological Park, described below).

Kinlock Rock Shelter is one of the largest cliff shelters in the Bankhead, having a mansion-size feel to it. The site was heavily used during the Mississippian Period, as evidenced by the *petroglyphs* (rock carvings) of birds' feet and strange symbols, including crosses representing the four corners of the earth.

The Kinlock area provides water to the short (but high-volume) Kinlock Falls located nearby, just inside the Sipsey Wilderness boundary.

DIRECTIONS: To reach the Montgomery Creek area, take AL 33 south from Moulton and turn right on FS 237. The gate may be closed, so walk the road west down into the creek bottom.

The Kinlock area is best reached by following Co. Rd. 6/60 west off AL 33 (about halfway between Moulton and Double Springs). The turn is marked with signs for the Sipsey River Recreation Area. Stay on this road (past the recreation area) until you reach a T intersection. Take a right onto FS 210. Before the road makes a sharp left curve and crosses a significant creek, look for roadside parking on the right; Kinlock Falls lies behind this parking area. Continue over the creek bridge to a spring box on your left; just past this spring is FS 204. Park off to the side of the gate and walk until you see an old road going off to the right. This abandoned road leads to a canyon rim, where a trail takes you down to the Kinlock Rock Shelter.

33 Sipsey Wilderness and Its Wild and Scenic River

34°17'07.27"N
87°23'56.22"W

At nearly 26,000 acres, the Sipsey Wilderness is one of the largest wilderness areas east of the Mississippi River. Its official wilderness designation protects some of the wildest habitats (and inhabitants) in our state.

The canyons of the Sipsey Wilderness truly contain an "enchanted forest." Each canyon, with its steep sandstone cliffs, shows a waterfall at its head during the wetter times of the year; such a cool microclimate allows the eastern hemlock to thrive far south of its expected range. Standing in one of these canyons

West Sipsey Fork of the Black Warrior River, Bankhead National Forest

makes you feel as if you were looking at a set for a *Lord of the Rings* movie or the stage for a Wagnerian opera.

The Sipsey Wilderness has miles of trails and many places to visit, but one of the most interesting is the Thompson Creek–Bee Branch area. Following Thompson Creek on the northwest side of the wilderness, the trail corridor contains a unique mixture of sandstone cliffs (above) in close proximity with limestone outcrops (below). The limestone supports chinquapin oak and other alkaline soil–loving hardwoods, with a very rich springtime wildflower mix; a stone's throw away is beech-hemlock forest on acidic sandstone-derived soils. As you enter the wilderness on the

Thompson Creek Trail you can take a short cut (about three miles from the Thompson Creek trailhead) to the Bee Branch by taking a left on a rough trail up White Oak Branch (the first stream encountered). This trail soon drops over the ridge into the Bee Branch drainage. Follow the trail down the drainage and cross the branch. You will soon hit the main trail to the Bee Branch area. Take a left on the main trail and follow it to the head of the canyon.

Bee Branch is very special because it contains stands of virgin timber—giant hemlocks, white oaks, and a tulip poplar tree that takes the combined arms of four to six people to reach around. An adjacent canyon to the east, called Buck Rough, houses equally impressive ancient timber.

If you skip the short cut to Bee Branch and follow the Thompson Creek Trail toward the Sipsey Fork and the mouth of Bee Branch, you will see a hole in a cliff known as the Needle Eye. This hole or "window" was formed by erosion; as its top becomes thinner and the hole becomes wider, it could eventually become an arch or natural bridge formed by nonstream forces. (More details about these types of formations are contained in the Natural Bridge Park description later in this book.)

A much shorter hike to old-growth timber starts at the Sipsey River Recreation Area on the south end of the wilderness. While the partially paved trails of the recreation area traverse great examples of "enchanted forest" canyons, seeing the old-growth portion takes more work. Head upstream from the parking lot on the west side of the river and under the large road bridge, then take a left on a rough trail that follows a small tributary called Turkey Creek. While walking between the creek and the canyon walls on the south side of the creek, notice a cliff shelter with a mortar hole in a rock; the mortar was used by Native Americans during the Archaic Period to grind acorns into meal. An old stripped car (from the modern period) that went too fast on the nearby road lies close. The route passes by many examples of giant old-growth hemlock, although many have been damaged or killed by windstorms and possibly air pollution. Be sure to admire the two waterfalls near the head of the canyon, where tributaries plunge down.

With its headwaters in the Sipsey Wilderness and other forested lands farther north, the West Sipsey Fork of the Black Warrior River is Alabama's only federally designated Wild and Scenic River. This designation protects the river from being dammed or degraded. (Many of its larger tributaries have been given the Wild and Scenic designation as well.) The clean, free-flowing condition of this river (like the nearby but less protected Brushy Fork) provides vital habitat for many species of endangered mussels. The river is also a stronghold for the threatened flattened musk turtle, which is endemic to the upper Black Warrior River drainage. In addition, the threatened streak sorus fern grows only on the cliffs surrounding the streams of the Sipsey Fork drainage.

The river is best explored by canoe in the wetter times of the year. Canoes can be launched at the Sipsey River Recreation Area and taken out at an official (but steep) take-out where the river crosses AL 33. This stretch is about 10 miles long and mostly gentle, with one Class II rapid. A tributary area below the wilderness, Caney Creek Canyon, is well worth exploring by land. While the ridges have largely been converted to pine plantations, the canyons contain old-growth beech-hemlock forests, high cliffs, and waterfalls.

Just north of US 278, the Natural Bridge Recreation Area has a nice natural rock formation for the public to enjoy.

DIRECTIONS: The Sipsey Wilderness and Sipsey Fork can be accessed at several places. One of the easiest access points is the Sipsey River Recreation Area, whose location was noted above in the directions to the Kinlock area. Here are trails north into the Sipsey Wilderness, plus the above-mentioned canoe launch.

The Thompson Creek–Bee Branch area of the Sipsey Wilderness is reached by continuing north on FS 210 from the Kinlock area, then right onto FS 208. This road dead-ends at the Thompson Creek Trailhead.

The Caney Creek Falls area can be reached from Double Springs by going north and west on AL 195. Take a right on Co. Rd. 2; follow it until you encounter (on your left) a well-used roadside parking spot beside a gate on an old logging road. (There are several roads with gates, but this one stands out; if you drive past a chicken house, you have gone too far.) Once you have parked at the correct spot without blocking the gate, follow the old road behind the gate, which will lead down into the canyon and falls area.

The Natural Bridge Recreation Area is located off Co. Rd. 63 north of its junction with US 278, east of Double Springs.

34 Southern Bankhead National Forest

34°00'43.39"N
87°22'46.34"W

The Forest Service lands south of US 278 are highly fragmented. A few such areas contain remnant longleaf pine in an Appalachian Plateau environment, which is certainly unique. This general area also contains the Rocky Plains, which were scoured of their soil when the Tennessee River—blocked during the Ice Ages from flowing north—flowed south toward what is now Mobile Bay. Although other theories explain their origin, the Rocky Plains were once an extensive area of flat surface rocks full of prickly pear cactus and, most likely, rare sandstone outcrop or glade plants. While the uplands were desert dry, the stream corridors were just the opposite—bottomland swamps. Occupying one of these swamps, Kaiser Bottoms was the site of the slave-built plantation of the infamous Dr. Kaiser, who sent the Home Guard to capture and kill those who did not want to fight for the Confederacy. (Remember the Aunt Jenny Brooks story?) He was eventually killed by the people he persecuted.

Unfortunately, the unique Rocky Plains have largely been lost to strip mining. We cannot even tell you where you can find an example of the Rocky Plains today. A good conservation research project would be to examine the scattered Forest Service lands of the area to see if any of this unique rocky environment still exists.

Some of the Forest Service lands of the southern Bankhead National Forest are located along the banks of Alabama Power's Smith Lake hydropower reservoir, such as the Houston, Corinth, and Clear Creek areas. The Houston Jail can be seen on the roadside going into the Houston Recreation Area. This primitive jail is worth a stop in itself, and the recreation area beyond is a good place to enjoy the lake and the surrounding forest. The Clear Creek Recreation Area contains water activities as well as canyons and an interpretive trail.

Nearby, within the boundaries of the national forest, lies Camp McDowell, an Episcopal church camp offering environmental education programs. Sitting on the banks of Clear Creek, the camp contains trails leading to patches of virgin old-growth beech-hemlock forest. The bases of canyon walls feature an abundance of glow worm insect larvae (*dismalites*), which use their bioluminescence to capture nighttime prey. Contact the camp if you are interested in visiting, or if you have a child who would like to attend an environmental education session.

DIRECTIONS: Houston Recreation Area can be reached from Double Springs by taking US 278 east. After a few miles, make a right turn onto Co. Rd. 63, another right onto Co. Rd. 61, and a final right onto Co. Rd. 61A.

Both Camp McDowell and the Clear Creek Recreation Area are reached by taking AL 195 between Double Springs and Jasper; follow the signs off this route to each place. Co. Rd. 29, west of its junction with AL 195, will take you through some of the Rocky Plains country that is now largely strip mines and pine plantations. You will need a Forest Service map to explore the scattered Forest Service lands found around AL 195.

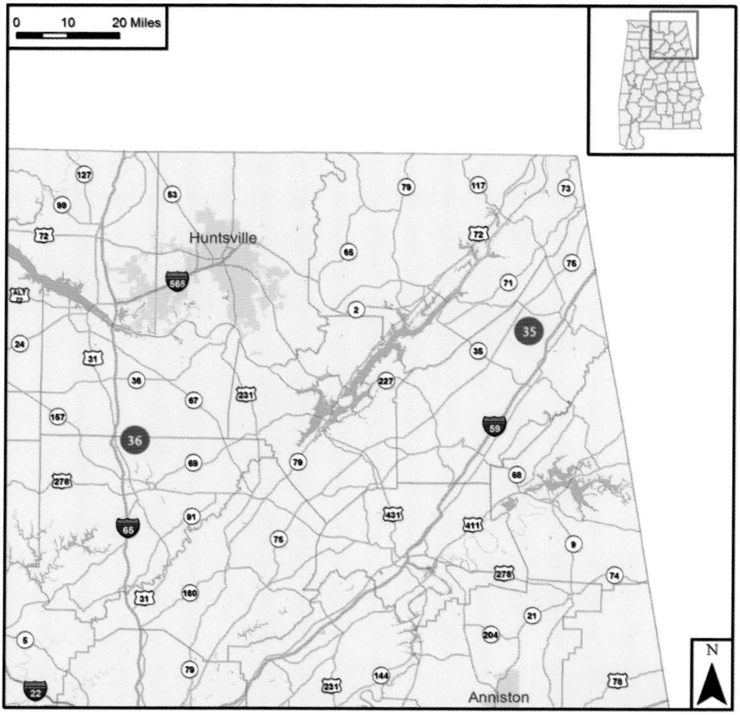

SAND MOUNTAIN AREA

Sand Mountain is the largest plateau in Alabama; some people say it is the largest unbroken section of plateau in the world. Starting at Raccoon Mountain near Chattanooga, Tennessee, it broadens greatly going south to near Birmingham and west to the Bankhead National Forest, where it fragments into a multitude of small, rugged canyons. Before the Civil War, most of the poor sandy soils on the flat top of Sand Mountain (and adjacent Lookout Mountain) remained thickly forested and were only used for running hogs and other farm animals.

The development of artificial fertilizers during the late 1800s created a farming boom on the sandy, easily tillable soils forming the broad tops of the plateaus. Railroads purposely developed agricultural boomtowns here; to create Cullman, those railroads "imported" German farmers, led by the Bavarian revolutionary, Johann Cullmann. (Yes, his last name was purposely misspelled for the town and county.) While much of the old farmland has since been converted to pasture, chicken houses and tomato farms still dominate the landscape of Sand Mountain.

Most of the remaining natural habitats on Sand Mountain are restricted to its sides and canyons, which cut into the mountain's top. While some of Sand Mountain's natural treasures were previously described in the Guntersville Lake section of this book, the majority will be covered below.

35 Chitwood Barrens Preserve (access is restricted)

This 53-acre preserve is owned and managed by the Nature Conservancy. Located on the top of Sand Mountain in DeKalb County, it was established to protect a population of the endangered green pitcher plant. Its sandstone barrens support many other rare species, including rose gentian, longleaf sunflower, Harper's love vine, and Little River Canyon onion. Large post oaks are distributed across the grassy barrens in a savanna-like fashion.

The barrens are based on sandstone rock lying close to or at the surface, which helps to inhibit thick tree growth; it also creates a dryness that encourages natural fire to eliminate other woody vegetation. The Nature Conservancy currently is restoring the site through periodic controlled burns.

Due to its sensitive nature, visiting Chitwood Barrens Preserve is controlled by the Nature Conservancy's Birmingham, Alabama, office.

36 Hurricane Creek Park

34°17'12.54"N
86°53'40.23"W

This formerly private, 67-acre park was established by the late conservation-minded William "Buddy" Rodgers. Donated to the state of Alabama, it is now administered by the city of Cullman. The park offers a few miles of hiking through some spectacular rock formations. Starting at the top, you will wind your way down into the canyon of Hurricane Creek, passing by a small natural bridge, giant boulders, and passages through the canyon wall. The park formerly had a cable-powered cart (resembling a mining car) that lifted you out of the canyon when you were ready to come back out. You'll certainly miss having the cable car on the steep return trek! If you plan to camp, call ahead for a reservation to make sure you can get one of the limited spots. And remember that the park is closed on Mondays and Sunday mornings.

Up-to-date information can be gleaned from the park's website.

DIRECTIONS: From downtown Cullman, take US 31 north out of town. The park is on the right.

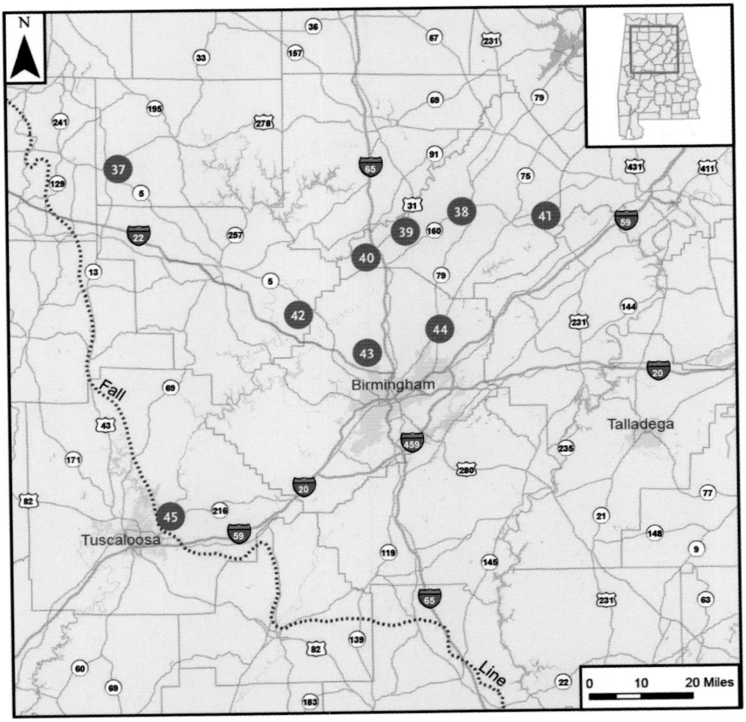

NORTH-CENTRAL ALABAMA AREA

The Appalachian Plateau of north-central Alabama is particularly rich in natural areas—public, private, historic, and riverine. Here are some more to check out.

37 Natural Bridge Park

34°05'36.27"N
87°36'07.05"W

Above: The natural bridge at Natural Bridge Park

Opposite: Indian Head peeks through the hemlocks, Natural Bridge Park

This small private park lies at the headwaters of the New River, which is in turn the headwaters of the true Sipsey River, which forms the Sipsey Swamp downstream before emptying into the Tombigbee River. (Be aware that the name Sipsey is applied to many places in northwestern Alabama, including the Sipsey Fork of the Black Warrior River and the Sipsey River proper.) The park has good beech-hemlock forest and prominent canyon walls, including Indian Head Rock. The park's centerpiece is the largest natural bridge in the state of Alabama (and possibly in the nation.) This unsupported rock span between canyon walls is truly impressive not only because of its size but its smooth, delicate-looking features. (Visitors are not allowed to climb on it, but they can view its splendor well enough from below.)

The natural bridge at Natural Bridge Park

Natural bridges are formed by water eroding the less resistant layers or types of rocks (like limestone) from beneath more resistant types (like sandstone). Similar-appearing formations, called natural arches—such as Needle Eye in the Sipsey Wilderness—are produced by other forces of erosion and weathering. Both natural bridges and arches are associated with the canyon country of plateaus. The landforms of the famous Colorado Plateau and our Appalachian Plateau are similar except that western landforms are larger and more exposed by lack of vegetation in a desert environment.

Directions: Natural Bridge Park is located on US 278 in the community of Natural Bridge, west of Double Springs.

Sweetshrub at Natural Bridge Park

Mayapples dominate the herb layer during springtime, Natural Bridge Park

38 Mulberry and Locust Forks

33°59'51.65"N
86°36'06.06"W

The Mulberry and Locust Forks of the Black Warrior River are two of the largest free-flowing rivers of our state. While both are prized by white-water enthusiasts, they also have more gentle stretches where canyon cliffs, boulders, and other scenery can be enjoyed from a canoe.

A great place to visit the Locust Fork is at Swann Covered Bridge. Here you will see the historic wooden bridge, cliffs, and water tupelo (a swamp tree) growing next to white-water shoals—a unique scene for sure. A mile-long walk downstream leads to a large waterfall in the river. If you canoe from Swann Bridge down to AL 160 (a little over two miles), be sure to portage around the falls. Below the falls is a cliff with an overhang, making you feel like you are canoeing into a cave. A large natural sandbar beach lies across the river from the overhang.

Near the Locust Fork in the Oneonta area is 83-acre Palisades Park, which contains some forest trails and exposed cliffs popular with climbers. Created by impounding the Blackburn Fork of the Locust Fork south of Oneonta, Inland Lake has some interesting cliff formations, including a large natural window/arch along its shore. Much of the land around Inland Lake is owned by the Birmingham Waterworks Board for the purpose of maintaining a water quality buffer. The lake can certainly be canoed, but a power boat will allow you to see more of it (and more quickly).

Directions: The Mulberry Fork can be viewed or canoed from the bridges around Garden City, which is reached by taking I-65 exit 287 and following US 31 northeast. River access is from US 31 and Co. Rd. 26.

To reach Swann Covered Bridge, go to the junction of AL 169 and AL 79 west of Cleveland. From this intersection, travel north on AL

A good canoe landing on the Locust Fork is found at the US 231 bridge crossing north of Cleveland

79 for one mile and make a left onto Swann Bridge Rd. If the gate is closed, park beside it and walk down the dirt road to the river. You can enjoy the river from this area or walk the trail downstream about a mile to the waterfall.

The Mulberry Fork and Locust Fork can both be canoed between various bridge crossings, including some of those mentioned above.

Palisades Park is reached by taking US 231 north from Oneonta to the park's turnoff sign.

The access area/boat landing on Inland Lake is easily found by going southwest from Oneonta on AL 75 and then following the signs to the boat landing. It happens to be on Boat Landing Rd.

39 Blount Springs

33°55'51.70"N
86°47'49.05"W

This mineral spring was the site of a popular resort during the 1800s, when people flocked to such springs for their supposed health benefits. The neat/disgusting thing about this particular spring is just how visible (and smelly) the sulfurous deposits are. Remains of concrete catchment basins can still be seen; some contain exotic-looking purple growths of sulfur-loving organisms.

Directions: Take I-65 exit 287 and follow US 31 northeast through the Blount Springs area to Co. Rd. 7. At this junction you will see a historic marker describing the spring's history. Turn right on Co. Rd. 7 and look for a crude pull-off on your left. Follow the old roadbed from the pull-off down into the creek bottom where the spring boxes are located.

Sulphur spring at Blount Springs

40 Rickwood Caverns State Park

33°52'28.73"N
86°51'38.60"W

This state park lies on limestone at the southern end of the Sequatchie valley formations. The park contains a natural cave with impressive formations; it also features albino blind cave fish and other life adapted to total darkness. The Fossil Mountain nature trail passes through a dry limestone karst landscape full of sinkholes and boulders covered with resurrection fern. The mixed hardwood–red cedar forest has an abundance of chinquapin oak, shagbark hickory, and red cedar, which are all lime-loving species.

DIRECTIONS: From I-65 take exit 284 to AL 160 west and follow the signs to the park.

Fossil Mountain trail, Rickwood Caverns State Park

Left and Opposite: **Fossil Mountain trail, Rickwood Caverns State Park**

Below: **Stalactites and stalagmites, Rickwood Caverns State Park**

41 Chandler Mountain

33°55'20.54"N
86°18'26.51"W

Chandler Mountain is a small peninsular extension off Sand Mountain. While the Chandler Mountain Plateau is best known for growing fine tomatoes, the mountain has some equally fine natural areas along its forested brows and slopes.

Horse Pens 40 is a private 120-acre recreation park with an impressive boulder field, all traversed by some short trails. (Some of the rocks in the park have small signs next to them that provide names based on what their shapes resemble.)

Nearby, the Nature Conservancy has established the 80-acre Gulf Creek Canyon Preserve. The preserve contains xeric (very dry) oak-hickory-pine forest on the upper slopes and canyon brow; more mesic hardwood forest grows on the lower sites. The old-growth forest provides habitat for Cumberland azaleas and decumbent trilliums. The area offers views of the spectacular scenery that Gulf Creek has created, carving into the south escarpment of Chandler Mountain as it plunges into the Ridge and Valley below. You can hear the rushing stream while admiring the rock cliffs across the canyon and the bucolic farmland in the valley below.

On the north side of Chandler Mountain is 1,700-acre Camp Sumatanga. Owned by the United Methodist Church, the camp is open to the public during daylight hours; it is available for group events as well. The camp has a lake at the base of the mountain, and its upper end supports a healthy array of marsh vegetation; several trails head up the mountain escarpment. And there are boulders in the Chigger Hollow portion that almost rival those at Horse Pens 40.

Directions: Horse Pens 40 and Camp Sumatanga can both be reached by taking exit 166 off I-91 near Ashville; follow US 231 northwest and take a right on Co. Rd. 35. To reach Horse Pens 40, follow Co. Rd. 35 until you turn right on Co. Rd. 42; at the top of the mountain you will see an entrance sign on your right. To reach Camp Sumatanga, continue on Co. Rd. 35 past Co. Rd. 42 and take a right on Co. Rd. 44 (Sumatanga Rd.). This road leads directly into the camp.

42 Blackwater Creek

33°43'43.46"N
87°05'24.89"W

Blackwater Creek runs through Walker County down to the Bankhead Lock and Dam impoundment on the Black Warrior River. The canyon of this free-flowing creek supports abundant fish and wildlife, as well as natural beauty. While that beauty can be glimpsed from bridges, it is best explored by canoe. And while most of the surrounding hills have been clear-cut and converted to pine plantations, the corporate landowners should be given credit for leaving a large buffer along the stream valley. The forest of the buffer has a cove hardwood feel about it, with lots of bigleaf magnolia.

Southwest of Blackwater Creek is the Horse Creek Rail Trail, running from US 78 to the city of Dora. Although the trail passes mainly through old pine plantations and rapidly developing lands, it still shows some natural values, especially around the lake of the city park. The northwest end of the trail is located near the Alabama Mining Museum, which houses important exhibits on the area's local history.

Directions: Blackwater Creek is reached by taking US 78 southwest from Jasper; take a left onto AL 69 and follow it to the creek. Here

Dora Municipal Park near the Alabama Mining Museum

you can either slither down the steep bank on the north side of the bridge to view the river or put in a canoe. Your take-out will be eight miles downstream (on US 78) at a boat launch on the Mulberry Fork.

Dora Municipal Park and the portion of Horse Creek Rail Trail behind it can be reached by following Co. Rd. 81 west off US 78. The turnoff is marked with a sign for the Alabama Mining Museum.

43 Lower Village Creek, Five Mile Creek, and Others

33°38'16.48"N
86°55'00.11"W

Village Creek runs through Birmingham—which means that it suffers from severe loads of pollution, litter, and other insults.

Everything winds up in Bayview Lake on the west side of town. Despite the pollution, Bayview Lake supports heron rookeries and attracts flocks of winter waterfowl. And the best stretch of Village Creek, nature-wise, lies below the dam that created the lake.

Below that dam, Village Creek flows through a different world. The creek carved a gorge containing the southernmost population of eastern hemlocks in the United States. Here the hemlocks reside with beech trees and other cove hardwood species, such as bigleaf magnolias. Fortunately, much of the lower Village Creek corridor or greenway is now protected by the Freshwater Land Trust and can be accessed at various bridge crossings.

Similarly, the greenway of the Five Mile Creek area (north of lower Village Creek) can be accessed from a canoe trail along that stream. Canoeists and "tubers" on Five Mile Creek will pass nice shoals, gravel bars, and low cliffs nestled in the surrounding hardwood forest. The city of Brookside believes in the importance of the greenway *so much* that they bought a canoe company to encourage your visit. Just call ahead to schedule a float trip.

DIRECTIONS: Lower Village Creek and Five Mile Creek are best accessed via bridge crossings, as described above. The city of Brookside maintains a website for its canoe company.

44 Turkey Creek Falls

33°42'09.61"N
86°41'48.63"W

Turkey Creek Falls is a 462-acre Forever Wild property in the Shale Basin of northeast Jefferson County. In addition to the low height (but high volume) falls, this portion of the creek has lots of cliffs, boulders, and scenic shoals. When facing downstream at the falls, you will notice a mostly dry stream channel to the left of a large boulder and the remains of a rock wall. The wall is all that's left of an old watermill that powered bellows from one of the area's earliest ironworks.

You can park at either end of the property or across the road from the falls. A paved trail passes through the woods by the parking area at the western end of the property. However, we suggest that you simply park at the east end and walk along the quiet road—just keep an eye out for the occasional car. This route parallels the streamside shoals downstream to the falls.

Another local conservation purchase governed by the Freshwater Land Trust includes a Turkey Creek spring run formed by Tapawingo Springs. This old recreation spring—an important suburban swimming facility during the 1950s—has crystal clear water filled with aquatic vegetation and snails. It is home to rare and threatened aquatic species such as the vermilion darter (endemic to Turkey Creek) and the watercress darter (transplanted there for its protection).

Directions: From Birmingham, Turkey Creek Falls is reached by taking AL 79 northeast toward Pinson. Take a left at Co. Rd. 131 and a right onto Turkey Creek Rd.

Tapawingo Springs is accessible by appointment with the Freshwater Land Trust.

45 Holt Lake

33°15'14.42"N
87°26'57.90"W

The southernmost end of the Appalachian Plateau lies just northwest of Tuscaloosa, Alabama. Here the plateau meets the Coastal Plain, and their biological resources mix. Tuscaloosa is located on the Fall Line where the older, tougher rocks of the uplands meet the largely low and rockless Coastal Plain. True to their name, Fall Line rivers and streams are marked by falls, shoals, and rapids. And because such falls are hindrances to navigation, cities and towns (like Tuscaloosa and Northport on the Black Warrior River) were founded at these places.

Over the past 200 years, locks and dams have been constructed at or near the Fall Line of most southeastern rivers in order to allow continued navigation. Impoundment has flooded the biodiverse rapids and shoals, eliminating the habitat needed by many aquatic species and driving them to extinction.

Although many shoreline habitats have been destroyed as well, some areas have been set aside and protected, especially along the Holt Lake section of the Black Warrior River. Rocky Branch Public Day Use Area is a true transition zone, with populations of both Alabama croton (Appalachian Plateau) and dwarf palmetto (Coastal Plain), plus healthy cove hardwood habitats. A nature trail through the park will give any visitor a good introduction to the rich cove habitats and shale outcrops; primitive camping sites are also available.

Across the river, Deerlick Park has hiking trails and camping too. Burchfield Branch Park (below Bankhead Lock and Dam) has no trails but contains scenic forests and a nice waterfall, and it is a good place to see bald eagles during winter.

A favorite stream for Tuscaloosa canoeists is Hurricane Creek, which empties into the impounded Black Warrior River below Holt Dam. Along this stream, Tuscaloosa County has established the 259-acre Hurricane Creek Park. The park offers canoeing and swimming opportunities as well as hiking trails along beautiful shoals and rock formations, including some boulders with bands of conglomerate rock. Bigleaf magnolia grows in this small canyon environment, with an understory of river cane and mountain laurel.

Across the Black Warrior from Hurricane Creek lies the Yellow Creek drainage, which contains Lakes Nichol and Harris, which are the city of Tuscaloosa reservoirs. This area also has a mixture of Appalachian Plateau and Coastal Plain species.

The Bankhead Lock and Dam area, which is upstream from Holt Lake, currently has publicly accessible lands only at various fishing camps and at the Mulberry Fork WMA (acquired through a 94-year Forever Wild lease). Bankhead Lake lies in the Shale Basin and has some nice sandstone cliffs and forested slopes. The 33,000-acre Mulberry Fork WMA contains some mining areas and extensive pine plantations, but the drains, hollows, and the slopes along the river feature rocky bluffs, natural hardwood forests, and mixed forests that are well worth visiting.

Directions: To reach Rocky Branch Public Use Area, take AL 216 north from Tuscaloosa toward Brookwood and look for the sign marking a left turn into the park.

To reach Deerlick Creek Park, take US 82 (McFarland Blvd.) through Tuscaloosa to Northport; turn right on Rice Mine Rd. and follow the signs to the park entrance (about 14 miles from US 82).

To reach Burchfield Branch Park from I-20/59, use exit 115 (Allison-Bonnett Memorial Dr./Warrior River Rd. in Hueytown); head northwest to Lock 17 Rd. and follow the signs to the park.

To reach Mulberry Fork WMA from Jasper, follow AL 69 south and then take a left onto Co. Rd. 6, which passes through the WMA before reaching the river. Just southeast of the WMA, a marina offers good boat access.

INTERIOR LOW PLATEAU

The Interior Low Plateau stretches from Alabama to southern Illinois, all at elevations between the Appalachians and the Coastal Plain. Much of the Interior Low Plateau is underlain by highly erodible limestone that forms valleys, basins, and karst or sinkhole landscapes full of caves. Other portions are less worn down and more rugged due to the presence of erosion-resistant chert.

The Alabama portion of the Interior Low Plateau is largely flat to rolling Tennessee valley lands. Much of the original valley forest was dominated by various oaks; the clearing of those forests created the valley's vast red-soiled farmlands. Remnants of that forest are found in woodlots and protected areas like Wheeler National Wildlife Refuge. Also, there are limestone cliffs, springs, and caves that retain calcium-loving cove hardwood forests with a great diversity of wildflowers. Open, rocky limestone environments feature glades or barrens supporting prairie-like environments of red cedar, grasses, and succulent plants. Other sites, including bottomland hardwoods and tupelo swamps, retain natural vegetation because they flood frequently or are kept wet by springs. Some areas, like the upper Elk River drainage and the extreme northwestern tip of Alabama, have cherty hills with stair-step waterfalls; these landscapes are covered with upland hardwoods and pines.

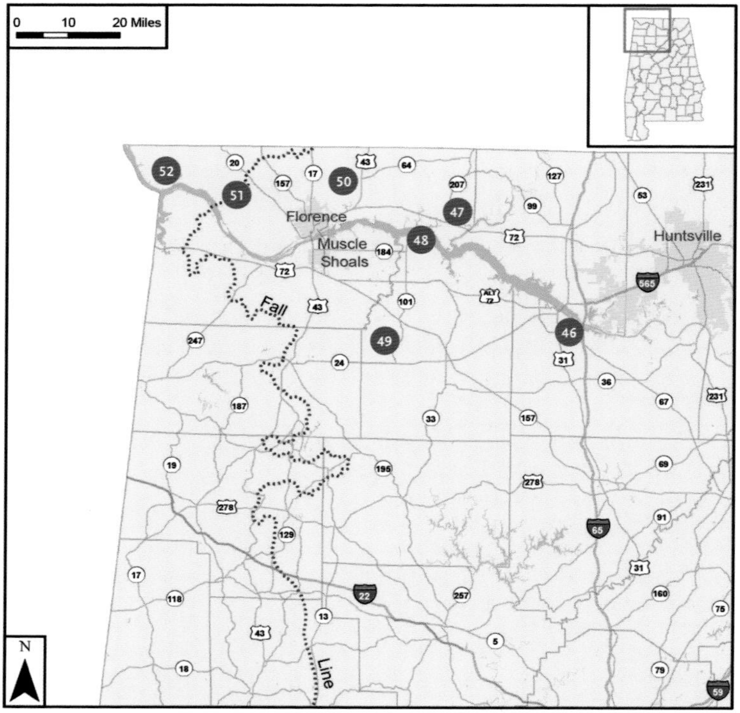

HIGHLAND RIM AND TENNESSEE RIVER VALLEY AREA

This area offers a healthy mix of outdoor adventures, from observing waterfowl to seeing bats and exploring caves. Along the way, be sure to check out the strange assemblage of prairie plants at various limestone glades.

46 Wheeler National Wildlife Refuge

34°32'49.06"N
86°57'04.12"W

The 35,000-acre Wheeler National Wildlife Refuge includes the lands around the middle of Wheeler Lake, a TVA hydroelectric reservoir created in the 1930s by the impoundment of the Tennessee River. The refuge comprises 19,000 acres of land and 16,000 acres of water, supporting the largest and most diverse concentration of waterfowl in the state. Backwater sloughs are drained in the summer to encourage the wetland plants favored by these birds; the sloughs are reflooded in the winter to facilitate their feeding. And 3,500 acres of the refuge are actively farmed, with farmers paying their rent by leaving 25 percent of the harvestable crops in the field to be consumed by the waterfowl.

Creation of the reservoir drowned much of the Tennessee valley's bottomland hardwood forest, although some still remains as part of the 10,000 acres of bottomland and upland forests of the refuge. The refuge also contains about 3,000 acres of pine plantations planted on old farmlands. The refuge's varied landscape provides habitats for a variety of upland and wetland animal species, including the rare mourning warbler, which is seen during times of migration.

The short observatory trail at the refuge's visitor center and museum follows the border between upland and bottomland hardwood forest types. The trail leads to a climate-controlled waterfowl observatory with spotting scopes and speakers piping in the surrounding sounds of nature. Early morning and late afternoon are usually the best times for waterfowl viewing. During the winter months, you can see thousands of ducks blanketing the refuge's impoundments, including the one by the observatory. Duck species include mallard, American widgeon, pintail, ring-necked, canvasback, green-winged teal, and American coot. The surrounding fields support migratory Canada geese, snow geese, great blue herons, great egrets, marsh hawks, kestrels, and thousands of sandhill cranes. If you're lucky, you just might spot an endangered whooping crane among its sandhill crane cousins. These huge birds—the result of reintroduction efforts including the re-creation of migratory routes—are starting to winter at Wheeler Refuge.

Birding enthusiasts visiting the Wheeler Refuge/Decatur area should walk the dikes of the refuge's dewatering units. For example, the White Springs dewatering area is a great place to see canvasbacks, buffleheads, and black ducks. The best place to see both Canada and snow geese is from the boat launch on Limestone Bay. A large flock of white pelicans populates this area as well, plus some nesting bald eagles.

Different wetland habitats can be viewed at several places in the refuge. The Tom Atkins Cypress Swamp boardwalk takes visitors through a small cypress swamp planted in 1939. (Although not native to this specific area, cypresses are found on the Tennessee River not far downstream.) The cypress trees fit in well and have successfully reproduced around this man-made reservoir. The boardwalk is named after Tom Atkins, a remarkable man who worked on the refuge prior to World War II but lost his hands and eyes in an accident while training for the war. He returned to the refuge and performed his duties with the help of an assistant, who Atkins himself paid. Atkins eventually became refuge manager.

A natural tupelo swamp-bottomland hardwood forest can be viewed at the Beaverdam Boardwalk Trail on the north side of Wheeler Refuge. This swamp is fed by a spring that contains the rare pygmy sunfish. The misnamed Blackwell Swamp—really a treeless marsh—was created by the combination of humans and beavers flooding a tupelo forest. The upper end contains a dying tupelo stand whereas the rest is covered with giant lotus pads, fragrant water lilies, and other aquatic plants. To avoid thick vegetation, the area is best canoed in the winter. You will see plenty of beaver lodges and dams. Don't be surprised to hear their warning (to other beavers) of your approach, a strong tail slap on the water's surface.

If you canoe Blackwell Swamp you may see a member of the local population of alligators. A number of the formerly endangered reptiles were brought from Eufaula National Wildlife Refuge to Wheeler in the 1980s; the goal was to establish a population that would help control the beaver population. Some of the alligators have grown to 12 feet in length, and they have definitely reproduced. While there is a debate as to whether alligators ever naturally occurred at Wheeler, they fit in well with the local environment and now constitute one of the species' northernmost populations.

The uplands of Wheeler Refuge contain some limestone bluffs and caves, including the Rockhouse. Located on the north side of the Tennessee River, the Rockhouse was used in the filming of Disney's *Tom and Huck*. (The nearby antebellum town of Mooresville, which was also used in the film, can really add to that feeling of being in Mark Twain's world.) Some of the refuge's caves, such as Cave Spring, provide habitat for the endangered gray bat.

Near Wheeler Refuge lie the Swan Creek and Mallard-Fox Creek WMAs. These TVA-owned, state-managed lands contain wetland habitats similar to those in Wheeler. Swan Creek has tupelo swamps, bottomland hardwoods, and dewatering units while Mallard-Fox Creek has more open sloughs surrounded by planted bald cypress trees.

Another site worth seeing in the Decatur area is the Cook's Natural Science Museum. It features wildlife from the Tennessee valley, including threatened species, as well as more exotic displays. The museum's insect collection is used in training the employees of Cook's Pest Control Company.

North of the refuge in Athens is the start of the Limestone County rails-to-trails project. This trail runs north to the Tennessee state line, offering a long walking/biking opportunity.

Directions: The Wheeler Refuge Visitor Center is easily reached by taking exit 334 off I-65. From this exit take AL 67 west toward Decatur; the entrance to the visitor center will be on your left.

To find the Cook's Science Museum, continue on AL 67 west through Decatur. Take a right on US 31, then turn left onto 13th St. SE. The museum is located at the junction of 13th St. SE and 5th Ave. SE.

To reach the north side of Wheeler Refuge, continue going north on US 31 and cross over the Tennessee River. Just after the bridge you will see some picnic tables on your right. This is the western edge of Swan Creek WMA. Continue on US 31 and follow the signs to reach the heart of the WMA.

Across the highway from the above picnic area is the White Springs Unit of Wheeler Refuge. You can reach White Springs from Decatur by going north on US 31 across the previously mentioned bridge and then briefly continuing east on US 72. On your right you will see a gated road leading over a ditch and into an open field; the site is marked with one of the North Alabama Birding Trail signs. Park on the hard ground to the side of the road, making sure not to block the gate. From that point you can walk down the road a couple of hundred yards to the dikes of the Whitewater dewatering unit, which will be the marshy body of water on your left.

To find the goose viewing area at the boat launch on Limestone Bay, continue going east on US 72 from White Springs. This road will become I-565 when it passes under I-65; get off at exit 2 to Mooresville. Take a right off of the exit, and another right on the main road in front of Mooresville. After crossing the Limestone Creek bridge, look for Arrowhead Landing Rd. (marked with a "boat" symbol) to your left. Follow the gravel road down to the boat launch.

To reach the Rockhouse area, continue east from Mooresville on I-565 to exit 3. Take a right onto Greenbrier Rd., then a left on Swancott Rd. You will shortly cross Beaverdam Creek and make a right onto Rockhouse Rd. This road goes down to a rocky bluff line where you can park and walk into the Rockhouse, located just down the slope to your left.

To find the Beaverdam Swamp boardwalk, continue east on I-565 to exit 5. Take a right onto County Line Rd. and you will soon see a frontage road to your right. Follow this road west until it dead-ends into the parking lot for the boardwalk.

To reach Blackwell Swamp, continue going south on County Line Rd. and pass through its intersection with Swancott Rd. Continue on County Line Rd. until you see Blackwell Run Rd. This road passes by the north side (upper end) of the swamp; a road fork to the right leads to its south side (lower end).

To locate Cave Spring, take AL 67 east from I-65 exit 334, then turn left onto Bethel Rd. Take a right on Upper River Rd. and then a left on Mussel Camp Rd. The cave and spring are shortly to your right, just as you pass the refuge boundary.

To reach Mallard-Fox Creek WMA, take Alt US 72/AL 20 west out of Decatur until you cross the Morgan/Lawrence County Line, then turn right on Co. Rd. 400. This road passes over the open slough of the WMA.

The trailhead for the Limestone County rails-to-trails project is located on Piney Chapel Rd. just north of Athens. The trail ends in Veto, Alabama, at the Tennessee state line.

47 Blowing Springs Cave (access is restricted)

This 60-acre property in Lauderdale County was purchased by the Forever Wild program to protect vital gray bat habitat. Due to the sensitive nature of the bats, the property (as well as the bats' mass exit at dusk) can only be viewed by special arrangement with the State Lands Division. The site is serenely beautiful, occupying a floodplain along a creek that merges into a wooded limestone hillside where the cave is located. The namesake spring of the property flows out of a small opening at the base of the hill. Cool air blows from this opening, and the clear spring water flows across the floodplain to the creek.

For more information and permission to visit, contact the State Lands Division. (See References and Websites.)

48 Joe Wheeler State Park

34°47'27.35"N
87°22'55.29"W

This state park includes a short nature trail that passes through a diverse hardwood forest; along the trail are some majestic black walnut trees. The park has some great views of the forested limestone hills meeting the coves of Wheeler Lake, an impoundment of the Tennessee River.

The state park and lake are named after General Joseph E. Wheeler, a famous Confederate cavalry commander in the Civil War. He later served in the US Congress and as a general in the Spanish–American War. General Wheeler's home and plantation, Pond Spring, are located near the state park in the broad valley on the south side of the river. The house and grounds are well worth visiting. The family cemetery is shaded by a stand of giant trees possibly left over from the virgin forest of the area. You'll also note that the stones used for the walkways are full of fossils.

The rest of the Wheeler plantation includes farmland and an abundance of bottomland and upland hardwood forests, including some huge Native American marker trees. These areas can be visited by special arrangement.

Directions: The main portion of Joe Wheeler State Park is reached by going west from Rogersville on US 72 and following the signs.

For the Wheeler house and plantation, take Alt. US 72/AL 20 east from Courtland; look for signs marking the right turn into the plantation house area.

49 Prairie Grove Glades

34°30'57.66"N
87°30'21.12"W

Prairie Grove Glades is a 191-acre Nature Conservancy preserve in the Moulton Valley of southwest Lawrence County. The preserve contains the largest intact cedar glade complex in Alabama. Cedar glades occur in the Interior Low Plateau where large limestone outcrops appear on relatively flat terrain. The dry, poorly developed soils on and around the outcrops encourage almost pure stands of red cedar. Some of the soils are too thin for good tree growth—it is these areas that look and feel like open prairies. These rare, isolated habitats are home to various grasses and rare plants. In early to mid-spring, the glades are covered with the sweet aroma of the white glade cress, while lyrate bladderpods bloom on the deeper soils at glades' edges. Other rare flowers appear in much anticipated sequence as the growing season progresses.

These glades provide us with a glimpse of the past, when extensive areas were covered with similar habitats, known as "barrens." Largely lacking tree cover and dominated by prairie grasses and wildflowers, barrens once covered much of the Interior Low Plateau, from southwest Ohio to northwest Alabama. (The open, treeless areas of the Bluegrass Basin and around Mammoth Cave, Kentucky, were barrens much valued for hunting, first by Native Americans and then by European settlers.) Fire suppression has led to the loss of many of these rare habitats (and their rare

Entrance to Prairie Grove Glades

species); without frequent fires, woody plants can safely invade and dominate. So don't be surprised (or upset) to find evidence of recent controlled burns at Prairie Grove Glades. Such burns are part of good glade management practice.

Directions: From Moulton, take a left onto AL 24 and head west for about 13 miles. Turn right and follow Co. Rd. 43 north for about one mile. Bear right at the fork and continue for another one-half mile to the parking area (and preserve sign) on the left.

50 Shoal Creek Preserve

34°54'46.77"N
87°36'58.98"W

The Shoal Creek Preserve is a 298-acre purchase by Alabama's Forever Wild land acquisition program. The area contains broad

Prairie Grove Glades, Lawrence County

uplands underlain by chert. The flatter, less rocky, and deeper-soiled areas of the property were cleared for agriculture in the past and are now in an early stage of forest succession. These old fields provide us with an opportunity to watch the area succeed, as the years go by, to mature hardwood forest. In addition, some of the old agricultural land is maintained as wildlife food plots.

The main attractions of the preserve are its slopes and streams. The steep slopes and stream gradients have created a multitude of waterfalls and shoals. The slopes show an abundance of rock outcrops, while the rich soils of the drainages support diverse hardwood forests with an abundance of spring woodland wildflowers, including spring beauty and Jacob's ladder. Walking along Shoal Creek (which makes up the eastern border of the property) and its tributaries (like Jones Branch) is a good way to see spring wildflowers, waterfalls, and shoals.

Directions: Take US 72 east from Florence and turn north on Co. Rd. 61. After passing through the small community of St. Florian, continue on Co. Rd. 61 for about three miles until you see an unmarked gravel road with a gate on your right. (You must keep a keen eye out for this road or you will miss it.) If the gate is closed, park to the side of it and walk along the road through private lands until you reach the Forever Wild boundary signs at the first creek bridge. Continue on the central road through the old fields of the property and down the slope to where the road ends in creek bottoms. If you walk upstream along the small cascading creek you will end up back at the bridge on the property boundary; if you walk downstream you will reach the Shoal Creek embayment on Wilson Lake.

51 Natchez Trace / Rock Spring Trail

34°52'37.35"N
87°53'40.19"W

The Natchez Trace Parkway is a national park unit that follows the route of the old trail that flatboat men followed north from Natchez, Mississippi, to Nashville, Tennessee. The boatmen used this route to get back to their greater Ohio River valley homes after they had floated their farm products down to markets in Natchez on the Mississippi. (This was an age before steamboats facilitated upstream travel.) The parkway corridor, including the short section that runs through northwest Alabama, is full of natural and historical sites.

Sections of the original trace can be seen in the woods at the Colbert's Ferry site in Alabama. The ferry was run by the mixed-blood Chickasaw chief George Colbert. A nice trace site within Alabama's section of the Interior Low Plateau is the Rock Spring Trail. This interpretive nature trail passes by a spring run (which has been impounded by beavers) and some upland forest containing beech trees. Sadly, some of these beeches have been killed by the excessive carving of names in their smooth gray bark. *So please keep your knife in your pocket!*

DIRECTIONS: To reach the Alabama portion of the Natchez trace, take Co. Rd. 14 west out of Florence until it intersects with the Trace. Going right takes you northeast to Tennessee; going left takes you southwest past Rock Spring Trail. Continue southwest on the trace to other Alabama trace sites and Mississippi beyond.

52 Lauderdale County WMA

34°55'05.52"N
88°03'51.33"W

This 11,106-acre, multiunit WMA contains some of the Flint (actually chert) Hill forest country of Alabama's Interior Low Plateau. Most of the land is in pine plantation, but it has great potential for restoration. Along with land purchased by Forever Wild, the WMA contains acres leased from the TVA along the Tennessee River. The more naturally forested TVA acres contain chert outcrops exposed along stream drainages full of hardwoods, including sugar maple.

DIRECTIONS: To reach the most scenic portion of the WMA (along the Tennessee River), take Co. Rd. 14 west out of Florence. Continue past the Natchez Trace and the historic Gravely Springs area to Waterloo. (This area usually has abundant wintering bald eagles.) From Waterloo go northwest on Pea Ridge Rd., then take a left onto Union Hollow Rd. Follow Union Hollow Rd. into the WMA and down to the hollows along the river. Other area roads weave in and out of the WMA. It is best to consult a WMA map (see References and Websites) before exploring too far.

RIDGE AND VALLEY

When Africa and North America collided in the distant past, the land that is now the Appalachian Ridge and Valley Province folded upward—like someone pushing on opposite ends of a piece of paper. Over the succeeding eons, the folded landscape was reshaped by erosion, leaving more resistant sandstone ridges and broad valleys underlain by less resistant rocks, such as limestone and dolomite.

The resulting landscape appears as long, narrow, unbroken ridges of uniform height, plus valleys containing streams that run parallel to the ridges. These streams sometimes cut across the ridges forming "gaps," which have proved to be quite useful as travel corridors for both critters and humans. Some of the limestone areas show karst landscapes with caves; others contain rather diverse hardwood forests featuring white ash. The limestone has also weathered into the rich soil of the Coosa River valley, which is extensively farmed. (The Coosa valley, by the way, is the southern end of the Great Valley, which stretches north to the Shenandoah Valley and beyond.)

The majority of the province's higher ridges and associated narrow valleys lie to the west of the Coosa valley. This rugged country was originally heavily forested—dry ridge tops and south-facing slopes clothed with mountain longleaf pine, hardwoods along the streams and in moist hollows, and mixed forest transition zones in between. The higher ridges separate distinct parallel drainages such as Shades Creek and the Cahaba River; the former joins the latter as the dividing ridges play out near the four corners of Bibb, Jefferson, Shelby, and Tuscaloosa Counties. Today, the floodplains of the creeks and rivers are dominated by sycamore, river birch, box elder, and green ash, with more diverse cove hardwood forest tucked away from the central floodplain or along tributaries.

The following areas represent the Ridge and Valley's diversity in Alabama.

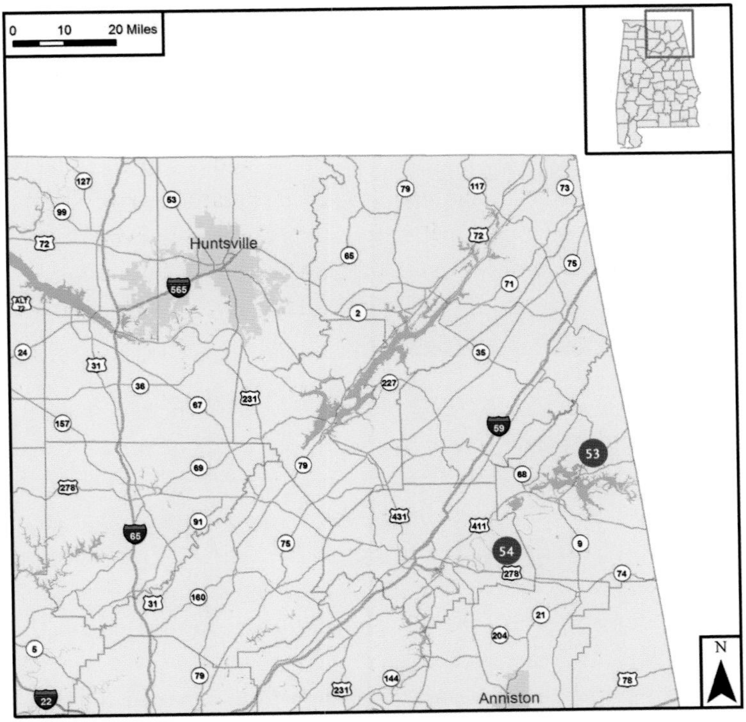

COOSA RIVER AREA

Two extremely rare and much diminished habitats, bogs and prairies, occur within Alabama's Ridge and Valley Province. Both are well known for their rare plant species.

53 Coosa Bog and Cornwall Furnace

34°14'25.23"N
85°35'07.28"W

Spindle-root at Coosa Bog

Coosa Bog is a Nature Conservancy preserve in Cherokee County that protects a single remnant of a once great habitat, the Coosa Flatwoods. Originally, the upper Coosa valley contained not only limestone-derived soil but broad, sandy river terraces that were dry or poorly drained, depending on the season. This environment fostered dry season fires and helped maintain a vast acreage of longleaf pine forest, including bogs dominated by the fire-dependent green pitcher plant.

The region's poor but easily tillable soil was cleared for farming in the early 20th century, when artificial fertilizers made such farming practical. At the same time, fires were suppressed. Consequently, longleaf pine has practically disappeared from this area, and the green pitcher plant is now endangered across its entire range (northeast Alabama and northwest Georgia).

The Alabama office of the Nature Conservancy was established in the late 1980s, and its first action was to purchase the Coosa Bog and thereby protect the world's largest population of green pitcher plants. This site also has a few remnant longleaf pines, which can hopefully be increased to reestablish the full structure of the flatwoods. Due to the endangered nature of the pitcher plants at Coosa Bog, you will have to contact the Nature Conservancy about visiting the site.

If you visit Coosa Bog, you may also want to go to the nearby Cornwall Furnace Memorial Park, located on the Weiss Lake impoundment portion of the Chattooga River. The park contains an old Civil War iron furnace similar to those at Tannehill State Park, but not yet restored. It supplied iron to the large Noble foundry in nearby Rome, Georgia, which churned out war supplies for the Confederacy. The park also contains the remains of an old canal used by the furnace, plus a nature trail.

DIRECTIONS: To reach Cornwall Furnace, take AL 9 northeast from Centre. Go past the town of Cedar Bluff and make a left onto Co. Rd. 92, which leads to the furnace park.

54 Coosa Prairies

34°02'46.17"N
85°48'20.83"W

Coosa Prairies are rare, grass-dominated communities associated with the sticky, calcareous (calcium-rich) clays of the Ridge and Valley. These prairies are small (no larger than 10 acres) openings within the Coosa Flatwoods. They feature rare plants such as Mohr's Barbara's buttons, Alabama leather flower, whorled sunflower, prairie milkweed, Virginia mountain mint, and barbed rattlesnake root. While the soil characteristics themselves inhibit tree growth, periodic fires tip the balance in favor of herbs (rather than trees) in these areas.

Very little Coosa Prairie habitat is currently protected within Alabama. Some protected (but not publicly accessible) habitat is located on the National Guard's Pelham Artillery Range in Calhoun County. Current management includes both intentional and accidental, artillery-generated fires, keeping woody vegetation from taking over and smothering the prairies.

Etowah County once had a significant amount of Coosa Flatwoods, with Coosa Prairie habitat within it. Unfortunately, this area was largely converted to pine plantations. Directions to one small remnant area follow. Use your binoculars to view this remnant from the road. *And please, don't trespass.*

DIRECTIONS: From Ballplay, travel south on Co. Rd. 71 and turn left on Tom Cat Rd. As you head southeast you will see a young patch of pine plantation on your left. There will be a private dirt road at the start of this plantation and another dirt road on the right side of the road about one hundred yards farther down. Pull into the first dirt road on the left. From the road's shoulder you can observe prairie milkweed in the pine plantation, and as you face the plantation you will notice an uncut patch of relatively mature pine-oak woods—possibly another property with Coosa Prairie openings. Confine your observations to this area, and *do not* walk up any side roads toward the woods.

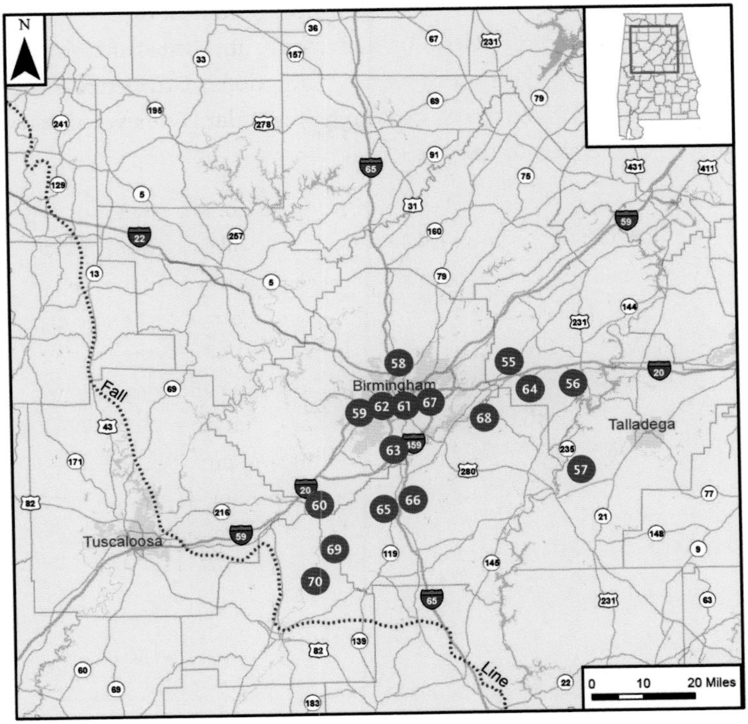

BIRMINGHAM AREA

The countryside around Birmingham features an array of habitats—wide valleys, steep ridges, fishing lakes, and free-flowing streams. Plus an abundance of parks and preserves, which means plenty of opportunities for hiking, camping, horseback riding, canoeing, biking, picnicking, rock climbing, and more. In other words, there are no excuses to stay indoors.

55 Dry Creek Preserve (access is restricted)

The 26-acre Dry Creek Preserve was established by the Nature Conservancy to protect one of the world's few populations of the Alabama leather flower. (The plant is known from only seven sites in northeast Alabama and northwest Georgia.) The preserve has no trail, but some of the best observations can be made along the road shoulders on the south and west sides of the property. Here you will find rose gentian and the large blades of prairie dock, as well as milkweeds and coreopsis. The tract contains some nice valley or low hill oak-hickory-pine forests of white oak, loblolly pine, and an understory of redbud. In the spring, the trees are full of the songs of migratory birds like the wood thrush.

DIRECTIONS: Due to the endangered nature of the plants at Dry Creek Preserve, you will have to contact the Nature Conservancy about visiting the site.

56 Coosa Lakes

33°33'01.70"N
86°16'09.08"W

The upper Coosa River runs through the Ridge and Valley Province. Unfortunately—at least as far as natural habitats are concerned—practically the entire river has been dammed for hydroelectric power. The free-flowing habitats and values of the river have been lost, and many of the aquatic species associated with it are now extinct or endangered.

Although the shores of the hydroelectric reservoirs have been developed for vacation homes and marinas, there are a few parks worth visiting for both their forest and water habitats.

(The James D. Martin Wildlife Park on the Coosa River near Gadsden was previously described in the section on Noccalula Falls and Black Creek.)

Ten Islands Historic Park is an Alabama Power Company park next to the dam that created Neely Henry Lake. This area offers short trails in the woods, picnic facilities, a swimming area, fishing, and a boat launch. As the park's name indicates, the area is richer in historical value than natural value. Ten Islands was a shallow area of the Coosa River, full of islands and shoals, which made it a natural crossing before European settlement brought bridges. The once biodiverse shoals are now deep under the lake, but a couple of the islands, including Rock Island, still exist. Neely Henry Dam was built across one such island and a now-dead river channel to the west.

During low flow times, you can see a large Native American fish weir in the river just below the dam. (Fish weirs are rock "Vs" built in rivers in order to bottleneck fish as they migrate; the bottleneck makes them easier to catch.) The west side of the river below the dam was also the site of Fort Strother, the first base Andrew Jackson used in his assaults upon the local Native Americans during the 1813 Creek War. A historic marker commemorates the site.

Pell City's Lakeside Park on Logan Martin Lake is one of the nicest parks we have ever seen on a hydroelectric reservoir. It is located on a slough opposite a ball field complex, and is connected to that complex by a short bridge. Lakeside Park's developers constructed recreation facilities with minimal removal of natural vegetation. It contains some bicycle/walking trails and a nature trail that passes through typical low hill forests of sweetgum, water oak, white oak, and loblolly pine. (Stay on the trail, and you will avoid the abundant poison ivy.)

The most impressive habitat of the park is a lake marsh, located at its northern end between the entrance road and the ball fields. This wetland contains trees and shrubs like black willow and buttonbush; it also supports a variety of grasses and other plants, including stands of purple swamp iris. Red-winged blackbirds are seen and heard throughout the marsh. A canoe can be launched from the boat launch/bridge area to further explore the marsh and the long slough downstream.

Beeswax Creek Park is a wooded Shelby County park on Lay Lake, located on land leased from Alabama Power. This park has walking/nature trails, recreation facilities, and easy access to the lake. Lay Lake has more stable water conditions than other Coosa Lakes, and the park has an interesting edge marsh because of that.

The Alabama 4-H Center, located off AL 145 near Columbiana, has trails, historical structures, and water-related recreation opportunities. The center offers environmental education, summer camps, overnight accommodations, and space needed for group retreats.

Further south off AL 145 is a public boat launch with great views of the lake and surrounding ridges, known as the Narrows. The launch offers good opportunities to explore the rocky lakeshore by boat or canoe. As you enter the area, be sure to admire the road cut exposures of (unexpected) metamorphic rocks. These rocks occur here because this is where the adjacent Blue Ridge Outliers/Piedmont Province transition zone meets the Ridge and Valley Province. Also, use your binoculars to view the Spanish moss festooning the trees along the cliffs across the river. This is a very unusual northern occurrence of that Coastal Plain plant.

Directions: Ten Islands Park is reached by taking AL 144 east from Ragland to the Neely Henry Dam site. The park is on the left just before the dam. (Other historic sites in Calhoun County, such as Janey Furnace and Lincoya Monument–Tallasahatchee Creek War Site, are found by continuing west on AL 144 from the dam and following the signs.)

To reach Pell City's Lakeside Park, take I-20 exit 158. Follow US 231 south through Pell City, then turn east onto AL 34. You will see the entrance to the park just after passing the Pell City Civic Center. The trail parking area will be on your left.

Beeswax Creek Park can be reached by taking Co. Rd. 28 southeast from Columbiana. Take a left on AL 145. You will shortly reach the bridge over Beeswax Creek; the park is on your right just before the bridge.

To reach the Alabama 4-H Center, take I-65 exit 238. Travel south on US 31 to AL 70, turn left, and follow AL 70 to Columbiana. Go through two traffic lights and take the right fork (by Shelby County High School) onto Co. Rd. 28. Follow Co. Rd. 28 for nearly seven miles (crossing AL 145) and turn left at the 4-H Center sign. Follow this road to the lodge.

The Narrows boat launch can be reached by following AL 145 south from the 4-H Center area. Turn left on Co. Rd. 47, then right on Co. Rd. 400, which dead-ends at the boat launch.

57 DeSoto Caverns / Kymulga Grist Mill and Covered Bridge

33°20'03.35"N
86°17'57.23"W

Even though the DeSoto Caverns site resembles an amusement park, the property's large cave is still worth seeing. The cave has some impressive formations, along with the carved name of a European trader from the 1700s. (BEWARE: Legend has it that the Creeks killed the trader for desecrating a site they held sacred.) The cave was associated with the mining of saltpeter (from bat droppings) for gunpowder during the Civil War and moonshining in more modern times. The Spanish explorer Hernando de Soto supposedly visited the site in 1540 when he wintered at a nearby Native American village in present-day Childersburg, which calls itself America's First City because of that event.

For a more natural above-ground experience, visit the Kymulga Grist Mill and Covered Bridge Park. Visitors will see a working grist mill on the creek, a supposedly haunted covered bridge, and a nice nature trail through some valley forest.

> DIRECTIONS: The Kymulga Grist Mill and Covered Bridge Park and DeSoto Caverns are located along AL 76 east of Childersburg. To reach the grist mill park, turn left onto Co. Rd. 175, which leads right to it. To reach DeSoto Caverns, continue east on AL 76; the park will be on your left.

58 Red Mountain

33°29'30.07"N
86°47'43.77"W

Red Mountain is not the highest ridge of the Birmingham area, but it is responsible for the growth of the city. Before mining began in the mid-1800s, large red outcrops of iron ore protruded from the ridges, giving the mountain its name. Limestone, the second basic need of the steel industry, makes up much of the north-facing lower slope of the mountain. The third component, coal, came largely from the Shale Basins of the Appalachian Plateau north of town.

Much of the industrial heritage of the area is preserved in the natural parks along Red Mountain. At 1,011 acres, Ruffner Mountain Nature Preserve is the largest city-owned preserve in the nation. (Ruffner Mountain is the name for the east-central section of Red Mountain.) Its 11 miles of hiking trails take you past many special sites. The start of the trail system (near the main parking lot and nature center) goes through a limestone slope forest with lots of white ash and one of the highest diversities of woodland wildflowers in the Ridge and Valley—trout lilies, blue phlox, shooting stars, and many more. Other trails take you up the mountain past rusty red iron ore rocks (and rusting

Springwater dancer at the constructed wetland, Ruffner Mountain Nature Preserve

iron mining equipment) to a limestone quarry; the top of the ridge offers superb views of Birmingham. Newly acquired lands on the south side of the mountain contain a wetland created by damming a mountain spring, as well as an adjacent trail through unusual rock formations.

Further west on Red Mountain is Vulcan Park, with its famous statue of Vulcan, the Roman god of the forge. The world's largest cast iron statue, Vulcan stands at the top of a 126-foot tower, which offers excellent 360-degree views of the city below. A museum, dedicated to the area's iron- and steel-making history, tells the Birmingham industrial story. The park also has the Vulcan Trail along its north slope. Once part of the mineral railroad connecting the various mines and the iron/steel mills, this one-mile trail passes through a heavily wooded corridor; plans are to extend the trail westward.

Nearby, the old Red Mountain Museum has a geology walk along the US 31/280 Red Mountain cut that explains the mountain's geologic history. Both the walk and the museum area are currently closed, and the museum's collections have been moved to the McWane Center in downtown Birmingham. The McWane

Center has an IMAX theater, science gizmos for children and adults, a growing Alabama fossil exhibit, plus large aquaria featuring life of the Cahaba River and marine environments.

Also nearby, the Birmingham Botanical Gardens sit on the southern toe of Red Mountain. They provide a great opportunity to see local natural habitats as well as more exotic vegetation. The forested sections of the gardens provide vital habitat for migrating birds, and thus are highly prized by Birmingham bird watchers.

Toward the western end of the mountain is the recently dedicated Red Mountain Park. This 1,100-acre tract features long, fairly straight trails (that parallel the ridge line) through a former mining area; a zip line and tree house add to the fun. The mixed hardwood-pine forest contains some longleaf pine; open habitats support bobwhite quail and kestrels. The mountain offers some great views of Jones Valley to the north and Shades Valley/Shades Mountain to the south.

It is interesting to note that Frederick Law Olmstead Jr., one of our nation's greatest designers of parks, developed a metro Birmingham park plan back in 1925. That plan called for the protection of large interconnected areas of floodplains and ridges. As a way to resurrect Olmstead's vision, several groups are currently working to connect the natural parks along Red Mountain. Check out the *Exploring Wild Alabama* website for updates.

DIRECTIONS: To reach Ruffner Mountain Nature Preserve, take I-20 exit 132 east of downtown Birmingham. Go north on Oporto-Madrid Blvd. and turn right onto Rugby Ave., then right on 81st St., which dead-ends at the nature center parking lot.

Vulcan Park can be reached by taking 20th St. South from downtown Birmingham and climbing up to the top of Red Mountain. You will see a parking lot on your right for the Vulcan Trail. Continue just a little further and take a right on Valley Ave.; the main park entrance is immediately to your right.

The McWane Center is located at the corner of 2nd Ave. and 19th

St. North (next to the historic Alabama Theater) in downtown Birmingham.

The Birmingham Botanical Gardens are reached by taking US 31/280 south from downtown Birmingham. At the US 31/280 split, continue on US 280 and take the exit for the gardens and Birmingham Zoo. Turn left on Cahaba Rd. to reach the entrance.

Red Mountain Park is located off Lakeshore Dr. in the western part of Homewood. Its entrance is clearly marked on the north side of the road.

59 Watercress Darter National Wildlife Refuge

33°22'30.28"N
86°57'45.81"W

The 23-acre Watercress Darter National Wildlife Refuge—one of the smallest federal wildlife refuges in the United States—is centered around some limestone springs in the Bessemer area of western Jefferson County. It was established to protect a key habitat area for the watercress darter, an endangered fish species found only in a few springs in the Birmingham area. While you will probably not see the darter during your visit, the short trail to the overlook of a spring pool is beautiful. The pool is surrounded by some small bald cypress trees, which are rare in the Ridge and Valley Province. Also, the West Jefferson County Historical Society protects the antebellum McAdory Plantation House complex next to the spring; and that, too, is well worth seeing.

Directions: From I-459 southwest of downtown Birmingham, take exit 1 and follow Eastern Valley Rd. northeast toward Bessemer. Keep going until you see the historic McAdory house complex on your left. The trailhead parking lot for the refuge is located on the left just after you pass the front of the house.

60 Tannehill Historical State Park

33°15'02.75"N
87°04'10.98"W

Upon entering Tannehill Historical State Park, you will see a sign stating that *this* is the southern end of the Appalachians. Actually (and technically), the Appalachian Ridge and Valley extends down into the middle of Bibb County to the southwest, but the park sits very close to the end of this province.

Before and during the Civil War, the short Appalachian ridges of this area were stripped of trees to make charcoal. The charcoal was used to produce pig iron from the local brown iron ore—the first iron made in the Birmingham area. The forests have come back, and the area has been made into an historical park with restored iron furnaces, a museum, lots of relocated pioneer structures, and plenty of nature trails.

Farther south, Brierfield Ironworks Historical State Park offers similar resources on a smaller scale.

Directions: Tannehill Historical State Park can be reached by taking I-59 exit 100 west of Birmingham and following the signs.

Brierfield Ironworks Historical State Park can be reached by taking AL 25 southeast from Montevallo. Turn left onto Co. Rd. 62; the park entrance will appear shortly on your left.

61 Shades Mountain / Shades Creek

33°28'25.78"N
86°46'01.50"W

Shades Mountain is the next major ridge south of Red Mountain, and the two are separated by Shades Creek valley. But Shades Mountain is geologically different from Red Mountain. Shades Mountain, the Oak Mountain complex, and the Ridge and Valley of Bibb County were folded from Pottsville Sandstone, the same type of rock that makes up the Appalachian Plateau to the north. Thus, Shades Mountain and its associated areas have characteristics of both the Ridge and Valley and the Appalachian Plateau. The ridges are generally long and narrow, but at some places (like Bluff Park in Hoover) they widen out into plateau-like tops with rock pavements, giant boulders, and steep escarpments.

The north-facing slopes of Shades Mountain support hardwood forests with a good assemblage of spring wildflowers. Some of this habitat, along with extensive floodplains, is protected in the following string of semiconnected greenway parks running along Shades Creek through various municipalities: Flora Johnson Nature Park, Irondale Furnace, Shades Creek Audubon Sanctuary, Jemison Park, Homewood Greenway, Homewood Forest Preserve, and Freshwater Land Trust properties.

The tiny Lover's Leap Park and adjacent Tip Top Grill overlook give visitors a feel for what the natural bluff top of Shades Mountain was like before development. The Homewood Forest Preserve offers the best opportunity on Shades Mountain to see mature, lower slope hardwood forest with a significant number of woodland wildflowers. The preserve is also the site of spotted and marbled salamanders' breeding migrations.

The top of Shades Mountain and its gentle south-facing slopes have been more heavily developed than the northern ones, but some steep areas remain, including the Vestavia and Boulder Canyon Nature Trail System. The largest protected area on either side of Shades Mountain is Moss Rock Preserve, which will be covered in the next section.

Bracket fungi, Freshwater Land Trust property, Shades Valley

Directions: The Flora Johnson Nature Park can be accessed by taking I-20 exit 132 east of downtown Birmingham. From this exit go south on Oporto-Madrid Blvd.; continue until you reach its intersection with Montclair Rd. Take a left onto Montclair Rd., then a right on Elder St. Follow Elder St. to the Shades Creek bridge at the base of Shades Mountain. Park your car off the road and walk to the park sign and trail entrance, located on the left after you cross the bridge. This trail traverses a mile or so of very scenic oak-beech slope forest along the creek.

The Irondale Furnace Park can be reached by following the just mentioned Oporto-Madrid Blvd. south across its junction with Montclair Rd. As you continue south you will soon reach Montevallo Rd. Take a right onto Montevallo Rd. and then a left onto Leech Dr. You will soon take another left onto Groover Dr., followed by a right on Stone River Rd. The park is located on the right just after Stone River Rd. crosses a small stream. Park your car and follow the park's trail downstream past the iron furnace to the stream's confluence with Shades Creek.

The 3.3-acre Shades Creek Audubon Sanctuary is located near the Irondale Furnace Park. Contact the Birmingham Audubon Society before visiting this tract.

Jemison Park can be reached by taking I-59 exit 19 southeast of Birmingham. Follow US 280 northwest to the Mountain Brook Pkwy. exit. Go northeast on Mountain Brook Pkwy. until you see the start of the park, just after the Cahaba Rd. intersection to your left. Continue on Mountain Brook Pkwy. and choose a curbside parking space on your right. If you follow the main portion of the park's paved trail northeast or upstream along the Shades Creek floodplain forest, you will pass close to a replica grist mill; continue over a low water crossing to an unpaved trail through a forest strip with old-growth trees. The park has some interpretive signs and labeled plants, including lots of bottlebrush buckeye.

The Homewood Greenway and Forest Preserve can be found by taking I-65 exit 255 south of downtown Birmingham. Go east on Lakeshore Dr. until you reach its intersection with Green Springs Hwy. (also called Columbiana Rd.). Take a right and cross the bridge over Shades Creek. (This is the site of a dam that once created Edgewood Lake, a popular recreation area until the 1940s; hence the name, Lakeshore Dr.) You will then see parking for the greenway on your left. To reach the forest preserve, continue on Lakeshore Dr. through the Green Springs intersection. After passing Samford University, turn right onto Old Montgomery Hwy. Then take a right onto south Lakeshore Dr. Follow this road, being extra cautious near the official salamander crossings. (The best time to view the migration is on the first warm, rainy night after New Year's Day.) Park in the lot behind Homewood High School and then walk back up the road a short distance until you see the nature trail on your right.

To reach Lover's Leap Park, take Alford Ave. to the west from I-65 exit 254. Follow Alford Ave. until you reach the T intersection with

Tyler Rd. Take a right onto Tyler, then a left on Shades Crest Rd. You will pass by historic houses from a time when this area was a summer resort or retreat from the heat of Birmingham proper. The Tip Top Grill will appear on your right. This is a good place to park, get a snack, and admire the view. The Lover's Leap historic marker and steps down to the leap are on your left. *Be careful of traffic on this busy road.*

The Vestavia–Boulder Canyon Nature Trail is found by taking I-65 exit 252 and following US 31 north. Turn right on Roundhill Rd. and park at the new Vestavia Hills Library. The trailhead provides access to the northern end of the trail, which drops off into some beautiful, steep hollows with cascading streams. If you keep following the trails downstream you will reach the Vestavia Nature Trail with its waterfalls.

62 Moss Rock Preserve

33°23'01.94"N
86°50'30.58"W

Moss Rock Preserve is a 350-acre park purchased by the city of Hoover in the 1990s. The park contains a variety of habitats in a small area, ranging from hardwood swamps to longleaf pine forests. However, the park is most significant in that it offers one of the best opportunities to see a Fort Payne type of sandstone glade.

When you enter the park from its south-central side, you will pass through a field of giant boulders ("The Boulder Field") reminiscent of Cherokee Rock Village on Lookout Mountain. Then drop down the hill through old-growth longleaf pine to Hurricane Branch, passing the White Trail which leads to the rest of the preserve's 10-mile trail system. Cross the stream and head toward the tall wet-weather waterfall that runs across a large

Boulder Field,
Moss Rock Preserve

natural pavement of rock. The glade occupies the sloping pavement of rock around and above the falls.

Because of its sensitive nature, the glade is not marked on the trail maps issued to the general public. However, we hope that you, the readers of this book, are more interested in ecology than the average visitor. *So tread lightly, and don't step on the islands of soil!* Shallow pockets of soil have developed in weathered depressions, and the few plant species adapted to these stressful conditions—literally, between a rock and a hard place—cannot survive much trampling. As you carefully make your way upslope across the glade, watch for spiny prickly pear cacti. These plants are well adapted to the droughty conditions of the glade, as is another succulent, Menges' fameflower. A third well-adapted glade plant is

Boulder Field, Moss Rock Preserve

Waterfall area, Moss Rock Preserve

Above: Sandstone outcrop, Moss Rock Preserve

Opposite: Rare snow event at Moss Rock Preserve

Nuttall's rayless goldenrod, whose flowers shine bright yellow in autumn. During that same season, small-head blazing-star turns the glade a lavender hue.

The preserve's Fort Payne sandstone is exposed in only about 25 locations stretching northeast from Birmingham to Fort Payne, Alabama. Moss Rock protects several good examples of this rock type, including the just described glade.

You will notice that most of the trees scattered about the glade are pines, and that many of these are small and stunted. These are natural bonsai trees that have been growing on these rocks for possibly 200 years. While some are Virginia pines, the typical "bonsai" species of cliff tops, many are longleaf pines, which is very unusual.

At the base of the previously mentioned waterfall, look for the faint fossils of horsetail plants. The horsetails grew here when this site was part of a sandy delta on the edge of the ocean. During that time, horsetails and ferns grew as big as dogwood trees, and club mosses were as tall as oaks. (These were also the days of giant dragonflies, cockroaches, and salamanders.) During the Carboniferous, the future coal deposits around Birmingham were deposited as dead wood, buried under mud, and later carbonized into rock.

The highest portion of Moss Rock Preserve lies along a power line that follows its northern boundary. From here, visitors can gaze across the old underground coal-mining country of the Cahaba River valley all the way to Oak Mountain State Park.

Recently, the city of Hoover added about 100 acres to Moss Rock Preserve. The orange trail of the Moss Rock system has been extended into the rougher sections of this very scenic land. These sections are known as Boulder Gorge and include a natural bridge, streamside boulders, a very high waterfall, some small rock outcrops, and some great views.

Directions: Take I-459 exit 10 southwest of Birmingham. Go east on AL 150 until you shortly reach Stadium Trace/Preserve Pkwy. Take a left and follow the parkway to its intersection with Sulphur Springs Rd.

There are three parking lots for Moss Rock Preserve. To reach the central access point, which leads to the Boulder Field–waterfall–sandstone glade area, keep going on Preserve Pkwy., which passes through the nature preserve, and follow it until you reach a traffic circle. Go through the traffic circle and park in the lot that has been carved out of the woods to your left. You'll find the trail head there.

To reach the eastern parking lot, which leads to both the main preserve and Boulder Gorge addition, continue past the above mentioned parking area and follow Preserve Pkwy. until it reaches a T intersection with Patton Chapel Rd. Take a left and look for a large lot on your left, with signs for Moss Rock parking, plus a preserve rules sign and map box. From here the White Trail follows Hurricane Branch into the preserve while the Orange Trail runs through the Boulder Gorge property.

To reach the western parking lot, turn left on Sulfur Springs Rd. (past Preserve Pkwy.) to a gravel parking lot surrounded by wood rail fencing on your right. The trails behind the Moss Rock rules sign and map box quickly lead to the Blue, White, and Red Trails.

63 Oak Mountain State Park

33°19'22.07"N
86°46'35.91"W

At 9,940 acres, Oak Mountain State Park is the largest public land area in metropolitan Birmingham and Alabama's largest state park. It sits mainly on Double Oak Mountain, which is part of the Oak Mountain complex. After starting as a small donated area around Peavine Falls, the majority of Oak Mountain's land was acquired by the National Park Service in the 1930s to serve as a recreation area. Plans to enlarge the area into a national park were never implemented, and the land was given to the state.

Oak Mountain State Park contains a wide range of habitats, including extensive stands of mountain longleaf pine. Some of this longleaf includes virgin old-growth forest that has been periodically burned. Sandstone glades in these open longleaf areas support the rare Confederate daisy as well as many other wildflowers and grasses.

Counterclockwise from top:
Small-head blazing star; Confederate daisy; and Menges' fameflower, Oak Mountain State Park

Autumn colors, Oak Mountain State Park

The park has lots of hiking and biking trails, fishing lakes, and various recreation facilities. The Oak Mountain Interpretive Center—a joint venture by the state's Department of Conservation and Samford University—has displays of the park's basic geology and wildlife, plus serves as a field station for outdoor education. The Alabama Wildlife Center is located close by, at the top of Tree Top Nature Trail, which displays injured birds of prey in open air cages. Unlike the center's other injured patients, these birds are unable to return to the wild. However, they serve to educate people about the importance of conservation.

Pine warbler, Oak Mountain State Park

Near the state park is an interesting gorge called the Narrows, where Yellowleaf Creek cuts through Double Oak Mountain on its way to the Coosa River. The high cliffs and white-water stream are very scenic to view from the roadside.

Directions: Oak Mountain State Park is easily reached by taking I-65 exit 246 (AL 119) south of Birmingham and following the signs to the park.

The Narrows is reached by taking I-459 exit 19 southeast of Birmingham. Follow US 280 southeast across AL 119 and over a big mountain (the true Oak Mountain), then take a right on Co. Rd. 280. This road passes through the Narrows. You can park on pull-offs beside the road. *Just watch for traffic!*

Gulf fritillary feeding on Blazing Star, Oak Mountain State Park

Fox squirrel, Oak Mountain State Park

64 Camp Winnataska

33°32'32.14"N
86°26'32.58"W

The 1,400-acre Camp Winnataska lies in the rugged sandstone country near the eastern end of the Oak Mountain and Double Oak Mountain ridges. This is a church/scout camp that offers environmental education sessions for children.

The natural setting of Camp Winnataska is one of the most spectacular in Alabama. The entrance road crosses Kelly Creek, which has been impounded by a very low dam to facilitate canoeing. You will next see a long pedestrian bridge on your right, which leads out over a wide, high-volume waterfall that forms the centerpiece of the camp. The trees are identified with signs, and here a water tupelo has two other species, pine and elm, growing out of holes in its swollen base. The falls drop down stair-step levels to a larger lake.

The camp has many forest trails in addition to the above. To schedule a visit or attend an environmental session, check the camp's website.

Directions: Take I-20 east of Birmingham to exit 147 near Moody. Turn left on US 78 and follow it for several miles, turning right on Cherokee/Winnataska Rd. Then turn right on Camp Winnataska Rd. to the camp's entrance.

65 Ebenezer Swamp Ecological Preserve

33°10'24.24"N
86°46'42.37"W

View from deep in Ebenezer Swamp

Ebenezer Swamp is a spring-fed tupelo swamp within the Appalachian Ridge and Valley Province. Because such swamps are normally found in the Coastal Plain, they contain unique Coastal Plain species within a more rock-dominated upland environment. Many of these small, isolated swamps have been lost to development, but this one has gone through several stages of protection.

The owners of Ebenezer Swamp donated most of its 60 acres to the University of Montevallo, which has a long-term history of using the swamp for teaching and research. The university then designated the swamp as an ecological preserve, open to

Southern rain orchid, Ebenezer Swamp

the public. The university built a boardwalk into the heart of the swamp, and designs are currently being made to develop an interpretive and research center.

As you first enter Ebenezer Swamp, you will cross through an upland or rarely flooded pine-hardwood forest before stepping up onto the boardwalk, which crosses the heavily flooded central portion. (The spring-fed tributaries keep this swamp very wet, even during times of severe drought.) The majority of the trees in this deepwater portion are water tupelo, but a good number of red maple can be found in higher sections of the swamp. Other wetland plants include golden club, with its bright yellow wands of tiny flowers, and the fragrant sweetbay magnolia, which is normally a tree of the Coastal Plain. There are clear signs of beavers in the swamp, with a large beaver pond/marsh to the north of the boardwalk. Bottomland bird species can be seen and heard here, including the Acadian flycather and prothonotary warbler.

Directions: To reach Ebenezer Swamp, take AL 119 north from Montevallo. Turn right on Co. Rd. 24 and cross over the swamp. Take the next left, where you will see an open field surrounded by a split rail fence and a large white sign for the preserve. A gate leads to a parking area next to a set of bathrooms and the trailhead.

66 Limestone Park

33°11'02.59"N
86°46'03.55"W

On the opposite or east side of I-65 from Ebenezer Swamp is Alabaster's Limestone Park, which lies off US 31 in the Saginaw community. The site includes an old farm and extensive surrounding beaver marshes, and it offers great wetland bird watching, with occasional sightings of moorhens, marsh wrens, and anhingas. There's a bird observatory overlooking the marsh and tupelo swamp, and the park's road offers opportunities for seeing grassland species like meadowlarks. Naturalists share the park with a remote-control airplane club, a community garden, and a police shooting range. *So please, stay out of their spaces* during your visit.

> DIRECTIONS: To reach Limestone Park, take I-65 south from Birmingham to exit 238. Cross over the interstate and follow US 31 south through the Saginaw industrial area for several miles. The park's gate will be on your right.

67 Metro Birmingham Cahaba Access / Parks

33°29'06.62"N
86°42'06.86"W

The Cahaba River is Alabama's largest (mostly) free-flowing river. True, the Cahaba has some low-level dams in its upper sections, but most of the river runs freely from St. Clair County to near the Alabama River around Selma—a distance of about 190 miles. In its journey southward, the Cahaba River crosses the Ridge and Valley to enter the upper Coastal Plain and Black Belt. Such physiographic diversity helps the river provide habitats for more fish species than any river its size in the nation. The river also enjoys a high diversity of mussels, snails, and other aquatic invertebrates. And in addition to such invaluable natural heritage, the Cahaba provides one million people with their drinking water.

Near Birmingham, the Cahaba is a pool-and-riffle stream with shoals and rapids breaking up calmer stretches of water. The river contains many large boulders and is often surrounded by scenic cliffs and mountain slopes with rich white oak–beech forest. Some stretches of the upper river are surrounded by flat floodplain forest dominated by sycamore, river birch, and box elder, with more diverse forest farther from the water's edge.

The upper Cahaba River is best explored by canoe during the wetter times of the year. There are several bridge crossings—including some with professional-grade canoe launches—that provide put-ins and take-outs. One of the river's most scenic segments is a seven-mile run from the canoe launch at Grants Mill Rd. to Old Overton Rd. Another good run (which retains water year-round) is from a park in downtown Helena on Buck Creek (which has a few Cahaba lilies) to Co. Rd. 52.

The Little Cahaba River below Lake Purdy offers a short float during the hot, dry days of summer. This trip goes from Cahaba Beach Rd. to the Birmingham Waterworks dam area (on the main Cahaba River) at US 280. (Confusingly, a different Little Cahaba River resides in Bibb County; a local business offers canoe rentals and trips on that river and the main Cahaba.)

If you are unable to canoe, there are still a few places to explore the banks of the Upper Cahaba, including large parks in Trussville, the Grants Mill Rd., and Old Overton access sites, a few parks in Hoover, and some tracts of Freshwater Land Trust property in between. The more extensive preserves found in Bibb County are described in subsequent sections.

The area behind the Trussville Sports Complex contains an extensive trail system that traverses the river's floodplain, plus forest trails passing large boulder formations. The city of

Irondale has developed a nice riverside trail at the Grants Mill Rd. access site.

Hoover East Park offers visitors a chance to cross the river at treetop level on a pedestrian bridge and then follow an old road/trail through floodplain forest with large sycamore, box elder, and green ash trees. Wildlife here includes the rare Swainson's warbler. In addition, Hoover has just developed a nature trail through the forest behind the Hoover Metropolitan Stadium's RV Park; the trail descends a short slope and follows tributaries down to the river. The route is particularly scenic.

Directions: From Birmingham, the Trussville Sports Complex can be reached by taking I-59 to exit 141. Turn right at the top of the exit, then left on Oak St. (You will see a brown sign pointing toward the Trussville Sports Complex.) Go to the second stop sign and turn left at Riverbend Rd. Look for trail entrances as you enter the complex, and park in the nearest sports field parking lot.

The Grants Mill canoe launch, which is surrounded by some Freshwater Land Trust property on the north side of the river, can be easily found by taking I-459 exit 27 (Grants Mill Rd.) southeast of Birmingham. Follow Grants Mill Rd. south until you reach the site's parking lot, which is to the left just before the Cahaba River bridge.

The Old Overton River access site is reached by taking I-459 exit 23 (Liberty Park). Go south from the exit and take a right onto Overton-Grants Mill Rd., then take a left onto Old Overton Rd. Follow this road until you see the parking area on your right.

Hoover East Park is reached by taking I-459 exit 17 (Acton Rd.) southeast of Birmingham. Follow Acton Rd. west until you reach Old Rocky Ridge Rd. Turn left and follow Old Rocky Ridge Rd. until you see the entrance to Hoover East Park on the left.

The trail behind the Hoover Metropolitan Stadium's RV Park can be reached by taking I-459 exit 10 southwest of Birmingham. Go east on AL 150 to Stadium Trace Pkwy. Take a right onto the parkway and follow it to the stadium. Turn into the RV Park just beyond the stadium (on the left), drive to the back, and look for the very visible trail leading out.

68 Lake Purdy / Little Cahaba River Corridor

33°28'50.53"N
86°37'43.94"W

The Birmingham Water Works Board owns several thousand acres of land around Lake Purdy, the Little Cahaba River below the lake, and the pump station reservoir on the main Cahaba. The main Cahaba River provides water to the pump station during the winter and spring, and Lake Purdy sends water down to the pump station reservoir during the drier summer and fall via the Little Cahaba.

The water works lands help buffer the water supply from development and associated pollution, and the lands also protect high-quality natural habitats. The stream terraces on these lands support rich forests that house Florida maple, white ash, black walnut, and American elm. Some of the floodplains along the Little Cahaba contain the locally rare dwarf palmetto palm, near the northern limit of this species' range.

The land around Lake Purdy includes a hilly limestone karst landscape with caves that support the endangered gray bat. (This gray bat population is farther south than most of the species' other colonies.) Lake Purdy also provides winter habitat for bald eagles, plus large deer and turkey populations.

The water works lands are best visited by personal canoe below Lake Purdy, or by required canoe or motor boat rentals on Lake Purdy itself. You can fish and walk along the banks, but stay out of posted "no access" areas and adjoining private lands. An old blocked road, on the south side of AL 119, is now part of Hoover's birding trail. This old road passes through hardwood forests bordering one of the lake's tributaries.

Another walking opportunity along the Little Cahaba can be found at Leeds Memorial Park upstream. This park has walking trails and picnic tables in seminatural surroundings along the upper end of this river.

DIRECTIONS: Take I-459 exit 19 on the southeast side of Birmingham, and follow US 280 briefly to the southeast. Turn right on Colonnade Dr. and right on Colonnade Pkwy./Blue Lake Dr. Veer right onto Sicard Hollow Rd. at the water works' historic brick pump station building. Follow Sicard Hollow Rd. over the Cahaba River and continue on this road until you take a right on Cahaba Beach Rd. Follow Cahaba Beach Rd. until it dead-ends at a blocked bridge. Park wherever possible but don't block the private drive next to this area.

Here you can enjoy a swim in the Cahaba River before launching your canoe for a short (1.6-mile) ride down to the dam of the drinking water pool at US 280. The whole float is very scenic, with water works' lands buffering much of this stretch. Your take-out can be reached by backtracking to US 280 and following it southeast; you will soon approach a bridge over the Cahaba River. Before crossing the bridge, turn right onto a very short connector road, then left onto Cahaba River Rd.; here you will see a parking area to your right just before crossing the bridge over the river and its dam, which impounds the Cahaba River for about three miles upstream.

Although you can launch a boat here, a better place is found by continuing over the Cahaba River Rd. bridge; an old road to your left heads under US 280 and into the forest upstream. Park on the wide shoulder to your left just past this road. You can carry your boat under US 280 to an open, grassy area and launch it there. If you are walking, continue into the rich hardwood forest ahead to the confluence of the Cahaba and Little Cahaba Rivers. If you are canoeing, stay away from the dam in times of high water—*or you could get sucked over and drowned!*

To reach the Lake Purdy area, continue southeast on US 280 from the Cahaba River bridge and take a left onto AL 119. After a few miles, this road will cross a slough of the lake; here are good access pull-offs for fishing and wildlife observation, including part of the Hoover Birding Trail, which is marked by a blocked road. If you continue another mile or so you will see the entrance to the boat rental/fishing center to your left with a supply store and picnic tables. If you continue on AL 119 you can turn left on Grant's Mill Rd. and cross the upper end of Lake Purdy.

If you stay on AL 119 you will soon enter Leeds, with Leeds Memorial Park (and the Little Cahaba River) on your right. The rather open and "civilized" park has some walking trails and picnic tables.

69 Cahaba WMA and Living River

33°10'39.87"N
87°01'19.31"W

This 41,500-acre area is leased by the state of Alabama for hunting and other outdoor recreation. While much of the area has been strip-mined for coal or converted to pine plantations, it also contains relatively undisturbed forests bordering a long section of the Cahaba River in Shelby and Bibb Counties.

Good access to the river, as well as some old roads suitable for hiking, are found at Boothton Ford, especially on the south or east side of the river. (Shelby County is currently working to make this area a county park.) Here Cahaba lilies grow in the shoals above and below the broken concrete slab of the ford. For better

Springtime Cahaba lilies at Hargrove Shoals, Cahaba River National Wildlife Refuge

or worse, the local armadillo population is tremendous. During winter they are forced to forage in the daytime, and you can get very close to these poor-sighted creatures.

Recently, Forever Wild acquired a 94-year hunting lease on about 70 percent of the Cahaba River WMA. Thus, the next two or three generations of Alabama hunters are assured access to this large tract of land.

Below Boothton Ford, adjacent to the western border of the Cahaba River WMA, is Living River, an environmental camp and retreat being developed by the Presbyterian Church (USA). The 440 acres of the camp occupy a bend of the Cahaba River that appears like an upturned hitchhiker's thumb. Although the

Woolly Dutchman's-pipe (left) and Alabama croton (right), Cahaba River National Wildlife Refuge

camp's physical facilities are just now being put in place, a canoe launch has been built at the front end of that thumb, allowing a four-mile float to the downstream end of the property.

That downstream end once housed the Marvel Slab, a concrete ford that allowed coal-mining trucks to cross the Cahaba River. As part of the camp's development, the slab has been removed, which in turn removed a serious impediment to migration for fishes, mollusks, and other aquatic creatures in this area.

Directions: Boothton Ford is reached by taking Co. Rd. 17 north out of Montevallo and turning left on Co. Rd. 10. Continue on Co. Rd. 10 through several road meetings until you take a right onto Boothton Rd., which leads down to the old ford.

To reach Living River, continue down Co. Rd. 10 past Boothton Rd. and take the next significant right turn.

Little Cahaba River at Kathy Stiles Freeland Bibb County Glades Preserve

70 Cahaba River NWR

33°04'36.33"N
87°04'21.30"W

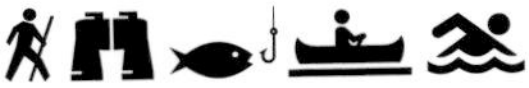

The area protected by the 3,577-acre Cahaba River NWR is one of the most biologically diverse sections of the river corridor, full of endangered aquatic species and rare plants. The refuge is a stronghold for the Cahaba shiner, goldline darter, round rocksnail, and cylindrical lioplax; it also houses the world's largest population of Cahaba lilies.

The refuge provides an important buffer for this biodiverse section of the Cahaba River, helping protect its water quality and habitats. While the surrounding ridgetops have been logged and converted to pine plantations, the refuge plans to restore them to the original (and now rare) mountain longleaf pine.

A few miles southeast of the refuge, on the north bank of the Little Cahaba River, is the Nature Conservancy's Kathy Stiles Freeland Bibb County Glades Preserve. Part of the larger Bibb County Glades complex, this area contains outcrops of Ketona dolomite, a rare type of limestone containing high levels of magnesium. The magnesium discourages the growth of trees and fosters the maintenance of grassy glades; natural fires (and now, controlled burns) help to keep the glades open and tree free. Many unique plants, adapted to this extremely harsh environment, have evolved here, including newly named species of rosinweed, blazingstar, prairie clover, and Indian paintbrush.

The Bibb County Glades area contains the highest concentration of rare plants (61 species) in the southeastern United States. When you combine those numbers with the many rare aquatic species in the river, the area becomes the most biologically diverse place in Alabama. And it is uniquely beautiful, especially where the blackish rock of the glades meets the shoals of the Little Cahaba River.

A little farther south, on the main Cahaba River, is the Nature Conservancy's Pratt's Ferry Preserve. This area includes limestone bluffs that are home to the Alabama croton, a rare shrub that is found only in a few places in Tuscaloosa and Bibb Counties. Here it grows in forests of lime-loving species like chinquapin oak, shagbark hickory, and red cedar. This section of the river is also a good place to see the periodical cicadas or "locusts" when they emerge, all at once, after 13 years of underground living. Their bulging red eyes and jungle-like sounds are something not to be missed. (The cicadas' next performance is scheduled for 2024.)

Directions: The Cahaba River NWR is reached by following Co. Rd. 24 east from West Blocton. Just before crossing the Cahaba River bridge, turn right on River Trace. This road, either in gravel or dirt

Counterclockwise from left: Alabama pinkroot; Cahaba prairie-clover; and Mohr's Barbara's buttons, Kathy Stiles Freeland Bibb County Glades Preserve

form, follows the river downstream; the further downstream that you venture, the larger the Cahaba lily populations will become. The road's drivable portion ends at Caffee Creek, but you can easily wade across on foot. The world's largest population of Cahaba lilies is found at Hargrove Shoals below Caffee Creek.

The Bibb County Glades are reached by taking AL 25 southwest from Montevallo. Turn right onto Co. Rd. 65 and travel about three miles, crossing the Little Cahaba River at Bulldog Bend. Continue for about a mile beyond the bridge and turn left onto an unnamed dirt road; this road dead-ends at the preserve's parking area. Follow the nature trail down to the Little Cahaba River.

The Pratt's Ferry Preserve is reached by continuing southwest on AL 25 past the Bibb County Glades turnoff (Co. Rd. 65). Turn right onto Co. Rd. 26 and travel about three miles to the bridge over the Cahaba River at Pratt's Ferry (also called Riverbend). The Nature Conservancy property is on the south bank of the river, on both sides of Co. Rd. 26.

BLUE RIDGE OUTLIERS

Whether or not Alabama truly contains a part of the Blue Ridge—the "true" Appalachian Mountains—is a debatable point. The authors of this book (along with many others) subscribe to the argument that if some more northern mountains, with similar partially metamorphosed rocks and lifeforms, are considered to be part of the Blue Ridge, then our Talladega Mountains should be considered southern outliers of that range.

After the Blue Ridge disappears in north Georgia, a set of quartzite mountains reappears along the Alabama–Georgia line near Piedmont, Alabama, and head southwest. These mountains straddle the boundary between the Ridge and Valley and Piedmont Provinces, just like the Blue Ridge does farther north. These mountains are characterized by different types of local quartzites, which formed when sandstones were slightly metamorphosed by the extreme heat and pressure associated with the formation of the Appalachian highlands.

Quartzite is very erosion-resistant rock and forms the highest mountains in Alabama: Cheaha, Dugger, and Choccolocco. These so-called Talladega Mountains stretch from the town of Piedmont to Sylacauga, with outliers in Coosa County. The Talladega Mountains form a stronghold for mountain longleaf pines, while their streams (especially the greater Choccolocco Creek drainage) are home to many endangered fishes, mussels, and snails.

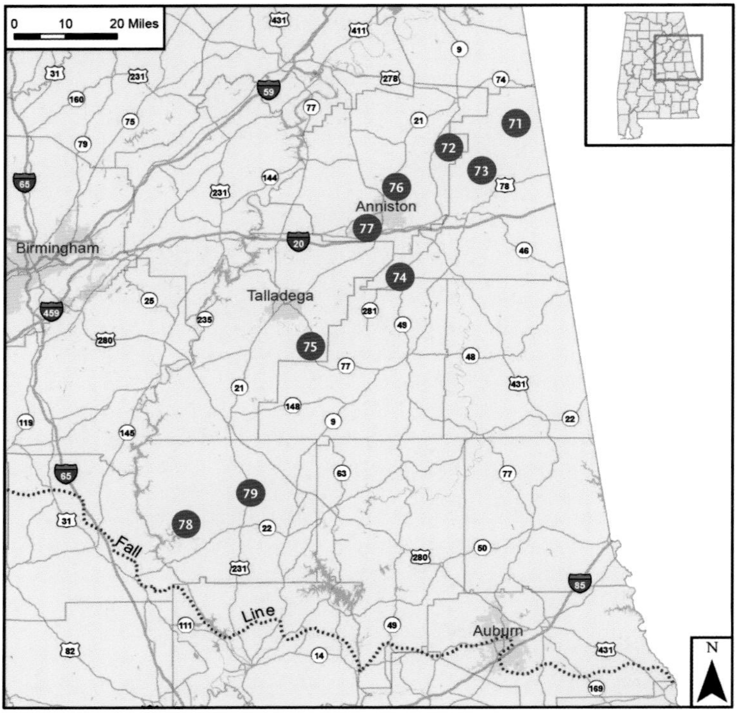

TALLADEGA UPLANDS AREA

Most of the Talladega Mountains are included within the Talladega division of the Talladega National Forest, providing many publicly accessible places to explore. The majority of Alabama's roadless areas are found here, plus two areas (Cheaha and Dugger) dedicated as wilderness. And most of this vast area can be accessed via the Pinhoti Trail.

At 130 miles (and still growing), the Pinhoti is Alabama's longest hiking trail. Additional sections of the trail have been constructed in Georgia in an effort to connect it to the Appalachian Trail; there are proposals to link the Pinhoti with the Florida Trail as well. The ultimate goal is for people to have the opportunity to walk from Quebec to the Florida Keys, passing through Alabama along the way.

The northern end of the Alabama portion of the Pinhoti Trail is located on the Georgia state line within the 594-acre Indian Mountain Tract, purchased by the state's Forever Wild program. From there the trail passes southwest through private land (thanks to a very generous easement) and then enters the Talladega National Forest at the US 278 trailhead. From that trailhead the Pinhoti goes south along razorback ridges with 360-degree views. After passing through Terrapin Creek Valley, the trail traverses a mixture of landscapes—hills, hollows, and the highest mountains in the state. The trail currently ends at Bull's Gap east of Sylacauga. As described below, there are many special areas along the Pinhoti Trail corridor that are worth seeing.

71 Terrapin Creek Valley

33°55'23.68"N
85°36'37.24"W

Surrounded by undulating ridges, Terrapin Creek valley more closely resembles the Blue Ridge than any other landscape in Alabama. The Pinhoti Trail runs perpendicular across this valley, while the Chief Ladiga Rail Trail runs down its length.

The Chief Ladiga Rail Trail is the state's longest rail-to-trail project. (Rails-to-trails involve transforming abandoned railroads into walking/bicycle paths.) The Ladiga Trail starts in Anniston and runs to the state line in Cleburne County, where it becomes Georgia's Silver Comet Trail, which leads to Atlanta. The Alabama portion is named after a local Creek chief who went to Washington, DC, in the 1830s to fight for his people's right to stay in their homeland.

The Ladiga Trail runs parallel to Choccolocco Mountain from Anniston into the Terrapin Creek valley. Walking or biking the Ladiga through the valley offers spectacular views of the shoal-strewn creek, valley forests, pastures, and rocky ridges. These ridges include the 6,017-acre Oakey Mountain Roadless Area to the south. This roadless area and the adjacent Dugger Mountain Wilderness make up the pristine watershed of the South Fork of Terrapin Creek. The high quality of that stream helps threatened mussels, such as the Coosa creekshell, to survive.

Directions: The Terrapin Creek valley can be reached by taking Co. Rd. 70 (Vigo Rd.) east from Piedmont. Just after crossing the large bridge (over Terrapin Creek), look for a road to your right, which will take you to a blocked bridge. The old railroad bed to the south of this road is the Chief Ladiga Trail.

To access the other end of the Terrapin Creek valley and the Pinhoti Trail, continue straight on Co. Rd. 70 after crossing Terrapin Creek. Proceed over the mountain and then take your first right, which will lead to the western end of the valley. Look for the rail bed and walk it going west until you reach the Pinhoti Trail crossing. To the left, the Pinhoti Trail heads south into the Oakey Mountain Roadless Area. To the right, it heads north toward US 278.

72 Dugger Mountain Wilderness

33°49'57.93"N
85°37'29.57"W

The 9,200-acre Dugger Mountain Wilderness preserves Alabama's second-highest mountain. Stream valleys on the mountain's lower slopes produce a rich assortment of wildflowers, including bloodroot; some of its pristine streams contain the threatened blue shiner. And the top of the mountain has a small but unusual stand of pure basswood. The extension of the Dugger

Mountain ridge to the southwest supports high-quality forest that is worthy of continued protection, too.

Directions: The Dugger Mountain Wilderness can be accessed by taking AL 21 south from Jacksonville, Alabama, and then turning left onto Co. Rd. 262. Continue across AL 9 and the road becomes Co. Rd. 55 (Rabbittown Rd.). Follow this road past King's Gap Rd. until you see a cleared area on your left. This is the old homeplace of Pinky Burns, a local hunter, trapper, and renowned storyteller. Park here.

If you are facing the road from the parking lot, the Pinhoti Trail crossing of east-west Rabbittown Rd. is a short walk to your left. On the south side of the road, the Pinhoti leads to Choccolocco Reservoir and its beautiful free-flowing tributaries beyond; on the north side, the Pinhoti takes you into the Dugger Mountain Wilderness Area.

To see streams and wildflowers within the Dugger Wilderness, continue east on Rabbittown Rd. and take a left onto FS 500. As you head north on FS 500 you will pass FS 500-K on your left. (Some great views of the Dugger Wilderness are found at the end of FS 500-K.) Continue north on FS 500 until you reach another crossing for the Pinhoti Trail. To the left, the trail leads into the Dugger Wilderness by way of a stream valley full of wildflowers; to the right, it leads into the Oakey Mountain Roadless Area. If you continue north on FS 500 you will shortly see a blocked old road to your left. You can hike this road to the top of Dugger Mountain.

73 Choccolocco WMA

33°46'58.17"N
85°33'36.90"W

This area takes up a large, practically solid block of National Forest land covering the low, broad, and rugged plateau between Dugger Mountain and Blue Mountain. From the 1960s to the

1980s, many of the ridgetops here were clear-cut and converted to loblolly pine plantations. Fortunately, management practices are now focused on restoring mountain longleaf pine forest to this area. Existing pine stands are being opened up and burned to restore their herbaceous diversity. Such open pine stands also provide habitat for the endangered red-cockaded woodpecker.

An old-growth loblolly pine stand near Coleman Lake provides habitat for this woodpecker and the rare red crossbill. A hollow along the Pinhoti Trail just east of nearby FS 540 contains some giant old-growth trees—tulip poplars, oaks, and even a few shortleaf pines. The hardwoods are hollowed out from past fires.

To the west of FS 540, the Pinhoti passes by cascading streams as they race through a deep hollow down to Choccolocco Reservoir. This section of the trail passes by a seepage slope full of maidenhair ferns and one of the largest chestnut oaks you will ever see.

South of Coleman Lake are the Shoal Creek Log Church and the creek that gives it its name. This clean, free-flowing stream supports several rare and endangered fishes and mussels, like the holiday darter and southern pigtoe. The Pinhoti Trail follows the creek past Pine Glen Recreation Area for much of its course.

Shoal Creek forms a horseshoe bend just before it leaves the national forest. Inside the bend you will see huge old-growth pine trees (complete with red-cockaded woodpecker holes), some giant tulip poplar trees, and white-water shoals all around. This out-of-the-way place is well worth seeing.

In this general area, a walk along an old road off of FS 522 gives you scenic views of Alabama's highest mountains, with Dugger Mountain to the north, Choccolocco Mountain to the west, and Cheaha Mountain to the south.

Directions: To reach the various areas of Choccolocco WMA, take I-20 exit 191 east of the Anniston-Oxford area. On the north side of this exit, take a right on US 78 and travel east, then a left on AL

9. Continue north on AL 9 until you reach its intersection with the Joseph Springs Motorway, where the headquarters office for Choccolocco State Forest is located. (To the left, the motorway leads through the state forest to the Mountain Longleaf NWR.) Take a right on the motorway and pass through a short section of the state forest (with the Frog Pond Observatory to your left) before you climb the hill into the Talladega National Forest. Here the road becomes FS 522. In about a half-mile you will see an unmarked, blocked road to your left. Park here to see the horseshoe bend of Shoal Creek. Walk in and stay straight when you reach a point where the road splits. This road will continue north until it starts curving east toward the bend in the creek. The walk is about three miles round-trip.

Other sites can be reached by continuing on FS 522 and taking a left on FS 500. You will pass by the Pine Glen Recreation Area. FS 500 subsequently meets FS 553, and if you take a right you will shortly reach 553-D on your left, which leads to Shoal Creek Log Church. After the previously mentioned intersection, FS 500 becomes paved, and you can keep following it past its sharp turn to the turnoff for the Coleman Lake area. At the sharp turn, continue straight on unpaved FS 532 and make a right turn onto FS 540. The Pinhoti Trail will cross this road. The trail to the right goes immediately into the hollow with many old-growth hardwood trees, then through the open pine forests next to Coleman Lake. The trail to the left leads down to the cascading headwaters of Choccolocco Reservoir.

74 Cheaha Mountain

33°28'42.81"N
85°48'34.69"W

The highest land mass in Alabama includes Cheaha State Park, the Blue Mountain Roadless Area (to the north), and the Cheaha

Rock Garden, Cheaha State Park

Wilderness (to the south). The Talladega Scenic Drive—Alabama's version of the Blue Ridge Parkway—has scenic overlooks in and around these areas. Overlooks provide views of the Ridge and Valley landscape to the west and the rolling hills of the Piedmont to the east.

The valley of the 4,797-acre Blue Mountain Roadless Area protects a pristine watershed that feeds Hillabee Reservoir, which provides water for the Anniston-Oxford area. The roadless area can be seen from the Talladega Scenic Drive overlook just north of the state park.

The 2,799-acre Cheaha State Park contains an observation tower marking the state's highest point at 2,407 feet. While the views from the tower are adequate, more spectacular views and experiences can be gained by walking the trails to Bald Rock, the

Pulpit Rock, Cheaha State Park

Rock Garden, or Pulpit Rock. The trail to Bald Rock includes a handicapped-accessible boardwalk. As you walk the interpretive trail, notice the stunted nature of the mountaintop trees, especially the oaks. These trees are small because the soil is rocky, poor, and dry, and the winter climate is harsh. (Such stunted stands are called "orchard oaks" because of their resemblance to fruit orchard trees.) You will see no longleaf pines here because the top of the mountain is above the altitudinal limit of that species. The boulders along the brow of the mountain also produce a microclimate supporting dwarf specimens of sweet birch, a species normally found farther north.

The Rock Garden and Pulpit Rock are good places to see the sunset and the Talladega Mountains continuing to the south. The Rock Garden area has a wet-weather waterfall stream surrounded

Cheaha Creek, Chinnabee Silent Trail, Cheaha Wilderness Area by an abundance of azaleas. These shrubs bloom in early summer, which is much later than in lower areas. Pulpit Rock is considered to be quite a romantic place, *so be extra careful!*

The 7,245-acre Cheaha Wilderness has many trails (including the Pinhoti) that can be combined to form loops. As you hike the wilderness, you will notice white crystalline rocks on and around the trails. This is the erosion-resistant quartzite that makes possible the continued existence of these high mountains.

The southern end of the Odum Scout Trail and, to a lesser degree, the Nubbin Creek Trail, have nice waterfalls during the wetter times of year. The Silent Trail leads from the Caney Head (the longest lasting source of water on top of the mountain) down Cheaha Creek and out of the wilderness to the best waterfalls in the forest, above Chinnabee Lake. These cascades include Wildcat and Devil's Den Falls. (The Silent Trail is named in honor of its builders, who were deaf Boy Scouts from the Alabama Institute for the Deaf and Blind in Talladega.) The largest waterfall in the area is Salt Creek Falls, which is hard to access since only the downstream side of the falls is in public ownership.

Directions: Take I-20 exit 191 east of the Anniston-Oxford area. To the south of the exit, take US 431 southeast until it intersects with AL 49 or the Talladega Scenic Dr. Take a right onto the scenic drive and follow it southwest toward Cheaha State Park. You will pass a few overlooks on both sides of the road. After you pass Co. Rd. 24 and a subsequent utility right-of-way clearing, you will see a road entrance to your right that has been blocked. Park here and follow this old CCC road down to Hillabee Creek in the Blue Mountain Roadless Area. You can also continue southwest on the scenic drive to an overlook on the right that looks across that area.

If you take a left on AL 49 when it splits off from the scenic drive, you can follow it down the mountain until you see signs for the Nubbin Creek and Lower Odum Scout Trails, which lead into the west and south sides of the Cheaha Wilderness, respectively.

Continue southwest on the scenic drive until you see a large parking lot on your left at a curve. Park here to access the north end of the Cheaha Wilderness. There is a trailhead from this parking area into the wilderness area, and the Pinhoti Trail crosses the scenic drive a short walk to your left (if facing the road from the parking lot). To the left of the drive, the Pinhoti Trail passes through Cheaha State Park to the Cheaha Wilderness beyond. To the right, the Pinhoti goes through the park to the Blue Mountain Roadless Area.

Continue on the scenic drive into the main portion of Cheaha State Park, then south a short distance until you make a right turn onto Co. Rd. 43. This road will take you down the mountain. Make a left turn onto FS 646 to reach the Chinnabee Lake Area and the waterfalls of the Silent Trail above it. You can also reach the Silent Trail by staying straight on the scenic drive past the Co. Rd. 43 turnoff; if you go down the mountain, the parking lot will be on your left. The Silent Trail (to your left) leads up through the Cheaha Wilderness to the Caney Head spring and trail junction. The trail to the right leads first to Wildcat Falls and then to the waterfalls above Chinnabee Lake.

The scenic drive continues to the Adams Gap Area where the Pinhoti Trail crosses the road again.

75 Southern Talladega Mountains

33°19'02.62"N
86°01'19.93"W

South of the Cheaha Wilderness, the Talladega Mountain range extends to Rebecca Mountain east of Sylacauga. This area has nice old-growth longleaf and the impressive Sherman Cliffs. Some of this area's national forest lands, along with private lands, are included in the Hollins WMA. This WMA has some fine examples of longleaf pine that were periodically burned; thus, it contains great herbaceous diversity. You can see some of this diversity from the roads of the area.

DIRECTIONS: The Southern Talladega Mountains can be traversed by following FS 600 south from the Talladega Scenic Drive area at Adams Gap (mentioned in the previous section). FS 600 (which, we must warn you, has some rough spots) runs south to a junction with AL 48/77; take a left and go west to Porters' Gap. (At Porters' Gap, AL 48/77 intersects with AL 77, which leads west to Talladega; this makes a good access point for the area as well.) Porters' Gap has a Pinhoti trailhead. To the south of the AL 48/77 and AL 77 intersection, FS 600 continues along the top of Rebecca Mountain. The Sherman Cliffs are located to your right about a mile and a half beyond the fire tower site.

FS 600 continues south to the Pinhoti Trailhead at Bulls Gap (and to AL 148, which leads west to Sylacauga). From Bulls Gap you can explore the lowlands of the Hollins WMA.

76 Choccolocco Mountain

33°41'47.57"N
85°49'12.99"W

Choccolocco Mountain stretches from the town of Piedmont to the Anniston-Oxford area. The northern end of the mountain is called Hurricane Mountain, and it contains a significant amount of national forest land. While such lands become more scattered in the middle section of Choccolocco Mountain near Jacksonville, they pick back up in the mountain's south-central section, within the Mountain Longleaf NWR.

Jacksonville State University has worked hard to improve the

Mountain Longleaf pines at Mountain longleaf refuge

conservation of and access to Chimney Peak, which provides good views of the Jacksonville area in a forest setting. The university's astronomical observatory is located there as well.

The Anniston Museum of Natural History is one of the largest city-funded natural history museums in the country. It offers exhibits on seemingly everything—dinosaurs, caves, Alabama wildlife, North American wildlife, African wildlife, natural communities, and Egyptian mummies. The museum is located in Lagarde Park (named after a major museum patron, John B. Lagarde), which contains some interpretive nature trails that pass through pine-hardwood and bottomland forests. The bottomland forest includes the second-largest loblolly pine in the state—truly a giant of a tree. The trails also feature permanently injured birds of prey in outdoor structures. A backyard wildlife habitat is located beside the museum building. Other areas of Lagarde Park contain the impressive Berman Museum of World/Military History and mountain bike trails by the community center.

The Anniston Museum of Natural History also developed a long, unmarked nature trail up the slope of the portion of Choccolocco Mountain known as Blue Mountain. The mountain trail can be reached by entering the Lagarde Park's road system from the main highway and then taking a right at the fork. Follow the right fork until it quickly ends at a cul-de-sac near picnic pavilions and a walking trail. A faint trail into the scrub passes an old construction cut with some beautifully colored clay formations. The trail becomes more defined as it starts to climb the mountain in a series of loops. It passes a surface-cut iron ore mine and continues through mixed pine-hardwood forest to a power line crossing near the top of the mountain, which offers superb views of surrounding mountains, forests, and towns. This area is also a good place for spotting colorful migrating warblers in the fall and spring.

The Mountain Longleaf NWR is the jewel of Choccolocco Mountain and the whole Talladega range. The refuge includes 9,000 acres of the old Fort McClellan military base. When the base was decommissioned, conservationists worked to retain the portion of the base that has the finest examples of mountain longleaf pine in the world. Although longleaf pine is typically thought of as a Coastal Plain or lowland species, it once dominated fire-prone Appalachian uplands in central Alabama, northwest Georgia, and some Piedmont areas to the east. Due to the fire suppression mentality of the mid-20th century (popularized by the Forest Service's Smokey the Bear campaign), most stands of the fire-dependent mountain longleaf were not burned as they once had been by lightning strikes, Native Americans, and European settlers. The forests grew up in pine-competing scrub, and the diverse herbaceous layer was lost. As the older trees were cut, the longleaf disappeared, to be replaced by faster-growing loblolly pines. Ironically, the military maintained high-quality longleaf forest on Fort McClellan by using some of their lands for target practice. Cannons and machine guns often caught the forest on fire, maintaining a somewhat natural cycle.

The military's accidental land-use strategy preserved stands of old-growth longleaf (200 years old or more) with a diverse herbaceous layer of grasses and wildflowers, including asters and legumes. Rare plant species on the refuge include the white fringeless orchid and ground juniper. The area supports a large population of fox squirrels, and the old fort property is rich in archaeological resources, including a prehistoric effigy mound where rocks are formed into the shape of a snake. Many people hope that the effigy mound will be added to the refuge.

Opening the various areas of the refuge to public access has been a gradual process. The refuge managers must first make sure that the risk of visitor contact with unexploded shells is minimal. Therefore, present access is limited to the high scenic ridgeline area, which is often covered in a hoar frost during cold winter days. (A hoar frost occurs when clouds condense and freeze on trees and other vegetation, giving them a sparkly winter wonderland appearance—a rather rare sight in semitropical Alabama).

Although most of the longleaf areas are not currently accessible, you can see some longleaf stands on the west side of the mountain while driving Bains Gap Rd., which crosses from the Choccolocco valley to Anniston. Since the risk of unexploded shells has not yet been minimized here, you are not allowed to get out of your car. In fact, it's always a good idea to check to see which areas are open to the public prior to making a trip to the refuge.

The adjacent Choccolocco State Forest is currently more accessible, and it contains an impressive waterfall, diverse terrace-floodplain hardwood forests with large trees along Choccolocco Creek, and the Frog Pond Wildlife Observatory. As part of the Choccolocco WMA, the state forest serves an important role in connecting the habitats and hunting lands of the Mountain Longleaf NWR with Talladega National Forest.

Despite past abuses of chemical contamination, Choccolocco Creek provides habitat for numerous rare and endangered aquatic species. The creek starts on the south side of Dugger Mountain and picks up biodiverse Shoal and Cheaha Creeks before finally flowing into Logan Martin Lake. The lower portion of the creek can be canoed between its bridges, but be conscious of the creek's contaminated sediments.

Directions: Chimney Peak is easily accessed from Mountain St. in Jacksonville. Mountain Street becomes Chimney Peak Tower Rd., and pull-offs near its terminus provide good views.

The Lagarde Park/Anniston Museum of Natural History area is located at the junction or split of US 431 and AL 21 just north of downtown Anniston.

The Mountain Longleaf Refuge/Choccolocco State Forest Area can be reached by taking I-20 exit 191 east of the Anniston-Oxford area. On the north side of this exit, turn east on US 78; continue east until you take a left onto AL 9. Continue north on AL 9 until you reach its intersection with the Joseph Springs Motorway, where the headquarters for the Choccolocco State Forest is located.

To reach the Frog Pond Wildlife Observatory, take a right onto the motorway and you will shortly see the observatory's parking lot on the left.

To reach Choccolocco Creek and the Mountain Longleaf refuge, take a left onto the motorway and pass over a bridge through the bottomland hardwood forest along Choccolocco Creek. There is parking along the roadside in several places as well as old roads to explore. Continue on the motorway until you reach Co. Rd. 55. Take a right and then the first left, which is the road heading to Bains Gap. This road climbs up the mountain; you will see and hear a waterfall through the woods on your left before leaving the state forest and entering the Mountain Longleaf NWR. After you cross into the refuge, continue to the top of the mountain where there is a crossroads with an information/map station. You can take a right to a scenic viewing spot or take a left and go south past more rugged mountain country. Until more of the area is checked for unexploded ordnance, you must confine your exploration to the east side of this mountaintop road.

77 Coldwater Mountain

33°37'11.33"N
85°52'56.03"W

Coldwater Mountain is a relatively isolated quartzite mountain that includes a 4,083-acre conservation area acquired by Forever Wild with assistance from the Anniston Water Works Board. The conservation area is named the Doug Ghee Nature Preserve and Recreation Area in honor of the state senator who was pivotal in crafting the legislation to establish the Forever Wild program.

The property protects key buffer lands around Coldwater Springs. This huge spring system is the main water source for Anniston. It also happens to be the world's only home of the threatened pygmy sculpin. An arranged visit to the spring will quite easily reveal this tiny fish, which may be the state's most abundant vertebrate per square foot of habitat. However, the fish is only found in this particular spring and spring run, making it vulnerable to extinction.

Because of the sensitive nature of the sculpin, its spring, and Anniston's water supply, access to the area is very limited. If you would like to take a swim in the clear, spring-fed waters of Coldwater Creek, you can visit a small park downstream maintained by the city of Oxford on US 78.

Recently, a new public access road, trailhead, and 11 miles of hiking/mountain biking trails were dedicated within the Doug Ghee Preserve. These miles consist of an easy, one-mile loop for inexperienced riders and a far tougher, 10-mile one for the more experienced (and adventuresome).

DIRECTIONS: To visit Coldwater Springs proper (and properly), contact the Anniston Water Works Board. To reach the trailhead in the Doug Ghee Preserve, take I-20 exit 179 and turn north on AL 202. Go about two miles before turning right on Co. Rd. 109/Coldwater Pump Rd. The new public access road will appear shortly on the right.

78 Flagg Mountain, Weogufka State Forest, and Coosa County WMA

32°53'38.43"N
86°22'11.83"W

Flagg Mountain is the southernmost peak in the Blue Ridge Outliers of Alabama. The mountain was once a state park where the CCC built a beautiful stone lookout tower and cabins. The state abandoned the park and the area became the Weogufka State Forest. Visitors to the state forest will see large old-growth longleaf pine trees on the sunny slopes of the mountain. Dry to moist

Road traversing Weogufka State Forest

hardwood forests occur along the drains, which include some springs. Because the top of the mountain is subjected to severe wind and cold, it is occupied by dry oak-hickory forest. Lumber company land on the south slope of the mountain contains some well-managed examples of mountain longleaf pine forest that are easily observed from the road as you travel over the mountain.

The old tower and cabins are being restored by a local conservation group. Because the group holds the lease on the mountain's peak, it is not currently accessible to the public.

At the junction of the main forest road and the spur road leading uphill to the tower, you will see a yellow sign with "AT" in big letters. While those two letters usually stand for the Appalachian Trail, in this case they mean Alabama Trail. The Alabama Trail is planned to link the Appalachian Trail to the Florida Trail by way of the Pinhoti Trail and extensions south toward Conecuh National Forest. One of the first sections of the Alabama Trail to be built is this four-mile loop in Weogufka State Forest. To hike this section, just park in the wide shoulder of the road and head downhill. You will pass the bases of some giant longleaf pines along the way.

Forever Wild recently purchased a 762-acre addition to Weogufka State Forest. This purchase is extremely significant because it will allow the rerouting of the Pinhoti Trail to Flagg Mountain; if all goes as planned, Flagg Mountain would then become the southern terminus of the Appalachian Trail. Check our book's website for updates on this project.

To the south of the Weogufka State Forest is the Coosa County WMA. While much of this management area is privately owned pine plantations, Forever Wild has acquired about 10,000 acres of high-quality longleaf pine forest within the WMA. The Forever Wild lands are adjacent to mature longleaf stands (owned by Alabama Power) that form the southern end of the WMA along the Lake Mitchell hydroelectric reservoir. Combined, these longleaf stands support numerous colonies of the endangered red-cockaded woodpecker.

One of the best ways to see this area is by boating the impounded sections of Weogufka and Hatchet Creeks. However, there is at least one relatively easy foot access area into the longleaf stands listed in the directions below. Also, if you have a boat you can follow the north shore of Hatchet Creek to where it meets the impounded Coosa River. This area contains several Coastal Plain influences, including Spanish moss along the banks and water tupelo in the shallows.

DIRECTIONS: To reach Flagg Mountain, go to Kellys Crossroads on AL 22 between Rockford and Verbena and take Co. Rd. 29 north. Turn left on Co. Rd. 16, then right on a dirt road known locally as CCC Camp Rd. On top of Flagg Mountain is a locked gate of the approach road to the observation tower. You will see a sign for the Alabama Trail to the right of the tower road.

To reach some of the new Forever Wild purchases in the Coosa WMA by land, take Co. Rd. 29 north from Kellys Crossroads and cross Hatchet Creek, then take the first left turn into the WMA. If the gate is locked, walk down this road into some nice longleaf pine forest.

If you have a boat, you can launch it at a nearby fishing camp. It can be reached by continuing southwest on AL 22 from Kellys Crossroads for a few miles, then taking a right on Co. Rd. 27, which dead-ends into the camp on an impounded section of Hatchet Creek. You will need either a lake or WMA map to navigate from this point.

79 Hatchet Creek

32°56'37.93"N
86°12'11.09"W

Hatchet Creek is one of the most pristine free-flowing streams in the Coosa River drainage. The creek's headwaters lie in the Talladega National Forest, but its main stem runs through some well-managed private forest land. Due to its clean water and low sediment load, Hatchet Creek is home to several threatened mollusks and fishes, including the coal darter. The creek also has large populations of walleye and Cahaba lilies.

The creek's bottom sparkles brightly due to the presence of tiny flakes of mica, which is an igneous (volcanic) mineral. The sparkling mica is characteristic of stream sand in some regions of the main Blue Ridge and Piedmont.

The only way to properly experience and enjoy Hatchet Creek is by canoe, using bridges for put-ins and take-outs.

Directions: Hatchet Creek can be reached by taking US 231 north of Rockford to the bridge crossing over the creek. For canoeing information consult *Alabama Canoe Rides and Float Trips* in this book's set of References and Websites.

PIEDMONT

The Piedmont is a region of rolling hills composed largely of metamorphic rocks. Ancient geologic processes applied heat and pressure to most of the rocks of the Piedmont and metamorphosed them into "new" types of rocks. For example, limestone became marble. The Sylacauga mines, located in the Blue Ridge Outlier–Piedmont Province transition area, now send marble across the globe.

The Piedmont also includes limited outcrops of granite, which is an igneous rock derived from molten rock or magma. The Piedmont's granite was formed in the ancient past when an ocean basin between continents was being closed. Along the continental margin of that time, portions of the earth's crust from one continental plate moved beneath another. The resulting friction melted huge bodies of rock called *plutons*, which oozed their way toward the surface in the Piedmont and eastern Blue Ridge Provinces. This magma cooled before it reached the surface, forming granite with large crystals. Some granite plutons were later exposed as domes, such as Stone Mountain, Georgia. More commonly, the granite appears as flat rocks. As mentioned in the last chapter, river sands in portions of the Piedmont sparkle due to the presence of tiny fragments of mica, another igneous mineral.

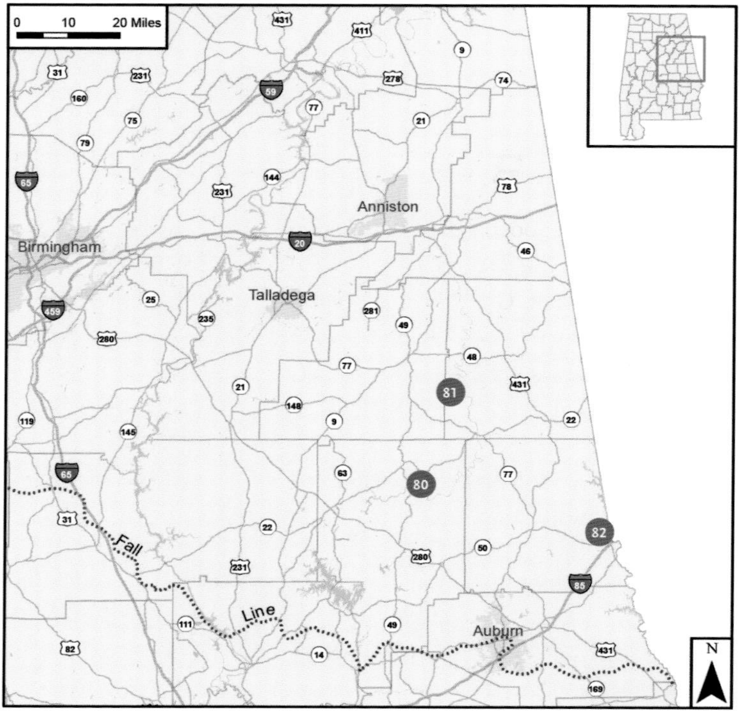

ANNISTON AREA

The natural vegetation of the Piedmont south and east of the city of Anniston is mixed pine-hardwood with some longleaf pines on especially dry sites; sycamore, box elder, and other hardwoods occupy the floodplains. The most unique vegetation of the area can be found on its limited granite outcrops. Although most of the Piedmont has been farmed and/or converted to pine plantations, there are several natural areas well worth investigating.

80 Tallapoosa River

32°58'09.81"N
85°44'22.00"W

The upper Tallapoosa River is largely a free-flowing river broken up only by the Harris Lake impoundment. The uppermost segment, from the Georgia state line to US 431 (44 miles), can be accessed by the Lloyd Owens Canoe Trail, composed of good canoe launches at bridge crossings. Canoe rentals and shuttle services are available in this area on the weekends. Along their journey, canoeists can see egrets, large gravel bars, low bluffs of metamorphic rocks, and scenic farmland. Particles of mica shimmer in the sand of the gravel bars, but not quite as much as they do downstream.

The free-flowing segments of the river below Harris Lake can be accessed at bridge crossings as well. The river level below Harris Lake is dependent on releases from that lake, so you might want to check water levels before doing a float trip below the dam.

Anyone who just wants to walk along the river can visit the 2,040-acre Horseshoe Bend National Military Park. This site is where the forces of Andrew Jackson defeated the Creek Indians who were resisting the encroachment of white settlers upon their lands. The battlefield lies in and around a horseshoe-shaped bend of the Tallapoosa River. This beautiful forested park has several trails, and the river bottom glistens with mica. There is a boat launch on the downstream end of the park that is useful for float trips or just paddling upstream into the park.

Wind Creek State Park is located on the Tallapoosa River's Lake Martin hydroelectric reservoir. The state park offers trails along the lake through rocky uplands as well as many other recreational activities. An exciting new conservation project on Lake

Unusual boulder formation along Deadening Alpine Ridge Trail near the Tallapoosa River

Martin is Russell Forest. The Russell Lands Development Corporation has set aside a sizable area along the lake as greenspace, with about 80 miles of hiking, biking, and horse trails. While this greenspace makes their adjacent developments more attractive to potential buyers, it also helps protect the lake's natural resources. Be aware that upon arrival at a trailhead in the forest you must call the corporation's security office to register.

Another new conservation project on Lake Martin is the Cherokee Ridge Alpine Trails. This project is located on Alabama Power Company land that is being managed for conservation and recreation in the form of an 11-mile hiking trail system. The trails pass by the lake, boulder formations, scenic vistas, and shoal-filled streams. The vegetation includes some mountain longleaf pine and dwarf rhododendron, plus deciduous magnolias in more moist environments. Bald eagles are sometimes seen on the property. The Deadening Alpine Ridge Trail has lots of dwarf rhododendron and particularly impressive boulder formations and cliffs. This 3.6-mile loop passes through an open mountain longleaf pine forest on top of the ridge and then drops down along its slopes following a set of switchbacks. The route offers great views of the lake and its rocky islands; the best rock formations are at the end of the loop route. Because it is rather strenuous, with little shade, the Deadening Trail is best avoided on hot summer days.

DIRECTIONS: To reach Horseshoe Bend National Military Park, follow AL 49 north from Dadeville in Tallapoosa County; the highway bisects the park. If you continue north on AL 49 and take a left onto AL 22, you will see an historic marker for the Battle of Emuckfaw, where the Creeks caused an earlier Jackson expedition to retreat.

To reach Wind Creek State Park, take US 280 southeast from Alexander City and follow the signs.

To reach Russell Forest, follow AL 63 south from Alexander City and turn right on the Willow Point Cutoff; one of the major trailheads can be accessed to the left off this road. Remember that you must call the security office and register once you reach the trailhead.

To reach the Cherokee Ridge Alpine Trails System, follow AL 63 south from Alexander City, then turn left on AL 229; follow this road until you reach its junction with AL 50. Turn left and travel east on AL 50 for a few miles, cross the Tallapoosa River and then turn left onto Overlook Dr. (0.3 mile past the bridge). Look for trailhead signs. Parking for Cherokee Ridge is one mile on the left; parking for the Deadening Trail is three miles on the left.

81 Granite Outcrops

33°13'05.78"N
85°38'06.62"W

Granite outcrops, like the previously described limestone and sandstone glades, are harsh environments. The plants that live on them have to be adapted to both flood conditions (in the short term) and drought conditions (in the long term).

Visitors to such outcrops catch a glimpse of the process by which seemingly lifeless bare rock is slowly transformed into a thriving natural community. Only lichens—mutualistic combinations of fungi and algae—can survive on bare rock expanses. But erosion produces depressions in the rock where sandy particles settle, and tufts of tough mosses soon sprout. These moss beds retain enough moisture that larger plants get a roothold—hardy grasses, cacti, and other succulents. Finally, shrubs and trees sprout, and their roots reach down into cracks in the depressions, pushing outward and breaking the rocky expanse.

Granite outcrops are characterized by a unique set of plants. During late winter and early spring, flooded pools turn blood red

Granite expanse at Flat Rock Park, with Harris Lake in background

Red leaves of stonecrop at Flat Rock Park

with a succulent annual plant called stonecrop. Other common granite outcrop plants include prickly pear cactus, one-flower stitchwort, southern reindeer moss (actually a lichen), and carnivorous terrestrial bladderworts. Trees found in the depression islands scattered across the outcrops include red cedar and scrub oaks, which can survive in the dry shallow soil.

The best granite outcrop in Alabama is Almond Outcrop, located next to the settlement of the same name in Randolph County. The outcrop is on private land, so it must be observed from the main highway and adjacent county road. The latter road is gravel and has much less traffic, making it easier to stop, park, and walk along. Hopefully, this unique natural wonder will one day become part of the Alabama public domain.

A granite outcrop with better public access is found at Alabama Power's Flat Rock Park on Harris Lake. This 25-acre outcrop was initially damaged when it was partially flooded by the impoundment; more damage occurred when it became a local hangout and party spot. Fencing the area, limiting car access upon the rocks, and making it an official family picnic area have reduced the impacts upon the outcrop. Flat Rock Park is open (only on weekends) May–September; in addition to a picnic area, it offers a nature trail, swimming, and bathrooms.

More undisturbed sections of Flat Rock (also known locally as Blake's Ferry) can be accessed outside the picnic area. But when walking on rock outcrop communities, remember not to step on the fragile plants and moss beds.

South of these granite outcrops is the Alexander City Pluton. A cross section of this volcano-wannabe can be seen in the road cut on the northeast side of US 280 on the southeastern outskirts of Alexander City. It can be viewed safely from a gas station across the highway. The round granite dome shape of the formation is unmistakable—truly a Stone Mountain–like formation on a miniature scale.

DIRECTIONS: To reach the Almond Outcrop, take AL 77 northwest from Wadley. Just before you reach Co. Rd. 15, coming in on your right, you will start seeing the granite outcrop. Park on a wide road shoulder and observe the outcrop from the road; or turn right onto Co. Rd. 15 and then take your next right, which is a county road as well. From here you can easily and safely walk the road and observe the outcrop.

To reach Flat Rock Park, take Blake's Ferry Rd. south from Lineville for approximately seven miles. This park is only seasonally open, so call before going.

82 West Point Lake

32°52'06.77"N
85°11'25.67"W

West Point Lake is a large impoundment on the Chattahoochee River, which straddles the Alabama–Georgia border near Lanett. Visitors will notice that the landscape around the lake and in surrounding areas is "more gentle" than sections of the Piedmont to the northwest, which border the Blue Ridge Outliers. West Point Lake is attractive to visit because it has so many public recreation areas on both the Alabama and Georgia sides. These recreation areas include trails, camping, and boat/canoe access.

One of the best trails on the Alabama side is the Interpretive Trail at Amity Campground. (Just tell the gateman that you are there to walk the trail and he will let you in for free.) The Interpretive Trail is largely made up of a boardwalk through a beaver swamp. The beavers have produced several open ponds as well as marshes and a buttonbush swamp. You can safely view wildlife (including the venomous cottonmouth) if you stay on the trail. The trail also passes through pine forest with some hardwood.

Other connecting trails traverse upland forest along the lake.

Hardley Creek Park offers views of cormorants fishing in the tailrace below West Point Dam as well as a walking trail along a more natural section of the river. A visitor center and museum on the Georgia side of the dam features local history.

Directions: Take I-85 exit 79 (Lanett) just west of the Georgia border. Follow US 29 north through Lanett, entering Georgia and the town of West Point. Take a left onto Co. Rd. 212 (State Line Rd.). You will reenter Alabama and pass by the dam area, Hardley Creek Park, Amity Campground, and other parks.

FALL LINE HILLS

The majority of Alabama lies in the Coastal Plain physiographic province, west and south of the Fall Line. The Fall Line meanders south from Florence to Tuscaloosa, then east to Phenix City. Its name comes from the waterfalls found along the border between the higher, rocky, upland physiographic provinces and the lower, relatively rockless Coastal Plain.

The Coastal Plain can be divided into many distinct subprovinces or physiographic regions, including the Fall Line Hills. This subprovince marks the transition between the various upland provinces and the Coastal Plain. Substantial hills occur in this region, plus large floodplain swamps in between. Because the region contains both upland and lowland elements, there are many interesting places to explore.

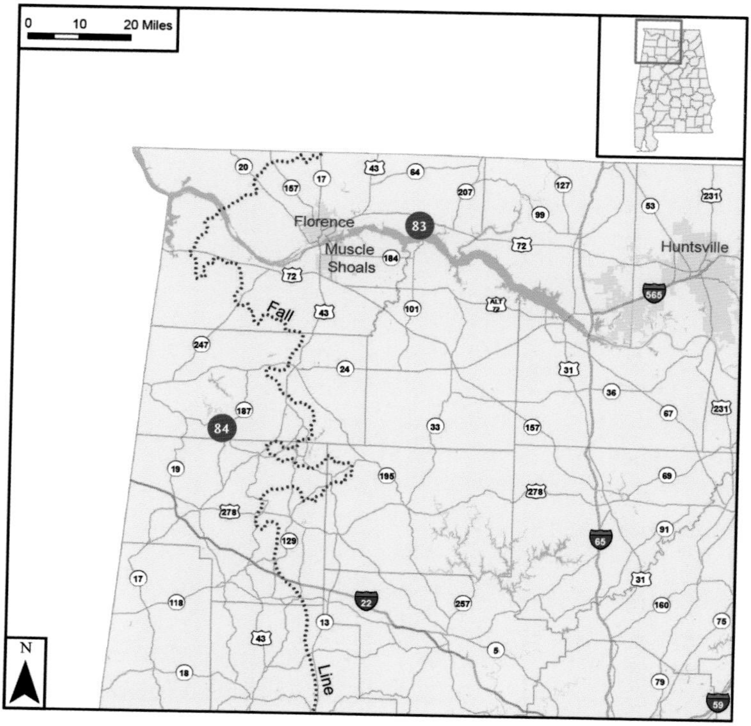

FLORENCE AREA

The area immediately surrounding Florence is dominated by the Tennessee River, with its bluffs, caves, and sloughs. Nearby are several contrasting areas of shady coves with hemlock trees.

83 Muscle Shoals / Coffee Slough

34°48'13.80"N
87°22'54.26"W

The Muscle Shoals once stretched for miles along the Tennessee River, from the city named after it upstream past the current site of Wheeler Dam. The grassy shoals once contained the greatest diversity of freshwater mussels in the world. The construction of Wilson Dam and Wheeler Dam virtually destroyed the shoals by placing them deep under water. However, a short stretch of rocky flowing river remains below Wilson Dam. This area has been restocked with several endangered mussels in an effort to expand their populations. Before 9/11, you could see the river from the Wilson Lock and Dam observation area and, at night, the bright lights allowed you to observe the riverside's many herons and raccoons. When boats and barges moved downstream, geysers of water expelled from the lock system forced the animals to retreat to higher ground. Hopefully this area will be reopened to the public in a safer future.

Across the river is the TVA's Muscle Shoals Reservation. This public greenspace has an excellent 10-mile-long trail system along the river bluffs. The dam area offers views of the remnant Muscle Shoals and a great blue heron rookery; bald eagles nest on the island downstream from the dam. The reservation includes the historic Old Quarters SWA, which features abundant wildflowers, plus the Lower Rockpile Campground.

Just downstream from the remnant Muscle Shoals is the Coffee Slough area. Coffee Slough is the mainland unit of the 4,685-acre, TVA-owned, state-managed Seven Mile Island WMA. A flooded and low-lying depression, the slough is named after one of Andrew Jackson's army officers who settled in the area after the local Native Americans were forced to cede their lands.

Coffee Slough has a unique diversity of habitats. The higher river bottoms and terraces contain fields that are farmed to provide food for game species. Lower floodplain areas support bottomland hardwood forest and a significant cypress swamp. Normal-sized cypress trees grow along the higher edges of the

Wilson Dam and the remains of the Muscle Shoals below it

slough, while dwarfed ones—stunted by the continuous flooding—are found toward its mouth. The scattered, stunted cypress trees form a very scenic watery savanna.

The most unique features of the Coffee Slough area occur where springs bubble out of the base of a limestone cliff along its border. This limestone cliff (with a few cave openings) is part of the Interior Low Plateau, and it forms a Fall Line border with Coastal Plain swamps. The lower slope of the cliff contains cove hardwood with lots of basswood. Fallen basswood leaves, along with weathered limestone, create a rich soil that supports a diversity of wildflowers, including Dutchman's breeches and columbine. The slope drops off into a spring-fed cypress swamp with pools chockfull of bream. This Fall Line location is one of the few places in Alabama where you can stand inside a limestone cave and look out at a cypress swamp.

Extensive walking trails at Muscle Shoals Reservation near Wilson Dam

On top of the bluffs above Coffee Slough is the 1,060-acre Key Cave NWR. The surface of this sinkhole-riddled land supports both active farmland and old farmland that is being restored to natural habitats, including the tallgrass prairie that was once common in this region. The refuge has a nice overlook platform and trails through some of this restored prairie, where you can see grassland birds such as savanna sparrows, northern harriers, and short-eared owls.

Not surprisingly, the refuge's namesake cave lies below this karst-sinkhole landscape. Key Cave is the only known home of the Alabama cave fish, which is blind since it needs no eyes in a pitch-black cave. (The fish is also albino since it has no reason to show color and needs no skin pigments to protect it from the sun.) The cave also supports a large colony of gray bats. Bat droppings provide the nutrients to the cave's water system that support the aquatic invertebrates eaten by the cave fish—a classic and simple example of a food chain.

Nearby, additional upland habitats are found upstream on Cypress Creek at the city of Florence's Wildwood Park. The park has a nature trail and mountain bike trails.

Directions: To reach the Wilson Lock and Dam observation area from the city of Muscle Shoals, take AL 184 east from US 72. Continue east on AL 184 until you reach AL 133. Take a left and head north to Wilson Dam. Cross over the Tennessee River and you will see the observation area next to the lock.

To reach the Muscle Shoals Reservation, take US 72 north in the city of Muscle Shoals; the entrance to the reservation will be on the right just before crossing the Tennessee River.

To reach Coffee Slough, continue north on US 72 and cross the Tennessee River into Florence, then take a left on AL 20. Follow AL 20 west until you cross over Cypress Creek. Almost immediately you will see the entrance to both the Seven Mile Island WMA and a municipal wastewater treatment plant. Turn left onto this entrance road. Park on the right outside of the treatment plant; do not block the road leading into the plant or the gated road on the right that leads into the WMA. Proceed on foot down the WMA road. You will see a long cypress swamp slough to your left running east to west. Follow the slough downstream; you will soon reach the spring run and limestone cliffs of the area.

To reach Wildwood Park, continue west on AL 20 and turn right onto Waterloo Rd.; you will soon see the park on the left.

To reach Key Cave National Wildlife Refuge, continue west on AL 20 and turn left on Co. Rd. 2 (Gunwaleford Rd.). Follow this road for about four miles and turn left on Co. Rd. 223. After about 1.5 miles, turn right on Co. Rd. 204. The refuge is located on the south side of this road.

84 Coastal Plain Hemlock Canyon Streams

34°19'38.20"N
87°46'47.32"W

In northwest Alabama, the Appalachian Plateau dips under the Coastal Plain. Some streams here have cut down into the underlying rocks and formed canyons similar to those in the Appalachian Plateau. Bear Creek is one of those streams.

The Bear Creek watershed shows some unique Coastal Plain habitats; its canyons also have beech-hemlock forest similar to adjacent areas of the Appalachian Plateau. To help you to better explore, understand, and appreciate this region, the watershed has several small TVA reservoirs and many developed camping grounds, both public and private.

Upper Bear Creek is a canoe floatway maintained by the Bear Creek Development Authority. Here there are several canoe launches as well as canoe rental and shuttle services.

In a very forward-thinking move, TVA acquired an easement along the creek to protect its beauty and streamside forest habitats. The creek has sections that feature gentle shoals, short cliff lines, tributary waterfalls, beech-hemlock forest, boulders, and sandy beaches. Other stretches have more challenging rapids including Factory Falls, which must be portaged around. A headwater dam provides water releases to the floatway on weekends. The effects of these releases on the creek's ecological health may be questionable, but it does allow the creek to be canoed in summer and fall when other streams are too low to float.

The Dismals is a private park/campground in the upper Bear Creek watershed containing old-growth forest. The protection of this area was an early focus for conservationists in the 1960s. The park entrance contains bluff top sandstone outcrops; below a mill

Canoe launch on Bear Creek at AL 13 crossing

dam there is a waterfall that plunges into the canyon. The canyon contains a variety of boulder formations with tight squeezes and some flat rocks used as dance platforms by the Chickasaws. Aaron Burr hid in the area after he fell from our country's favor.

The key attraction of the park is its tall, old-growth trees, including the state champion eastern hemlock. The state "winner" was originally part of a set of almost twin trees, but storms destroyed one of those giants, leaving the champion sadly alone.

The park gives its name to glow worms called *dismalites*, the larvae of insects which are known to glow on moonlit nights. A flashlight can induce them to do the same thing.

The nearby private Rock Bridge Canyon Park (also in the Bear Creek watershed) contains another Coastal Plain hemlock canyon as well as the small natural bridge that gives the park its name.

Bear Creek leaves Alabama to enter the bald cypress-lined rock canyons of Mississippi around Tishomingo State Park, then reenters our state and flows north toward the Tennessee River. Around the town of Red Bay, the lower portion of the creek becomes more typically Coastal Plain and is surrounded by bottomland hardwood forests and bald cypress stands. (To facilitate your visit, a canoe trail is located along this stretch.) Some of the bottomland hardwood and bald cypress along lower Bear Creek can be seen at stops in the protected lands of the Alabama portion of the Natchez Trace Parkway.

To the south of the Bear Creek drainage lies the Buttahatchee River, which also flows through great beech-hemlock canyon country before it enters Mississippi to join the Tombigbee River. The privately owned, publicly managed Sam R. Murphy WMA offers some public access along the river including the area known as the Buttahatchee River Bluffs, which contain hemlocks and side canyons with waterfalls. Fortunately, the timber company that owns the land around the bluffs has entered into conservation agreements with the Nature Conservancy to protect this special area.

Directions: To reach Dismals Canyon, take US 43 southwest from Russellville. The entrance to the park will be on the right.

To reach upper Bear Creek, continue southwest on US 43. A waterfall enters the creek on the south side of the bridge, and a canoe outfitter is located here. Various canoe launches and take-out points can be found upstream and downstream of US 43.

To reach Rock Bridge Canyon, continue southwest on US 43 to Hackleburg and take a left on AL 172. Continue northwest on AL 172 and turn right at Co. Rd. 45. About two miles down Co. Rd. 45 you will reach a curve to the left but keep going straight. An honor box for entrance fees is on your right. Proceed to the parking area at the end of the road.

To reach lower Bear Creek, continue on AL 172 northwest until it becomes AL 19; go on to Red Bay. There are canoe launches along the creek from here down to Pickwick Lake. Downstream of Red Bay, the creek crosses over into Mississippi before reentering Alabama, and you can follow it by taking a left off AL 19 in Red Bay onto AL 24, then right on MS 366 heading into Belmont, Mississippi. Take a right onto MS 25 and, before reaching the town of Tishomingo, you will see the Natchez Trace. Go north on the trace to the small canyons of Tishomingo State Park (the rockiest place in Mississippi). Continue north on the trace and back into Alabama. There are various historic and natural sites along this stretch of the Natchez Trace Pkwy., including picnic spots (just over the state line) along lower Bear Creek. You can continue north on the trace past Freedom Hills Overlook, Colbert's Ferry, Rock Spring, and other Alabama sites covered in earlier sections of this book.

The Buttahatchee River is reached by taking US 278 east out of Hamilton. The river can be canoed between various bridge crossings going downstream into Lamar County and Mississippi. The state-leased Sam R. Murphy WMA offers terrestrial access along the river, but this land is largely farmed. The riverside portion of the WMA is reached by taking the Co. Rd. 35 exit off US 78 and following this road south to its junction with Co. Rd. 16. Take a left; after you pass over the Buttahatchee River, the lands of the WMA (mostly farmland) are on your left. Use a WMA map to navigate the side roads in this area.

To reach the hemlocks and the Buttahatchee Bluffs portion of the WMA, continue east on Co. Rd. 16 until you turn left on Webb Loop Rd.; then turn right onto Oaks Rd. After a mile or so you will see a paved road on your left that forms a loop. Continue to the second entrance of this loop and take a left. Just before you enter the housing area along the loop you will see a fork of unpaved roads on the right. You can park here on WMA land (look for the small yellow signs) or continue on the right fork of the unpaved roads. By foot or by car, follow the right fork down the slope. You will see hemlocks in a side canyon to your left, but continue downhill to the river where more hemlocks grow along the bluffs. Walk back up the side canyons to its bluffs and wet-weather waterfalls.

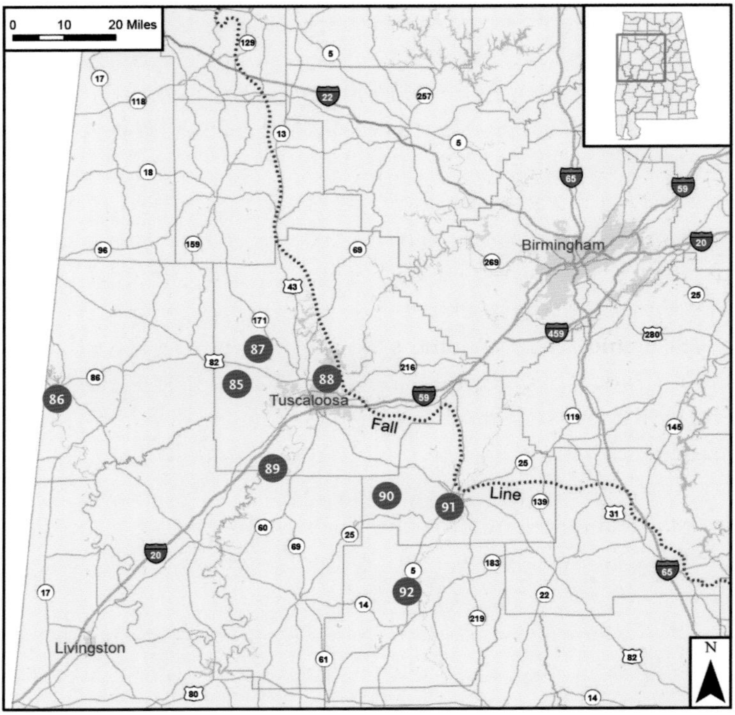

TUSCALOOSA AREA

The Tuscaloosa area offers a wealth of outdoor activities in a diversity of habitats. You can enjoy everything from hiking, camping, and fishing to the exploration of a huge Native American settlement.

85 Sipsey River Swamp

33°15'09.35"N
87°46'31.04"W

The Sipsey River Swamp has nothing to do with the Sipsey Wilderness, previously mentioned. The swamp is formed by the Sipsey River, which flows into the Tombigbee River; in contrast, the wilderness surrounds the Sipsey Fork, which flows into the Black Warrior River.

Sipsey is a Native American word for poplar or cottonwood, appropriate for both areas. The Sipsey Swamp has some large cottonwood trees scattered in it, and it supposedly once had more. The Sipsey River's headwaters lie in the Appalachian Plateau's beech-hemlock canyons and strip-mine country around Natural Bridge Park. This area drains into the New and Little New Rivers, which join to form the Sipsey River. By the time the Sipsey reaches the town of Fayette, it has formed a wide swamp containing numerous old river channels and islands. The swamp continues south and then bends southwest near Tuscaloosa to form the border of Greene and Pickens Counties before emptying into the Gainesville reservoir on the Tombigbee River.

The Sipsey River is one of the longest continuously free-flowing rivers left in our nation; it only suffers from impoundment near its mouth above Gainesville. The Sipsey has never been channelized, so it retains its natural meandering nature, abandoning and carving new river channels; it also floods the surrounding bottomlands on a regular basis, building up natural levees. Bald cypress trees grow on the river's banks and point bars, creating an unusual scene in this modern age of human-induced stream channel erosion. The river flows through a largely forested rural area, and its water quality is very good. These factors combine to make the Sipsey River Swamp the best example of a natural riverine bottomland hardwood ecosystem in Alabama.

These factors also make the swamp a stronghold for mussel species, such as the Alabama spike, southern clubshell, Alabama hickory nut, and Alabama moccasinshell, that are now threatened with extinction. These species lost most of their habitat due to the creation of the Tennessee–Tombigbee Waterway and other

Buttressed trunks of tupelos, Sipsey River Swamp Recreation Area

impoundments. The mussels are associated with the very stable gravel bars found along the lower river. The Sipsey River is also home to the threatened frecklebelly madtom, black sawback turtle, rainbow snake, and a species of aquatic fly found nowhere else in the state.

The lower section of the Sipsey River (below Co. Rd. 181) is unique in that it is surrounded by both floodplain and hills. Here the river has a more defined channel bordered by low, blue limestone cliffs. The tops of these cliffs are often wet with seepage and covered with bald cypress. Where tributaries cut though the limestone, low cave-like overhangs are formed. The gravel in such tributaries is a good place to look for fossil shark's teeth, from a time when this area and the related Black Belt were covered by an ocean.

The Sipsey River Swamp is not well known to most Alabamians. It can be visited and canoed using various bridge crossings as put-ins and take-outs, from Fayette to AL 14 in Greene and Pickens Counties. During the drier times of the year, the swamp can be explored on foot at two state-owned properties. The 500-acre Alabama Department of Transportation (ALDOT) Sipsey River Swamp mitigation preserve is located in two tracts where US 82 crosses the river west of Tuscaloosa. These tracts were purchased for ALDOT's wetland mitigation program. With ALDOT's permission, the tracts can be accessed by individuals and groups for educational purposes.

Downstream a few miles from the ALDOT property is Forever Wild's 3,500-acre Sipsey River Swamp Recreation Area. This property contains a network of old logging roads, which are maintained as a trail system. Large bottomland hardwoods and pines were removed from this tract in the early 1990s, but those cut areas are now covered with 20-foot-tall trees. Much of the property retains mature bottomland oak and bald cypress-tupelo swamps. Visitors entering the tract will first see only water tupelo, but as you reach the river and start heading downstream you will notice more and more bald cypress. This conservation area marks the northern boundary of bald cypress on the Sipsey River.

The main road through the property runs along the river in many places. If you walk the entire five-mile length of this road you will reach a spot known as the Fish Camp. This area has some very large cypress trees and oaks next to the river. Another Forever Wild tract lies to the south of this area, but that area is currently not accessible.

The US Army Corps of Engineers (hereafter, Corps) has lands along the short impounded section of the Sipsey River Swamp at its mouth. This property contains upland forests along slopes leading down to practically pure cypress stands, plus bottomland hardwood.

Directions: The upper end of the Sipsey River Swamp is accessed by taking US 43 east from Fayette, Alabama. You will soon reach the swamp and can observe it from the roadside, once you find safe road shoulder parking. The river can be canoed between the various bridge crossings heading downstream from here. However, the best canoe runs on the river are located far downstream.

To find the best canoe sections as well as other sites in the Sipsey Swamp/Tuscaloosa area, take I-20/59 exit 73 in Tuscaloosa and head northwest on US 82 (McFarland Blvd.).

For the Sipsey River Swamp Recreation Area, continue west on US 82 and turn left onto the road (Old Hwy. 82) leading to the town of Buhl. This turn is marked with a sign for the Sipsey River Swamp Recreation Area. In Buhl, you can access the northern tip of the recreation area by continuing west on Old US 82 and parking on the left just before crossing the river bridge. To reach the main portion of the recreation area, take a left off Old US 82 in Buhl onto Co. Rd. 19 (Sipsey Valley Rd.). Follow this road south until you see a sign for the recreation area. Turn right onto an access road and follow it to a large parking lot. From here, walk the gated road into the heart of the recreation area's cypress and bottomland hardwood swamps.

The best sections of the river—where you can canoe through the swamp in high water—are reached by continuing south on Sipsey Valley Rd. and then taking a right onto Co. Rd. 2. (Tuscaloosa Co. Rd. 2 will become Greene Co 156.) Just before Co. Rd. 2 crosses a bridge over the Sipsey River to Benevola, turn right onto a short access road down to a boat launch. From here it's a wonderful boat or canoe float down to Co. Rd. 181—about 12 miles. You can reach the take-out by going back east on Co. Rd. 2 from the river bridge; turn right and go south on Co. Rd. 208. Bear right onto Co. Rd. 183 where it meets Co. Rd. 208; the road then becomes Co. Rd. 60. When you reach a crossroads with Co. Rd. 181, take a right; follow this road to the river bridge. Access to the river is a little rough, though; it's better to try the west side of the bridge.

The next stretch of river is similar in length but less swampy, with more cypress trees along the banks and lots of low limestone cliffs. Its take-out is AL 14, which can be reached from the put-in by following Co. Rd. 81 east, back to its crossroads with Co. Rd. 60. Take a right and follow Co. Rd. 60 south to AL 14. Take a right and, just before you cross the Sipsey River, take another right and an immediate left; follow this road (running west and parallel with AL 14) to the river. The cave-like formation is visible on the left about midway downstream, where a tributary enters the river.

To visit the Corps's Sipsey Swamp property, continue west on AL 14 over the Sipsey River bridge and take a left onto Vienna Rd. This road passes by an old antebellum church where a bodyguard of George Washington is buried. (Many Revolutionary War veterans received Alabama land grants after the land was taken from the Native Americans in the early 1800s.) Once past the church/cemetery, you will start to see the red property boundary lines of the Corps, as well as the impounded river and surrounding cypress-bottomland hardwood forest, to your left. You can park on the wide shoulder of the road and explore the property on foot. The road continues to the site of the former town of Vienna, which is now a Corps boat launch and park on the Gainesville Lake portion of the Tombigbee River. You can put a motor boat in the lake here. Downstream is the impounded mouth of the Sipsey; upstream is the AL 14 bridge.

86 Tom Bevill Lock and Dam

33°12'41.70"N
88°17'08.36W

The visitors center at the Tom Bevill Lock and Dam features a reproduction of a mid-19th century plantation house. A short walk takes you down to the edge of the Tennessee–Tombigbee Waterway and a view of the bottom end of the working lock and dam. The site also features the paddlewheeler *MV Montgomery*, which spent its long working life yanking snags from our major rivers.

Birders especially enjoy the open areas surrounding the center, which attract a variety of species, including orchard orioles. Wading birds, waterfowl, and eagles frequent the river's edge.

Nearby is the Pickensville Recreation Area, a narrow park situated along Aliceville Lake. The park offers great birding opportunities, hiking, camping, and boating.

Directions: From Tuscaloosa, take US 82 west until you cross into Pickens County. Turn left on AL 86, passing through Carrollton (and its famous "ghost" in the courthouse window) to Pickensville. To reach the recreation area, continue on AL 86 for one mile; the entrance road is on the right. To reach the Tom Bevill Visitors Center, turn left on AL 14 in Pickensville and follow it south for a short distance, turning right on Lock and Dam Rd.

87 Lake Lurleen State Park

33°17'55.45"N
87°40'49.38"W

Near the Sipsey River Swamp, but within the Black Warrior River Basin, 1,625-acre Lake Lurleen State Park provides more upland hiking experiences. The park has nice trails around the lake through maturing upland hardwood forests full of white oak.

Directions: Lake Lurleen State Park is located off US 82 west of Northport, Alabama.

88 University of Alabama Arboretum

33°11'29.13"N
87°28'29.33"W

On the opposite or east side of Tuscaloosa from Lake Lurleen is the 60-acre University of Alabama Arboretum, which has trails through similar habitats as described above. Here, though, the plants are labeled! The arboretum also has a wildflower garden containing 250 species and experimental, ornamental, and children's gardens.

DIRECTIONS: To reach the arboretum in Tuscaloosa, take a right off of US 82 West onto Veterans Memorial Pkwy. (15th St. E.). The arboretum is located adjacent to the former university golf course (near the Tuscaloosa VA medical center) and the intersection of Veterans Memorial Pkwy. and Pelham Loop Rd. Enter through the arboretum/golf course gate and follow the signs down a dirt road.

89 Moundville Archeological Park

33°00'16.51"N
87°37'55.71"W

Moundville Archeological Park is known for its extensive earthen mounds built by the Native Americans during the Mississippian Period. It is one of the four great Mississippian mound centers in the United States. The tall, terraced temple mounds and surrounding plazas and artwork portraying plumed serpents indicate a Mesoamerican influence. The site has a museum and reconstructions of a temple mound house and its supporting village.

The park also contains a boardwalk nature trail over bluffs and ravines adjacent to the Black Warrior River. The boardwalk provides the rare opportunity to stand at canopy level with large tulip trees growing in the ravine below. During late spring, you can admire their tulip-like flowers up close, while still attached to the trees!

Further down the Black Warrior River drainage, the University of Alabama has a biological research station known as Tanglewood. A modest antebellum plantation home is located on the station grounds. The property has some maturing upland and bottomland hardwood forests but, unfortunately, much of the property was clear-cut in the recent past.

Directions: To reach Moundville State Monument, take AL 69 south from Tuscaloosa. The park is located on the right just before reaching the town of Moundville.

Permission to visit Tanglewood must be secured from the University of Alabama's Department of Biological Sciences.

90 Oakmulgee Division of the Talladega National Forest

32°45'07.30"N
87°06'52.62"W

The Oakmulgee Division of the Talladega National Forest is located in the relatively high Fall Line Hills southeast of Tuscaloosa. Roland Harper, long-time botanist at the Geological Survey of Alabama, called such scattered and unusually rugged hill ranges the "Pine Hills." That is an appropriate name because most of the area is dominated by upland longleaf pine forest. The hollows contain high-quality oak-hickory forest with an understory of bigleaf magnolia. Many of the streams of the area are surrounded by swamp tupelo wetlands.

Mating pair of Mitchell's satyrs, Oakmulgee Division, Talladega National Forest

These forests house Alabama's largest and healthiest population of the endangered red-cockaded woodpecker (over 100 colonies). This bird became endangered because of the cutting of old-growth pine forests and fire suppression. The Oakmulgee Division provides a relative abundance of woodpecker nest sites due to the presence of good-quality old-growth longleaf pine stands. These woodpeckers require open pine forest, and the longleaf forests of Oakmulgee are kept in their historically open state through aggressive controlled burns.

To see the woodpeckers, drive down Forest Service roads and

look for pines with wide white paint bands on them; the bands mark potential or active nest trees. If you see a woodpecker hole surrounded by a large collar of pine resin, then you have found a nest tree. The bird pecks holes in the tree all around the nest hole so that resin will run out and form the collar; the sticky, burning resin helps to keep snakes and other predators out of the woodpecker's nest. In addition, this species requires old-growth pines infected with red heart disease. The disease softens the wood of the living tree and allows the birds to carve their nest cavities.

The birds are most likely to be seen around nest trees in the early morning or late afternoon. A good place to see them is on the north side of FS 731, which crosses the Oakmulgee WMA. (This road is known as Co. Rd. 50 when you access it from AL 69 in Moundville.) Many of the older stands of longleaf grow around the Reed Brake Research Natural Area in the center of the WMA. You may walk in if the roads are closed by gates.

If you are looking for a more traditional hiking experience, go to the Payne Lake Recreation Area. This area contains a loop trail around the upper end of the lake through upland mixed forest, with large loblolly pines in the bottoms and swamp tupelo wetlands. A local garden club has labeled some of the area's ferns.

Near the southeast end of the national forest, close to Selma, lies Paul M. Grist State Park. This park contains a small lake and hiking trails through the surrounding hills that pass through relatively lush upland hardwood forests.

Directions: To reach the Oakmulgee Divison of the Talladega National Forest, take AL 69 south from Tuscaloosa to the town of Moundville. In Moundville, take a left onto Co. Rd. 50, which goes east into the national forest. If it is open, FS 723 (to the south of Co. Rd. 50) leads to the Reed Brake Natural Area and other nearby old-growth longleaf. You may also walk into this general area. Both Co. Rd. 50 and FS 723 pass by trees with the white bands denoting red-cockaded woodpecker nest trees.

Atamasco lily, along banks of Cahaba River below Centreville

If you continue on Co. Rd. 50 and take a right onto FS 726, and then take a left onto AL 25, you will see the entrance to Payne Lake Recreation Area on your right.

To reach Paul M. Grist State Park, take AL 22 north from Selma and look for signs directing you to the park entrance.

91 Fall Line at Centreville

32°56'40.29"N
87°08'19.51"W

In this book, the Lower Cahaba River is considered to stretch from the Fall Line shoals near Centreville down to the Black Belt chalk country near its mouth at the Alabama River. Below the Fall Line, the river is surrounded by bottomland hardwood swamps or Black Belt chalk cliffs, and it supports Coastal Plain species such as the threatened alligator snapping turtle—which, at over 200 pounds, is one of the largest freshwater turtles in the world. This rarely seen monster fishes by opening its mouth and wiggling its tongue, which has a projection that looks like a worm or insect larva. Its next meal is thus attracted to within snapping distance. The lower river, below the Fall Line, can be canoed year-round between the various bridges that cross it.

The actual Fall Line shoals over which the Cahaba River plunges can be seen at Centreville. If you can get to some of the gravel bars in this part of the river, you will discover an amazing number of empty mussel shells representing many species.

Public access to the shoals is limited to a riverside trail located beside a local economic development group's building on US 82. You will find adequate parking here as well.

DIRECTIONS: The riverside trail and its parking area are located in Centreville on the west bank of the Cahaba River just north of US 82.

92 Perry Lakes Park / Barton's Beach Preserve

32°41'47.16"N
87°14'18.54"W

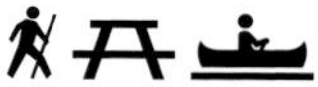

Downstream of the Fall Line, the Cahaba River becomes a more sluggish and meandering stream. The river runs through a flat, alluvial valley carved out and built up by the river's erosional power and flood-borne soil. Here the higher river terraces and floodplains are farmed; more frequently flooded areas support bottomland hardwood wetlands.

Perry Lakes Park in Perry County has fine examples of bottomland hardwoods, including Spanish moss-draped cypress swamps surrounding oxbow lakes of the Cahaba. Within a little over an hour's drive from the Appalachian Ridge and Valley of Birmingham, you can be in a place that looks like something straight out of a Louisiana bayou!

Coastal Plain streams naturally expend energy by meandering side to side, rather than cutting down into their gently sloping alluvial valleys. They constantly erode the outsides of river bends while depositing sand, gravel, and other sediments on the insides. This deposition of sediments forms sand and gravel bars at the

Barton's Beach is a popular swimming spot

bends. The largest such sand bar or "beach" on the Cahaba is located in the Nature Conservancy's 125-acre Barton's Beach Preserve, adjacent to and accessible from Perry Lakes Park. This section of the Cahaba River is home to many rare fishes, including freckled darters, skygazer shiners, crystal darters, and frecklebelly madtoms. Also, the area supports some mussels, butterflies, and turtles that are disappearing in other places around the state. Barton's Beach is a great place to sit back and enjoy the peace and quiet of nature, while watching the Cahaba River slowly flow by. *But be aware that there are alligators in the neighborhood!*

The centerpiece of the adjacent Perry Lakes Park is three oxbow lakes formed by the Cahaba's past meanderings. As the river wandered through the floodplain, it tried to straighten its course by cutting through bends, leaving abandoned river channels or

Above: One of several unique bathrooms built by the Studio for Rural Design at Perry Lakes Park

Opposite: Bald Cypress Pond at Perry Lakes Park

"oxbows" (shaped like an ox's yoke) before beginning the meandering process again. These old river channels retain water during the summer months and are often flooded by the river in late winter–early spring, restocking them with fish while gradually filling them with sediment. Over time, the shallow, silted edges of these lakes are colonized by very flood-tolerant trees like bald cypress and water tupelo. In the case of the Perry Lakes, multiple river course changes laid one oxbow across another, forming an odd, many-pronged formation rather than the more typical curved, horseshoe shape.

The Perry Lakes are surrounded by an extensive bald cypress–tupelo gum swamp, the trees festooned with Spanish moss. This is one of the northernmost populations of Spanish moss in Alabama. Here the "moss" (really a type of bromeliad) is concentrated on the lower limbs of the trees; it is especially thick over water, where the humidity is high and the temperatures are somewhat moderated during winter.

Perry Lakes Park has several old roads and new paths that have been combined into an interpretive trail system. These trails travel along the edges of the cypress swamp lakes and sloughs, through bottomland hardwood with luxuriant growths of dwarf palmetto palm, and mature loblolly pine–hardwood forests. A trail with some giant old-growth tupelo is located to the left of the road as you near the lakes.

However, the best way to see the swamp is by canoe or small boat. An old canoe/boat launch is located on the shallow lake at the end of the park's entrance road. For deeper water, and to see more swamps and lakes, you will have to find a place to get through a line of cypress trees on the back side of that lake, diagonally to the left from the old boat launch. Once you make it into deeper water you can follow waterways to the left or straight ahead. Straight ahead takes you through beautiful cypress swamps before reaching higher bottomland hardwood with a thick understory of dwarf palmetto palm. The waterway to the left leads through the swamp to a large open lake (Round Lake) before higher land is met. A more sure way to reach the back lakes is to drop your canoe off at the roofed foot bridge you will see on your left as you drive in. Then walk your boat over the bridge on the trail leading to the edge of Round Lake near the birding tower. This old fire tower, refurbished by Auburn University's Studio for Rural Design, provides great views of the valley.

The CCC built picnic facilities on the property back in the 1930s, which are still quite functional. Recent improvements include a pavilion and stylish, open-air bathrooms by the same Studio for Rural Design.

The fish ponds seen when entering the park—once part of the Marion Fish Hatchery—provide excellent bird–watching opportunities; the drained ponds are especially rich, often full of shorebirds. Eagles nest at Perry Lakes Park as well.

DIRECTIONS: From Centreville, travel south on AL 5 toward Marion. Take a left on AL 175 and follow this road until you see a sign on the left for Perry Lakes Park, just as you come up on the old fish hatchery.

Barton's Beach can be accessed by parking at the end of the road in Perry Lakes Park and walking along the old road to the sand bar.

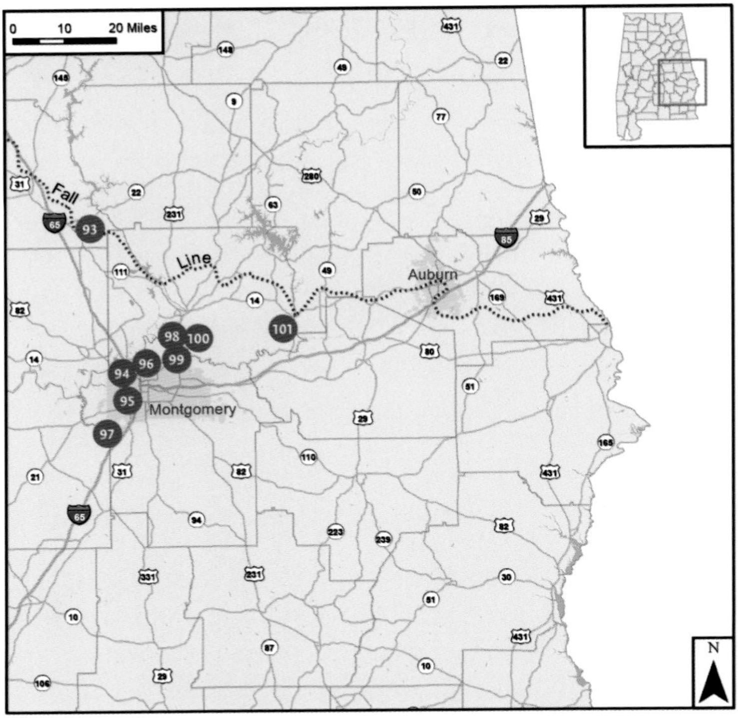

MONTGOMERY AREA

The Montgomery area offers a number of outdoor adventures, especially those involving water and history. Nearby, the Coosa and Tallapoosa Rivers join to form the Alabama River itself, a vital fact in the location of our state's capital.

93 Confederate Memorial Park

32°43'21.45"N
86°28'32.25"W

This 102-acre park is located in extreme southern Chilton County. The park was created to preserve the site of the Old Soldiers Home for Confederate veterans. The home operated around the turn of the 20th century to serve the needs of poor and aging veterans who had served in the Confederate Army. The home contained a hospital, dining hall, running water, carbide lighting, dairy, farmland, fishing pond, cottage style accommodations, and cemetery.

Today, all that remains are the cemetery, building foundations, and other ruins. A historic post office and church have been moved to the site, and a Civil War museum has been built as well.

The park features both natural and historical features. Naturalists can enjoy the one-mile long interpretive trail, which has some special features. The trail identifies the forest trees and describes various aspects of forest ecology and management, including the display of a soil core. The forest is maturing upland hardwood forest that was partially cleared for farmland and a fishing pond during the time of the Confederate soldiers' home. Farming terraces and an old dam can still be seen in the woods along the trail. The trail passes the natural spring and associated storage tank and pumping station ruins that supplied the home with running water. A tree has grown around one of the small water supply pipes, making the pipe look like a tap used to collect sap from a sugar maple.

DIRECTIONS: From I-65 N, take exit 186 to US 31; from I-65 S, take exit 205 to US 31. From either direction, follow the signs to Confederate Memorial Park.

94 Roberta Case Pine Hills Preserve (access is restricted)

The Nature Conservancy's 363-acre Roberta Case Pine Hills Preserve in Autauga County was acquired to protect the threatened canebrake pitcher plant. One of the rarest pitcher plants in the world, it is only found in a few counties within the Fall Line Hills of central Alabama. The preserve is named in honor of Roberta Case, who, with her husband Fred, discovered the plant and worked for its conservation.

The canebrake pitcher plant grows in hillside seepage bogs, which are similar to many pitcher plant habitats found in the Lower Coastal Plain. (Pitcher plants make up for lack of nutrients in these poor, wet soils by attracting, drowning, and digesting insects.) In fact, this particular environment supports disjunct populations of plants normally associated with the Lower Coastal Plain like yellow-eyed grasses, hatpins, and spreading pogonia orchids. The preserve also protects a population of Harper's heartleaf, which is endemic to this part of Alabama.

The canebrake pitcher plant bogs historically occurred among fire-maintained longleaf pine savannas. After purchasing the preserve, the Nature Conservancy has worked hard to restore the natural community. Fire has been reintroduced to the system in order to keep the pitcher plants from being shaded out.

You will have to contact the Nature Conservancy of Alabama to arrange a visit to this fragile site.

95 Cooter's Pond

32°25'47.05"N
86°24'01.62"W

Cooter's Pond is an old Corps park now run by Autauga County. The present Cooter's Pond was formed when water from an Alabama River impoundment (Lake Woodruff) flooded some of the surrounding bottomlands and oxbow lakes. The park has a short trail through a picnic area along some bluffs supporting a hardwood forest full of Spanish moss. While the site does not offer

Water view of Cooter's Pond

much for hikers, it makes a nice picnic spot and offers great canoeing opportunities.

From a canoe you can explore the islands and shores of Cooter's Pond. (Motorboats are common, so make sure you are prepared for a few wake waves.) Working your way to the head of the slough, you will pass under a cart bridge for a golf course and then through a spadderdock lily marsh with scattered bald cypresses. The head of the slough is bordered by a thick cypress swamp draped in Spanish moss. When the water is high, you can canoe from the boat launch east across the pond through side sloughs, swamps, and marshes to a large cypress-lined oxbow lake on the east side of I-65. Anybody who sees this beautiful lake from the interstate will want to canoe it!

In nearby Prattville is an unusual place known as Wilderness Park. The 26-acre area is maintained as a wilderness with a nice trail—well worth exploring. The trees are very large; in fact, Alabama's second largest beech tree lives here. Unfortunately, the park also has a most unnatural feature in that the understory of much of the forest is dominated by giant oriental bamboos. The native understory plants, as well as tree seedlings, have been choked out by the bamboos. This area reminds us why exotic bamboo should never be planted in the wilds of Alabama. Yet, it is hard not to enjoy the exotic feel of the place when you visit.

Directions: To reach Cooter's Pond, take I-65 exit 179 and follow US 82 west. Take a right onto US 31. You will soon see signs directing you to turn left to reach the park.

Wilderness Park is located on Upper Kingston Rd. in Prattville.

96 Alabama Nature Center

32°28'28.02"N
86°22'56.31"W

The Alabama Nature Center is located off I-65 close to Prattville. The property features an extensive system of hiking trails, including boardwalks that pass spring-fed cypress swamps and sweetbay magnolia bottoms, plus more typical upland habitats and manmade ponds. The property contains the old Lanark Plantation House, which is in the process of being restored. Isabel and Wiley Hill donated the property to the Alabama Wildlife Federation for the purpose of creating a nature center. Subsequently, the federation created a great trail system that it uses for environmental education projects. The federation has developed a butterfly garden and built a very large pavilion and small snack/gift shop to serve those who visit the center. The center is open to the public on the third Saturday and third Sunday afternoon of every month.

DIRECTIONS: From I-65, take exit 179 (Prattville/Millbrook) and go east on Cobbs Ford Rd. for one-quarter of a mile and turn left on Edgewood Dr. At the T in the road, go right for one-half mile and turn left onto Lanark Rd. (This is a dirt road with a small white sign that says "To Lanark.")

97 Montgomery County Sites

32°21'04.57"N
86°28'19.55"W

Despite being the place where many of our state's conservation decisions are made, Montgomery County contains limited outdoor recreation opportunities and very little conserved natural land. There are a few small sites to visit, such as the city of Montgomery's Lagoon Park, which has an exercise trail that borders forested portions of the park. A nice canebrake is located near the exercise trail, plus the park's namesake lagoons and wetlands.

One of the county's few nature trails is found at the Corps's Gunter Hill Campground. The campground is located on a peninsula formed by an embayment of Antioch Creek, which feeds into Catoma Creek and subsequently the Alabama River. All of these streams are impounded by the Lake Woodruff reservoir.

This area has campsites, suitable for both trailers and tents, and a boat launch. The campsites are tucked into a scenic upland hardwood forest draped in Spanish moss. In some places, the campsites slope down to bottomland hardwood forest which includes a few young bald cypresses and a dwarf palmetto palm understory. Day users can pay to launch their boats here, and they can get a permit to hunt in a 250-acre area to the west of the campground. However, the other facilities, including the hiking trail, are available only to campers.

If you are camping at the park and want to go hiking, take the paved trail located in the grassy area behind and to the left of the bathhouse. When the trail forks, take the fork to the left and cross a road/parking lot leading to the boat launch, then follow the trail over a long footbridge that is mounted to the top of a utility pipe. The trail continues into the forest in a paved form and passes through loblolly pines, shagbark hickories, and other upland hardwoods. The rich soils support woodland wildflowers such as jack-in-the-pulpit. The path passes close to a low bluff that drops off into a floodplain dominated by bottomland hardwood with dwarf palmetto palms.

At Gunter Hill Campground, you can pay a launch fee to put your canoe into the embayment of Antioch Creek. Wildlife here includes egrets, herons, kingfishers, and (occasionally) endangered wood storks. There is a bulrush marsh area to the left of the boat launch that you can also explore. However, be careful to watch for cottonmouths and alligators—and give them plenty of room, if seen.

If you canoe out into the embayment from the boat launch, you will see upland hardwoods and some loblolly pines on the surrounding slopes with some bottomland hardwoods; young bald cypresses dot the shoreline. Dwarf palmetto palms and moist soil herbs, like cardinal flowers, grow along the water's edge. If you follow the right shoreline you will curve around the peninsula that the campground sits on and ascend up another finger of the Antioch Creek embayment. The shoreline of this narrow embayment, opposite the eastern side of the campground, makes for some interesting exploring by foot.

Besides Gunter Hill Campground, the Corps owns scattered parks and lands along the Alabama River lakes from near Wetumpka to Claiborne. These are open to various forms of recreation including camping, canoeing, and hunting.

DIRECTIONS: The Gunter Hill Campground area is reached by following US 80 west from Montgomery for nine miles. Turn right on Co. Rd. 7, then follow the signs.

98 Coosa River Fall Line

32°37'05.18"N
86°15'25.52"W

The mighty Coosa River has its headwaters in the mountains of north Georgia and joins the Tallapoosa River near Wetumpka to form the Alabama River. The Coosa River drainage once enjoyed the greatest diversity of aquatic life in the world. It was the world's center for aquatic snail diversity and also home to many endemic species of fish, mussel, and crayfish.

The damming of the lower Coosa River for hydroelectricity caused one of the greatest mass extinctions in United States history. The majority of species that depended on the river's shoals immediately and completely disappeared; others are now threatened with extinction, restricted to remnant populations in the river's few remaining clean and free-flowing tributaries. USFWS biologists are working with landowners, industries, and environmentalists to help these remaining species. Their most promising efforts are found on the last free-flowing stretch of the Coosa near Wetumpka.

The lower seven miles of the Coosa is known as the Devil's Staircase. Fortunately, this Fall Line section was not dammed; instead, the waters from Lake Jordan were routed through a side hydro reservoir called Bouldin. The waters of Lake Bouldin flow back into the river system downstream of Wetumpka, bypassing the Coosa's original channel.

As this system was established, water flow in the Devil's Staircase was drastically reduced, especially when it was needed most by aquatic life. Recently, scientists discovered a remnant population of the endangered tulotoma snail here, and an agreement between the federal government and Alabama Power Company was forged to provide additional water during critical seasons.

Increased water flow has also benefited local paddlers, making the lower Coosa (and the Montgomery metro area) one of the best summer white-water canoe and kayak areas in the state. The river contains some Class III rapids, including Moccasin Gap. Boaters can put in below Jordan Dam and take out at the Wetumpka River park. Canoes and shuttle services are available from local outfitters, too.

This last remaining natural section of the Coosa River may have always been its most unique section. Its Fall Line environment has a mixture of upland and Coastal Plain elements. The hills, cliffs, and boulders in the river's shoals are best associated with the Piedmont, while the bald cypresses growing in the shoals represent the Coastal Plain. There are few environments that feature white-water rapids surrounding islands of cypress trees! If you cannot boat, you can still observe this unique environment from the walking trail in Wetumpka's river park.

If you are interested in a hike in this area, consider tackling the 12-mile Swayback Bridge Trail. This hiking and mountain biking trail is located along Lake Jordan, which is upstream from the free-flowing section of the Coosa.

DIRECTIONS: To reach the park/canoe take-out on the Coosa River, start at the junction of AL 14 and AL 212 in Wetumpka; go east on AL 212 and cross over the Coosa River; the park will be to your right.

To reach the put-in for the Coosa and the Swayback Bridge Trail, take US 231 north out of downtown Wetumpka, then turn left on Co. Rd. 667. This road will lead you to signs to the Swayback Bridge Trail.

Edge of the meteor crater, Wetumpka

To reach the canoe put-in, veer left when you reach a Y in the road a few miles after turning onto Co. Rd. 667. You will soon see a dirt road (Rapids Rd.) to the left, leading down to the river put-in.

99 Meteor Crater

32°32'37.30"N
86°12'43.10"W

The Fall Line area north of Wetumpka is the site of a gigantic crater produced by an ancient meteorite. Although its five-mile diameter is larger than the more famous Meteor Crater of Arizona, Alabama's crater is more subtle because it is covered with

Edge of the meteor crater, Wetumpka

forests. However, the level rim and steep slope of the crater clearly show that this is not a normal landform. The impact of the meteorite altered the geological formations in the crater area; therefore, the crater's outline is easily seen on a geological map.

The crater can be viewed from several places in the Wetumpka vicinity. One of the best places to see its rim and wall is the old Jasmine Hills Gardens. (The garden is currently closed but is sometimes reopened during springtime.) A panoramic view of the highest point on the crater rim (Bald Knob) is visible from routes into Wetumpka. From the Bibb Graves Bridge, you can easily see the upturned rocks tilting in the direction of the crater. Outcroppings of dramatically upturned rock formations are also visible along the east side of US 231; a commemorative marker (on the west side of the highway) provides details.

The Coosa River flows across the western edge of the Meteor Crater. Look for signs of impact at Wetumpka's river park, mentioned in the previous section.

DIRECTIONS: The historic and picturesque Bibb Graves Bridge is on AL 14 in the heart of downtown Wetumpka. Head south on US 231 for other viewing spots.

100 Fort Toulouse / Jackson State Historic Park and Bartram Arboretum

32°30'13.32"N
86°15'31.90"W

Fort Toulouse Park is located at the confluence of the Coosa and Tallapoosa Rivers, where they form the Alabama River. The park protects the area's historic significance.

This area was home to prehistoric natives who built the mound in the park. Later, during the 1700s, the Alabamas—the most influential group of the Creek Confederacy—lived here, and the French established a trading post (Fort Toulouse) to court their favor. This tribe and the adjacent river gave our state its name.

After the French and Indian War, the fort came under the jurisdiction of the British, who soon abandoned it. The famous naturalist William Bartram visited the ruins of the fort during the American Revolution period and commented on how this land at the rivers' junction would make a grand city site. (Such a river town was later built on higher ground downstream and named after General Richard Montgomery.) After defeating the Creeks at Horseshoe Bend, Andrew Jackson reestablished the fort, renamed Fort Jackson. Chief Red Eagle surrendered here; the site of his surrender is part of 254 acres that were added to the park through the Forever Wild program.

Today, the area's historical and natural resources are preserved in the park's 434 total acres. Fort reconstructions and period reenactors bring alive the relationship between human beings and this beautiful natural area.

The park contains a short nature trail along hardwood bluffs that border the floodplain—the Bartram Arboretum. The trees of this area are festooned with an abundance of Spanish moss, and signs provide natural history information.

Longer walks are possible along the trail system located behind the Fort Jackson reconstruction. These trails, composed of old roads, lead to the junction of the rivers.

DIRECTIONS: Take US 231 south from downtown Wetumpka. You will see a sign directing you to turn right down a side road to the park.

101 Yates Lake / Coon Creek / Tallassee Falls

32°32'08.76"N
85°53'35.68"W

The shoals of the lower Tallapoosa have been dammed to create small impoundments, such as Yates Lake, for hydroelectricity. Forever Wild recently acquired 3,518 acres on the western side of this lake. The property contains three miles of lakefront and a mixture of hardwood ravines and pine-hardwood ridge tops with some remnant longleaf pine. The Channahatchee Creek ravine is particularly beautiful.

A smaller Forever Wild purchase, the Coon Creek Natural Area, is located downstream from the above ravine. Here the Yates Lake impoundment backs up into Coon Creek; the natural area occupies steep slopes leading down to the lake. North-facing slopes contain a rich upland forest with various oaks and beeches; Carolina silverbells decorate the understory with white, bell-shaped blossoms in the spring. There are some small cascades on wet weather tributaries and outcrops of metamorphic rocks. The forests surrounding these outcrops have more wildflowers, including hepatica and trillium, than other habitats on the site. The tract also contains some bottomland hardwood with dwarf palmetto palm in the understory. Young bald cypress trees have germinated along the lake's shore and among the marsh vegetation at the head of the creek's impounded section.

There are no trails on the property, but the road leading down to a boat launch on its south side provides a good walking experience. The boat launch offers opportunities for canoeing along Coon Creek—probably the best way to see the property. And a picnic area is located on the north side of the creek.

Downstream on the Tallapoosa River, below Thurlow Dam, lies a remnant of the once mighty Tallassee Falls. When power is not being generated at the dam, the falls are largely dry; however, "good" falls can be seen with water release. Interestingly, cypress-bottomland hardwood wetlands appear along the river just below the falls, creating the sharp contrast between a rocky upland Piedmont stream and a lazy, swampy Coastal Plain one.

DIRECTIONS: The Forever Wild land along the western shore of Yates Lake is accessed by following AL 229 north from Tallassee. Turn right onto Co. Rd. 44 and then take any one of the series of roads to the left where you see yellow state land signs; Dean Order Rd. is a particularly good access point. The Forever Wild property is mixed in with private land, so pay attention to the signs and stay on state-owned land.

To reach the boat launch of the Coon Creek tract, take AL 14 east from downtown Tallassee. Turn left on Macedonia Rd., left on Hicks Store Rd., left on Gravel Pit Dr., then right on Coon Creek Landing Rd. The picnic area can be reached from the north via Sulphur Springs Rd.

To reach the Falls from downtown Tallassee, take AL 14 east to the river bridge. An access road will be found on the right.

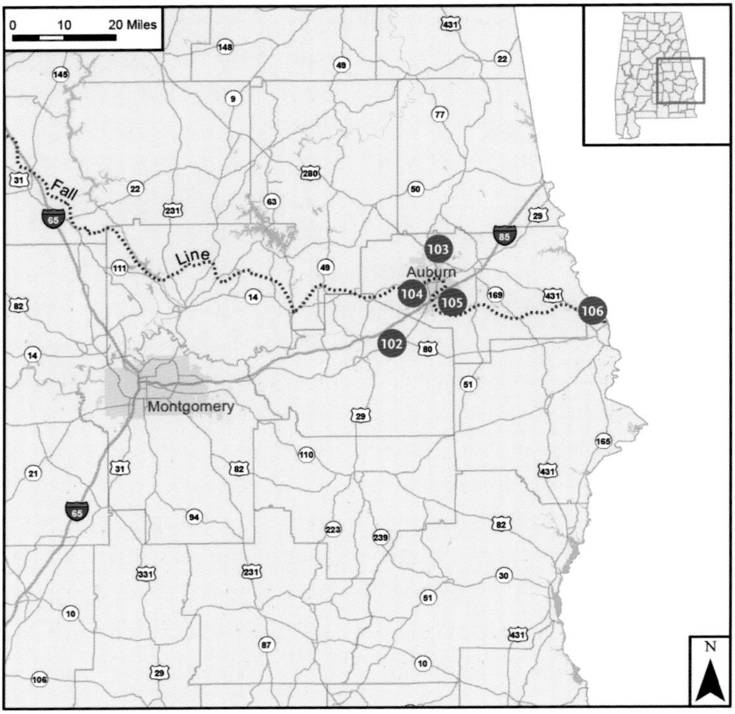

AUBURN AREA

Auburn is located near the junction of the Piedmont and Fall Line Hills. Hence, the area enjoys a wide variety of habitats, from Fall Line shoals to unbroken forests.

102 Tuskegee National Forest

32°28'38.80"N
85°36'37.06"W

At 11,000 acres, Tuskegee National Forest is one of the smallest national forests in the nation. But despite its small size, it features a great diversity of habitats. The sandy ridges contain longleaf pine stands with associated wildlife, such as fox squirrels. Stream valleys house beech-magnolia forests and bottomland hardwood forests. Some of the beech-magnolia forests contain rare six-foot-tall needle palms, giving the forest a tropical feeling.

The primary hiking trail through the national forest is the Bartram Trail, whose name commemorates the nearby visit of the famous naturalist in the late 1700s. This 7.5-mile trail connects all of the above forest habitats. The most scenic section of the trail is the Bartram Botanical Area at the southwest side of the forest. Here, the trail traverses some of the best beech-magnolia forest in Alabama. (This is one of the northernmost areas where the beautiful, evergreen southern magnolia grows in abundance.) Other species found within the Botanical Area are the needle palm and shade-tolerant spruce pine, which looks like a northern white pine. The botanical area also has bottomland hardwood wetlands that front Choctafaula Creek.

Directions: To reach the Bartram Botanical Area from Tuskegee, travel east on US 29, then north on Co. Rd. 53. As soon as you cross Uphapee Creek, turn right; the trail's parking lot is on the left.

The rest of the Bartram Trail can be accessed by continuing northeast on US 29. Take a left onto AL 186, pass the Forest Service headquarters, then take another left onto FS 900. Follow this road until you see a parking area for the trail.

103 Louise Kreher Forest Ecology Preserve and Nature Center

32°39'38.91"N
85°29'19.08"W

This 110-acre preserve is owned and managed by Auburn University's School of Forestry and Wildlife Sciences. The property has numerous hiking trails, pavilions, and a beautiful outdoor classroom. Environmental education programs are offered to school groups, and the property contains an orienteering course. Free trail maps are provided, and a great trail guide is available for loan or purchase.

The preserve includes the barn of the old Kreher farmstead, and much of the property is old farmland that has succeeded to loblolly pine forest, with wax myrtle in the understory. The forest is managed using controlled burns to help produce the herbaceous diversity associated with an open, sunny pine forest. Some hardwood-covered slopes and creek terraces have plantings of native wildflowers such as bloodroot, Catesby's trillium, and atamasco lily. The lower slopes contain metamorphic rocks of the Piedmont, and a small waterfall is located upstream.

DIRECTIONS: The preserve can be reached by traveling north on AL 147 from Auburn. The entrance is on the right.

104 Donald E. Davis Arboretum

32°35'43.81"N
85°28'58.45"W

The Davis Arboretum is a 15-acre botanical area in the heart of Auburn University's campus. The arboretum contains plantings of almost 200 trees native to Alabama and the Southeast, with a few exotic species as well. The multicolored native azaleas are particularly stunning in the spring. The accurate labeling of the plants makes this a great place to learn your trees and shrubs.

A small stream drains the property and has been dammed

to form a pond full of turtles. Above the pond is a planted cypress-tupelo swamp and marsh full of spring-blooming blue and yellow swamp irises. Other portions of the stream corridor contain largely natural forest. The arboretum has exhibits on the wildlife of the area; there is also a native vine trellis. Some plantings include examples of special vegetation types found in the various physiographic regions of the state, like seashore vegetation, pitcher plant bogs, and the Black Belt prairie.

Adjacent to the arboretum is the oldest experimental cotton rotation plot in the nation. The cotton is rotated with other crops, including nitrogen-fixing legumes, as part of research on sustainable agriculture.

DIRECTIONS: The arboretum is located on the campus of Auburn University at the corner of Garden Dr. and College St.

105 Chewacla State Park

32°33'03.07"N
85°28'29.91"W

The 696-acre Chewacla State Park offers many opportunities for hiking near the city of Auburn. The rare needle palm can be found in the bottoms within this hilly terrain on the Fall Line. However, the most scenic feature of the park is the waterfall below the lake, which plunges down a steep gorge to a larger creek below. The pines of this rocky area give it a mountain-like aspect. However, we are reminded that this is a southern Fall Line location by the abundant Spanish moss hanging from the pines and other trees.

DIRECTIONS: Chewacla State Park is located four miles south of Auburn just off I-85 exit 51.

The oldest rocks in Alabama are found at Chewacla State Park

106 Chattahoochee River Fall Line

32°29'03.30"N
85°00'02.94"W

The short trail of this park in Phenix City is well worth visiting for both its natural and historical values. Visitors will follow a walkway along the Chattahoochee River through a neatly maintained park (which has a wilder border on its landward side). The park affords great views of the Fall Line along the Chattahoochee River.

Here you can see the river flow over waterfalls and shoals. Large metamorphic rocks of the Piedmont are exposed as shoals on this edge of the Coastal Plain, especially during times of low water. However, don't be tempted to walk out on them. Water releases from dams upstream can cause the river to rise almost instantly, cutting off your way back to the bank. While the river is most impressive at times of high water, it is best viewed from the safety of the bank *rather than while being drowned.*

The park area contains significant wildlife viewing opportunities, including sandpipers, gulls, and large flocks of cormorants.

The Fall Line of the Chattahoochee has been the site of human settlement since prehistoric times. The portion of the Chattahoochee River from around the Fall Line downstream (toward Eufaula) was the heartland of the Lower Creek Indian subnation. Historical markers in the park note that the Creeks located their villages next to the Fall Line so that they could capture fish as they migrated upstream through the bottleneck of the falls—much like a natural fish weir.

The Fall Line was (and still is) the head of navigation on the Chattahoochee River, which helped Phenix City, Alabama, and Columbus, Georgia, spring up on opposite banks of the river at this location. The settlements grew as they took advantage of the water power that could be harnessed from the river's falls. Above the waterfalls and shoals is an old mill dam that powered textile mills like those seen across the river in Columbus. A trail follows the Georgia side of the river by that site.

If visitors are interested in additional historical and natural sites, they can follow AL 165 south from Phenix City toward Eufaula. There are several historical markers on this route, including one for Fort Mitchell, which was constructed during the Creek Indian War of 1813. (A park is being created on this site that will include a picnic area and a reconstruction of the fort.) A little farther south on AL 165 is a marker denoting the northernmost Spanish fort in eastern North America. AL 165 leads to Eufaula NWR, described in this book's chapter on the Chunnenuggee Ridge subprovince.

DIRECTIONS: The Phenix City River Walk is located in the downtown area on the west bank of the Chattahoochee River between the 14th St. and Dillingham St. bridges. There is parking on the north side of the Dillingham St. bridge just before you cross it to the east bank.

If you take AL 167 south from Phenix City toward Eufaula NWR and the city of Eufaula, you will see the historical markers for Fort Mitchell and the Spanish fort.

BLACK BELT

The Black Belt is a unique subprovince of the Coastal Plain underlain by white chalk. The chalk fostered the development of grasslands, and over many generations the grasses produced the fertile black soil that gives the region its name.

This region was a sea when dinosaurs walked the Earth, and the chalk is composed of the calcium-rich shells of tiny marine microorganisms (*coccoliths*), which settled out near its shore. In certain places abundant fossils can be found, especially shellfish, sharks' teeth, and mosasaurs. The latter are the most famous fossils of the Black Belt, being giant, crocodile-like sea creatures. Their huge size and imagined ferocity make modern great white sharks seem rather tame.

Some of the area's river cliffs look like the famous White Cliffs of Dover, England. That is to be expected, since the same coccoliths created both. The white color really shows up when the cliffs are dry and the sun is out. The chalk is so pure in places that you can break off a piece and write your name with it. Many of these chalk formations are quarried for their calcium (lime) content.

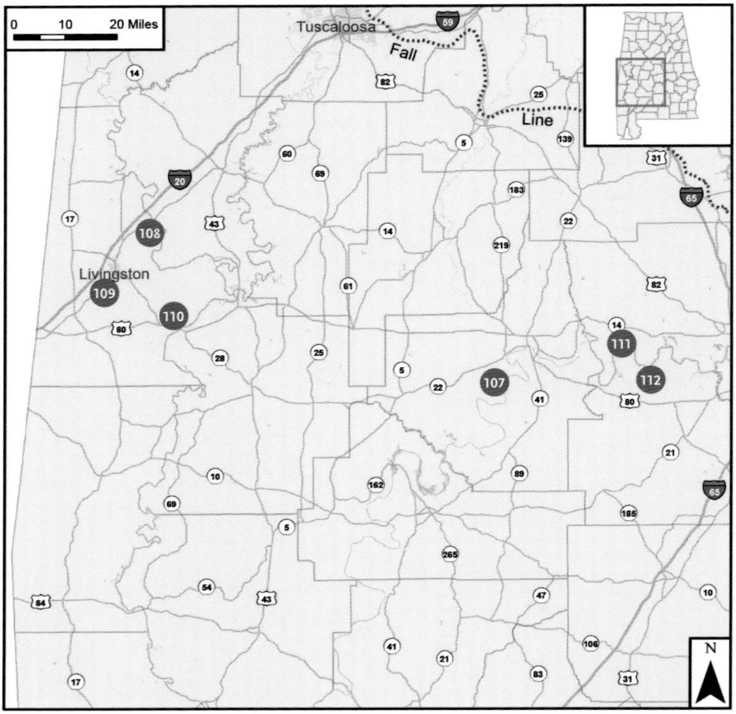

LIMESTONE PRAIRIE AREA

As hinted earlier, the underlying chalk has shaped the unique natural communities of the area. Acid-loving pines are largely absent from the alkaline soils weathered from the chalk. (In some places, though, other geologic deposits overlie the chalk, and there you will find an abundance of pines.) The forests of the chalk areas are dominated by lime-loving species like chinquapin oak and shagbark hickory. These areas also include the unusual Osage orange with its huge, green, brain-like fruits.

Chalk is largely impermeable to water, so when chalk is close to the surface, such as on hilltops, the growth of trees is hindered. The combination of dry, shallow soils and frequent fires helped to create and maintain significant areas of prairie and savanna in the Black Belt. Many of the wildflowers, grasses, and even trees (like bur oaks) that are common to the midwestern tallgrass prairies are also found in the Black Belt. In fact, the Black Belt may have served as these plants' Ice Age refuges when areas to the north were covered with glaciers and cold-tolerant vegetation.

The Black Belt prairie was once grazed by buffalo, elk, and wild horses. Today it provides important habitat for declining grassland birds such as the lark sparrow and bobwhite quail. The Black Belt also provides habitat for the painted bunting, which is normally found only on Alabama's coast. This little iridescent red, blue and green creature is among our most colorful birds, and it depends on the scrubland at the edges of Black Belt prairies.

The Black Belt was initially avoided by European settlers due to the perception that the region's soil was poor; they were also taken aback by the area's sparse tree cover. However, the soils were discovered to be excellent for growing cotton, and large plantations were built during the antebellum period using slave labor. Soon the majority of tallgrass prairies and savannas disappeared under the plow, just as they did in the Midwest. Prior to the Civil War, the Black Belt was the wealthiest region of Alabama. But after the war, the slave-based economy was replaced by a sharecropper system, and the price of cotton fell due to increased production elsewhere. The region quickly went from being the richest to (presently) the poorest area of our state.

The land went through some changes, too. Much of the Black Belt farmland was severely abused and eroded down to bare chalk gullies. Some farmlands were abandoned and are now succeeding toward forest. Much of the land has been turned from cropland to pastureland, restoring a prairie-like feel to the area. Now catfish ponds are increasing on the flat chalk lands because the chalk helps form an impermeable pond liner. (The Black Belt site of Emelle in Sumter County houses a toxic waste dump for these and other reasons.)

The Black Belt contains significant areas of upland and bottomland hardwood, but its unique prairies and savannas have been largely lost to agriculture and fire suppression. While much of the Black Belt looks like open prairie, these areas are actually no more than pastures of exotic grasses, with little wildflower or native plant diversity. However, prairie remnants and their associated wildflowers still exist in areas where the chalk is very close to the surface. As in other provinces of our state, it is these remnants that are well worth visiting.

107 Old Cahawba

32°19'10.84"N
87°06'17.18"W

The lowest portion of the Cahaba River passes through the Black Belt formation and contains some spectacular white chalk cliffs as well as low, seepy ledges covered with bald cypress trees and wildflowers. If you are floating this section, be forewarned that the flow of these final seven river miles can be affected by the Miller's Ferry impoundment on the Alabama River. Sometimes the river is moving swiftly; at other times the reservoir backs up the Cahaba, creating slack water that requires extra strenuous paddling.

There is a nice area of roadside wildflowers located on the north side of AL 22 where it meets Co. Rd. 9 near Old Cahawba State Historic Park. But more importantly, a chalk prairie is located to the east of Co. Rd. 9 just before you turn east onto Co. Rd. 2 to enter the park. This prairie is very important biologically because

Black Belt prairie at Old Cahawba

it contains the Old Cahaba rosinweed, which is only found in this area of Alabama's Black Belt. Fortunately, a 3,007-acre tract that includes this prairie was acquired by the Nature Conservancy (and subsequently Forever Wild). The tract also includes chalk cliffs along the Cahaba River, bottomland hardwood forests, and ravine hardwood forests covered in Spanish moss. From the roadside you will see that the prairie has been used as a pasture, but it still has lots of red cedars and prairie coneflowers, plus a prolific population of dwarf palmetto palms. (This dwarf palm will remind you of the prairies of central Florida.) Due to past grazing and fire suppression, some of the best patches of wildflowers occur along the sunny roadsides where the cows could not reach.

The actual Old Cahawba State Historic Park preserves a site rich in human and natural history. (Cahawba is the old-timey spelling of Cahaba.) The Old Cahawba site was picked as our state's first capital because of its central location at the junction of two major rivers, the Cahaba and Alabama. (Rivers were essential to transportation in the days before railroads.) Unfortunately, its location at the rivers' confluence led to flooding of the site's low-lying bottoms and ravines; for this and other reasons, Alabama's capital was moved first to Tuscaloosa and then to Montgomery.

River traffic also brought diseases from the Gulf Coast, as recorded in Old Cahawba's graveyards. During the Civil War, the area served as a prison camp for Union soldiers. Although conditions were rough, the prisoners' health was surprisingly good—at least when compared to other Civil War prison camps. Sadly, many of the Union soldiers who survived Cahawba died on their way home when the steamboat *Sultana* exploded on the Mississippi River.

After the Civil War, the city of Cahawba faded away. The state has acquired portions of its site to preserve the history of Alabama's first capital. Visitors can see historic features within the forest that has reclaimed the site—cemeteries, artesian wells, and columns from an antebellum mansion that overlooked the two rivers. Natural habitats within the park include upland and bottomland hardwood forests. There is a boat launch on a slough off of the Alabama River, which has a healthy cypress swamp at its head, and we have seen alligators there more than once. The park has several trails, a history museum, and nature center.

Directions: Take AL 22 west from downtown Selma and turn left on Co. Rd. 9. Shortly before this road reaches a T intersection with Co. Rd. 2, you will see the Old Cahawba Prairie on your left. Find a parking place (without blocking the gate on the left) and enjoy the roadside wildflowers. Then hike down the road behind the gate, through the prairie and pine plantations to the hardwood slopes along the river. The riverine chalk cliffs will be upstream to your left.

To reach Old Cahawba State Historic Park from the above, take a left on Co. Rd. 2 and follow it into the park.

108 Chalk Cliffs and Surroundings

32°31'03.33"N
87°50'11.61"W

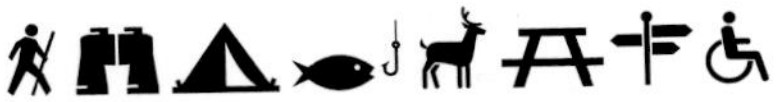

The most impressive landforms of the Black Belt are located where rivers have created white chalk cliffs. Of these, one of the tallest is Jones Bluff on the Tombigbee River near Epes, the site of the old French trading post, Fort Tombecbe. The fort was built in the mid-1700s as a wartime supply base, to assist the French and Choctaws in their unsuccessful effort to pull the Chickasaws out of the English sphere of influence. When the English defeated the French in a later war, the fort was abandoned. Then the Spanish claimed the area at the time of the American Revolution; the earthen walls of a later Spanish fort can still be seen at the site. The site has typical lime-loving tree species such as chinquapin oak, Osage orange, and hawthorns, plus prairie coneflowers within the fort's open grounds. The beautiful Cherokee bean is also present. The bluff top affords fantastic views of the white chalk cliff, the Tombigbee River, and the bottomland hardwood in the lowlands across the river. The site is owned by the University of West Alabama, and potential visitors need prior permission from the university.

Surrounding the fort is a heavily grazed Black Belt prairie. The University of West Alabama fenced some tiny plots of the

Chalk cliffs lining the Tombigbee River near Epes

prairie to prevent further grazing and determine how the vegetation changes. To see a small naturally ungrazed area, turn north off US 11 in Epes onto Co. Rd. 20, then stay straight through an unmarked intersection. The road continues as Co. Rd. 21, and the ungrazed area can be viewed on its right side just before you reach the I-20/59 overpass. Efforts are being made to permanently preserve this remnant prairie.

Flowing southeast from Mississippi, the Noxubee River enters the Tombigbee upriver from Epes. The Noxubee has an outstanding diversity of aquatic wildlife associated with its calcium-rich water, all produced in its chalk-based watershed. The river can be canoed between widely spaced bridge crossings in Mississippi and Alabama.

The Howell Heflin–Gainesville Dam Site West Bank is found on the Tombigbee upstream from the mouth of the Noxubee. A drive through these Corps lands reveals a variety of bottomland and upland habitats. The area is great for seeing riverine birds, including an occasional anhinga.

Further upstream is a Corps park known officially as the S. W. Taylor Overlook; unofficially, it's China Bluff. Although the park's facilities have declined due to recent budget cuts, visitors can still see some historic graves and an impressive view of the "dirty" chalk cliffs of China Bluff to the north. The park's forest includes some nice hardwood including large post oaks decorated with Spanish moss. The S. W. Taylor Overlook is closed frequently (including all winter), so check with the Corps before planning a visit.

Another Corps park, up the Tombigbee River at Cochrane, has likewise seen a decline in facilities, including the loss of a hiking trail. However, the area contains some interesting Black Belt red cedar savanna that may have arisen recently on old farmland. The area contains cedars scattered in a mixture of grasses and wildflowers. This site has great potential for restoration—if it were burned and planted with wildflowers characteristic of the Black Belt.

The Demopolis Chalk Cliff, on the grounds of historic Bluff Hall, is easy to access. Bluff Hall and Gaineswood (across the street) are both antebellum houses open to the public, and they are certainly worth a tour. Visitors can walk behind Bluff Hall to reach a magnificent view from the top of the chalk cliff, which towers above the Tombigbee River.

Demopolis has an extra colorful history, since it was founded by aristocrats and soldiers who had to leave France after Napoleon was defeated and exiled. They had little experience with farming and tried, quite naively, to grow French wine grapes and olives in Alabama's semitropical climate. To make matters worse, they first settled on the *wrong land grant* and had to move! While most of the French left for bigger cities, some stayed and prospered, and more traditional American settlers turned Demopolis into a thriving antebellum river port.

There is a famous painting of the Demopolis Chalk Cliff hanging on the wall of Bluff Hall. The painting was done in the antebellum period from a vantage point downstream from Buff Hall, possibly near the present chalk-mining operation. The view captured in the painting has changed surprisingly little. Bluff Hall and other structures still line the top of the cliff, patches of trumpet creeper vine still hang over the cliff, and the opposite bank of the river is still covered in a bottomland hardwood swamp that is now part of the Demopolis WMA. The biggest change is the impoundment of the river to form Lake Demopolis, making the cliff a little shorter.

If you are visiting the Demopolis area, you might want to stop at the above-mentioned Demopolis WMA. Its 6,952 acres are owned by the Corps but managed by the state. Some of the land was purchased as mitigation for the impacts of the Tennessee–Tombigbee Waterway. The WMA contains several sections on the Tombigbee and the Black Warrior Rivers, including the land between their confluence. The easiest way to reach these lands is by boat. However, the largest block of land, which lies across the river from Demopolis, can be reached by road.

The WMA has gated access roads that can be hiked. These roads pass through bottomland hardwood, which is periodically cut for timber. The main road leads to the river, where visitors can see the swampy junction of the Tombigbee and Black Warrior Rivers upstream. Within the bottomland hardwood, wisps of Spanish moss festoon trees and dwarf palmetto palms cover the forest floor. Bald cypresses grow in low areas, and a young cypress swamp is forming in a beaver pond of the area.

Also near Demopolis is Chickasaw State Park, which actually lies in the Chunnenuggee Hills. This small state park offers a picnic area and some hiking trails through upland forests. Wild turkeys are abundant and seemingly tame in this area. And there is a handicapped-accessible public hunting site nearby.

The Forever Wild program recently purchased about 3,300 acres on and around the State Cattle Ranch, an old prison farm close to Demopolis. The land includes mixed upland forests and flooded swamps as well as large areas of Black Belt pastures. These pastures have great potential to be restored to native grasses and flowers. The area was bought, in part, to provide a field trial competition location for bird (quail) dogs. Restoration of native prairie vegetation should help restore quail populations in this area. If bison were added to the mix, we could complete the Black Belt prairie scene!

As of this writing, public access to the State Cattle Ranch is still in the developmental stage. Check this book's website for updates.

DIRECTIONS: To visit Fort Tombecbe on the Chalk Cliffs of Epes (Jones Bluff), contact the president's office at the University of West Alabama. If you cannot plan your visit ahead of time, you can see the cliffs from US 11 on the east side of Epes where it crosses the Tombigbee River.

After you visit the Epes area, you can reach other sites on the upper Tombigbee by following Co. Rd. 20 west from Epes and across I-20/59 (at exit 23). Continue west on Co. Rd. 20 to AL 39. Take a right and follow AL 39 north to the historic antebellum town of Gainesville. In Gainesville, take a left onto AL 119, then a right onto Co. Rd. 85. Co. Rd. 85 runs parallel to the upper Tombigbee River, and between Gainesville and Cochrane it passes by the junction of the Noxubee and Tombigbee Rivers as well as the Heflin Lock and Dam, S. W. Taylor, and Cochrane recreation areas.

To reach the Cochrane Recreation Area you will need to take a right onto AL 17 when Co. Rd. 85 meets it in a T intersection. Then take a left at a sign for the recreation area.

To reach the Demopolis Chalk Cliff in Marengo County, follow US 43 through the city; you will see signs for Bluff Hall, which is across the street from the more famous Gaineswood antebellum home. Park at Bluff Hall and walk behind the building to stand on top of the chalk cliff above the Tombigbee River. The bottomland hardwood of the Demopolis WMA can be seen across the river.

To reach the Demopolis WMA, continue south on US 43 to its junction with US 80 and take a right. Follow US 80 west for a while, crossing the Tombigbee River well below Demopolis. Continue west on US 80 and then take a right onto AL 28, then another right onto Co. Rd. 23. Follow Co. Rd. 23 northeast to Belmont, then follow Belmont Circle southeast; watch for signs directing you to the WMA's gate, which will probably be closed. Walk the road into the heart of the area.

To reach Chickasaw State Park, follow US 43 south from Demopolis. The park is located north of the town of Providence.

109 University of West Alabama Blackland Prairie Restoration / Lake Livingston University

32°36'17.36"N
88°11'37.29"W

The University of West Alabama (formerly, Livingston University) offers the public the best chance to see the wildflowers and other plants associated with Black Belt prairie country. The university is restoring a significant area of old hay fields to Black Belt or Blackland Prairie. (Blackland Prairie is the name given

Restored prairie at the University of West Alabama

to this type of habitat by the Environmental Protection Agency; the Black Belt is what we call the region in Alabama.) This restoration lies within the nature trail system at the man-made Lake Livingston University.

The prairie restoration is being accomplished thanks to periodic burns, which control encroaching woody vegetation. The result looks like a midwestern tallgrass prairie, complete with waving grass, prairie coneflowers, and Indian paintbrush. Surrounding woody plants are red cedar, honey locust, and native plums. Adjacent nature trails run through shady red cedar forests and lakeside marsh habitats.

Directions: Take exit 17 from I-20/59. Follow AL 28 south and turn right onto Hwy 11 at the stop light. Follow this road to the back entrance of the University of West Alabama. Turn right into the university and proceed less than a mile; the lake and its parking lot will be on your right. Walk to the right along the lakeshore to the nature trail, which is behind and to the right of the baseball field. You will cross a short bridge over a marshy finger of the lake; a map board here will help orient you to the area. As you follow the trail to the right away from the lake, you will enter a relatively large open area—the prairie restoration site. Keep walking until you encounter the interpretive nature trail, which will take you back through a cedar forest to the entrance.

110 Bluffport Preserve (access is restricted)

Bluffport Preserve is a 30-acre site purchased by the Sumter County Nature Trust. It protects the unique biology, geology, and history of the now-vanished town of Bluffport.

Once a thriving river port, Bluffport moved itself west in 1940, probably to be nearer the railroads and highways that had become the dominant forms of transportation. The Old Bluffport site is located on the Bluffport Marl formation of the Selma Chalk, a mixture of limestone and clay. The marl is full of fossils that can be easily seen at bare spots on the land. Fossils of oysters and marine snails are abundant; those of nautilus, squid, sharks' teeth, and mosasaurs are here, too.

The prairie on the site, dominated by Indian grass and little bluestem, has not been significantly disturbed for about 100 years, and it shows a great diversity of plants. About 200 species have been documented so far, including many that are commonly associated with the midwestern tallgrass prairie ecosystem. Five such species are of special conservation concern at either the state or federal level.

Old Bluffport was a booming shipping point for steamboats carrying cotton downriver and goods from the rest of the world upriver. The remains of "slides" used to get the cotton down the bluffs to the steamboats can still be seen. The town also included a stagecoach inn, blacksmith shop, hotel, academy, and church. The most unique remaining historic feature is the milk cave, a room cut 25 feet deep into the front of the bluff. Shelves and counters were carved out of the chalk. Steamboats stopped at the cave so that passengers could wait in its coolness while enjoying cold drinks.

Directions: To visit the Bluffport Preserve, contact the Sumter County Nature Trust, which is governed through the University of West Alabama.

111 Jones Bluff and the Alabama River (access is restricted)

Jones Bluff is an old Corps park on the Alabama River in Autauga County that was recently closed due to budget cuts. The park includes Black Belt chalk covered by pines, hardwoods, and prairie. The site features trails through the forest that connect former picnic grounds. The trails pass through a Spanish moss-draped forest of upland hardwoods including white oak, chinquapin oak, ash, beech, and bigleaf magnolia. Bottomland hardwood forests grow along the area's creeks, and these forests include horsetails in the herb layer. At the old silted-in boat launch, the site borders a slough formed by the Lake Woodruff impoundment. The adjacent river/lake environment supports the rare Alabama map and black saw-backed turtles as well as bald eagles.

The park has many rare plants including Ashe's hawthorn, Great Plains ladies' tresses, creamflower tick trefoil, impressed nerved sedge, nutmeg hickory, three-flowered hawthorn, croomia, Alabama larkspur, and Canada violet. Some forest openings in this area support Indian pink and the exquisite Cherokee bean.

Much of this former park can be explored only through serious bushwhacking. You will need permission from the Corps to visit it.

112 Lowndes County Sites

32°19'38.47"N
86°42'44.21"W

Lowndes County is one of the most rural counties in Alabama. It contains large areas of Black Belt chalk and alluvial bottomlands along the Alabama River. There are several interesting natural history sites near the river.

The 11,118-acre Lowndes County WMA is owned by the Corps and the state of Alabama. Much of the site was purchased for bottomland hardwood restoration to help mitigate the environmental impacts of the Tennessee–Tombigbee Waterway. The terraces and floodplain on the site are old farmland that has been planted with trees; some day it will make a great bottomland forest. There are also mature tupelos, cypresses, and bottomland hardwood swamps along its streams and the Alabama River impoundment (Lake Woodruff). Upland hardwoods and pines occupy the slopes within the area.

The WMA can be accessed by land along its various roads, most of which are closed outside of hunting season. Visitors should see turkeys, barred owls, and beavers; there are some old pecan groves here as well. However, the best way to see this area is by boat or canoe. The boat launch of the Prairie Creek Campground is a great place to enter the reservoir backwaters that border the WMA. Canoeists and boaters can see alligators, swamp irises, and other wetland life. The bottomlands show the influence of the alkaline Black Belt chalk through the presence of lots of atamasco lilies in the spring. These white, Easter lily–like plants are so pretty that they look unreal. Needle palms also grow here.

Another good access point is the Corps' Holy Ground Battlefield Park. This park commemorates a nearby battle of the Creek War. The Creek Indians' prophets told them that this land was holy, so the soldiers could not hurt them. The soldiers proved them wrong. Chief Red Eagle had been skeptical of the prophets' claims, and when the battle was lost he escaped by swimming his horse across the Alabama River.

The Holy Ground Trail follows the river bluffs through terrain similar to the battlefield. The river can be seen through Spanish moss-draped oaks, and an abundance of atamasco lilies occur here, too. The trees have been labeled in this area for your edification.

DIRECTIONS: To reach the Lowndes County WMA and the various Corps parks on the Alabama River, follow US 80 west from Montgomery, then take a right onto Co. Rd. 29 at Lowndesboro. Follow Co. Rd. 29 through that historic antebellum town and take a left onto Co. Rd. 40. This road goes west and passes through the WMA and past its various access roads, as well as the sign marking the side road to Holy Ground Battlefield Park. Co. Rd. 40 continues to White Hall where another section of the WMA can be accessed to the north. If you continue west, the road becomes Jones Bluff Rd. and passes by Prairie Creek Campground.

CHUNNENUGGEE RIDGE

The Chunnenuggee Ridge subprovince of the Coastal Plain is characterized by its uplands, especially to the south and west. The Ridge, with its sandy soils, forms a topographic transition between the relatively flat Black Belt chalk to the north and the much more hilly Red Hills to the south. The western side of the subprovince, heading into Mississippi, is known as the Post Oak Flatwoods because of the area's unique, poorly drained forests containing a lot of post oak trees.

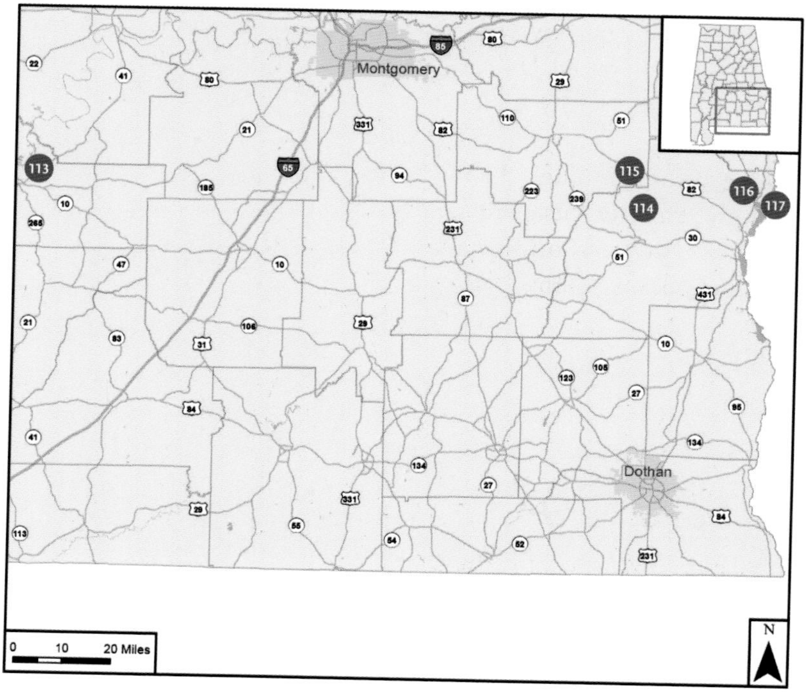

SANDY RIDGE AREA

According to some sources, "chunnenuggee" is a Native American word describing a "long, high ridge." As such, the Chunnenuggee Ridge has extensive areas of both low rolling hills and narrow ravines. The ridge tops were originally dominated by shortleaf pines and hardwoods, with longleaf pines on especially sandy and dry sites. While hardwood forest occupies most ravines, some poorly drained ravine bottoms support evergreen shrub swamp species. Upland swamps are usually dominated by swamp tupelo.

Much of the forest in this region was cleared to provide farmland. In recent decades, the open farmland has been converted to timber production involving fast-growing loblolly and slash pines.

The area around Union Springs is the "quail capital of Alabama," and the city even has a monument to champion bird dogs. A significant amount of land in this area is managed as pine savanna through the use of timber thinning and controlled burns. This benefits quail habitat and hunting. These quail plantations also help to maintain (now rare) open pine forests and their associated herbaceous diversity and wildlife habitat.

113 Roland Cooper State Park

32°03'23.76"N
87°14'42.56"W

The 263-acre Roland Cooper State Park is located at the Miller's Ferry or Dannelly impoundment on the Alabama River. The park lies along the border between the Chunnenuggee Ridge and the Red Hills. The park's uplands contain pine forests that appear to have been planted on old farmland back in the 1960s and 1970s when the reservoir was being built. These forests are more mature and open than the pine plantations on surrounding private lands, and they have the potential to become even better with proper burning and other management practices. This area of the park is traversed by the Chipmunk Trail, which can be accessed from the entrance road.

If you want to see the lakeshore environment, then hike the Lakeside Trail. This trail starts at the pavilion within the campground and runs through the hardwood forest behind it. The trail shows amazing beauty and diversity of habitats. The shoreline has some edge marsh (including the exotic water hyacinth) as well as a large number of bald cypress trees that have sprung up along the reservoir's shore. Despite their young ages, the cypresses have produced a lot of knees, which extend into the adjacent bottomland hardwood forest. The latter forest still naturally floods, as evidenced by some woody debris that settles on the land from time to time. Nice dwarf palmetto palms are found in the shrub layer here. Some slightly higher terraces and slopes are covered by rich bluff hardwood forest containing beech. Even higher lands contain mixed pine-hardwood forest that has been subjected to burning; shortleaf and loblolly pines are found in this area. The trail dips in and out of all of these habitats.

Nearby Corps parks on Dannelly Reservoir offer additional recreational opportunities.

Directions: From Camden in Wilcox County, follow AL 41 northeast and you will see signs directing you to the park.

114 Barbour County WMA

31°58'00.38"N
85°26'48.63"W

The largest public wildlife habitat in the Chunnenuggee Ridge area is the 18,924-acre Barbour County WMA. The WMA is made up of both state and private lands in Barbour and Bullock Counties. Here you will find thick pine plantations, lots of upland hardwood, mixed forests, and shrub swamps. The area also contains some pine savannas, which have been managed for bobwhite quail and other wildlife.

Directions: From Eufaula, take US 82 west to Comer and turn left onto Co. Rd. 49. Co. Rd. 49 runs through the WMA (and past various side roads of the WMA) to the Barbour County fishing lake. The WMA also borders the Wehle Nature Center, discussed below.

115 Robert G. Wehle Nature Center

32°02'20.70"N
85°28'09.18"W

The best place for nature enthusiasts to enjoy the Barbour County WMA is actually across the county line in Bullock County at the Robert G. Wehle Nature Center. The beautiful nature center's small collection of mounted animals and other items are geared toward school groups, but adults can certainly appreciate the center's trail system.

A nice interpretive loop trail around the center's lake leads from the nature center to an old-fashioned hand water pump and a petrified log. Near the upper end of the lake is an outdoor classroom pavilion (with a wetland animal display) overlooking a tupelo swamp, which was formed when a stream was impounded to form the lake. The trail passes through pine forest with a ground layer of cane. A marshy open area at the extreme upper end of the lake contains a planted garden of insect-eating pitcher plants. (The pitcher plants are slightly out of their natural ranges but still neat to see.) The lake is surrounded by gourd bird houses (used by purple martins) and plantings of bald cypress. The far side of the lake has some nice old oaks and a view of some horse barns and a pasture.

The Wehle Nature Center sits on 25 acres of a 1,500-acre tract that was one of the first purchases by Alabama's Forever Wild program. The land's owner, Robert G. Wehle, sold the property to the state at a discount; he also provided funds to build this nature center. The nature center is open to the public on a limited schedule, so it's best to call ahead.

DIRECTIONS: The Wehle Nature Center is located approximately five miles southeast of Midway, Alabama, on Co. Rd. 47.

116 Lakepoint Resort State Park

31°59'23.31"N
85°06'40.88"W

The 1,220-acre Lakepoint Resort State Park is located on Lake Eufaula, a Corps impoundment on the Chattahoochee River. The park features the most extensive facilities on the Alabama side of the Chattahoochee, which makes up the lower half of the border between Alabama and Georgia. The park offers good bird watching—even from the restaurant, which looks out over the surrounding Eufaula NWR. On a cold winter day you can enjoy a good hot meal while observing ducks, geese, herons, gulls, and huge flocks of cormorants chasing fish.

The campground and nature trails are set in a flat environment of Spanish moss, oaks, and stands of tall pines. Southern magnolias sprout up among the pines, and the area would eventually succeed to a magnolia- and beech-dominated hardwood forest if controlled burns where not performed to maintain the open pine forest. The park also contains some hardwood swamps, and small, stunted bald cypresses grow in the lake.

Directions: Take US 431 north from the city of Eufaula; the state park will be on your right.

117 Eufaula NWR

31°59'13.21"N
85°05'33.64"W

The 11,184-acre Eufaula NWR surrounds the middle portion of its namesake lake. It includes a mixture of pine, hardwood, mixed forests, farm fields, pasture, old fields, and wetlands, all of which

Wetlands at Eufaula NWR

are maintained and managed for the benefit of waterfowl and other wildlife. Wildlife Drive, with its observation towers and blinds, gives visitors a good survey of all of these habitats. Wetlands are found where the lake shallowly floods the land. The refuge's wetlands include lotus pad and grass marshes, plus some bottomland hardwood. Scattered bald cypress trees also occur on the refuge, with some of them apparently stunted by growing in near-constant water levels.

In addition, the refuge has diked some of the lake's sloughs. The dikes manipulate water levels to mimic a natural wetland's drying and associated vegetation growth in summer and subsequent reflooding in winter. This creates superb habitat for migratory ducks. During the winter, visitors can see numerous species of ducks including mallards, ringnecks, widgeons, and buffleheads. (Better bring a spotting scope because the ducks are often beyond the reach of binoculars.) The refuge supports a year-round population of Canada geese, and it is one of the best places in the state to see white-fronted geese in winter. Summer visitors

Wetlands at Eufaula NWR

will see common and purple gallinules (as well as alligators) in areas thick with lily pads. The refuge's lands in Georgia offer other wildlife viewing opportunities, including nesting herons.

Lake Eufaula is named after an adjacent city in Alabama that, in turn, is named after a local Creek Indian chief. Chief Eufaula is known for his address to the state legislature in which he recommended that the invading Anglos love one another and the land. He said this despite the fact that he and his people were being forced to move to Oklahoma. Coincidently, there is also a very large impoundment in Oklahoma known as Lake Eufaula in the area where the Creeks were resettled.

Directions: The Eufaula NWR headquarters and Wildlife Drive are located to the north of Lakepoint State Park. From the state park, get on US 431 N and then quickly take a right onto AL 165; next, turn right onto AL 285 (also known as Old AL 165). Signs will direct you into the refuge.

RED HILLS

The Red Hills make up a subprovince of the Coastal Plain characterized by red subsoil. The landscape is gently hilly in the east and almost mountainous in the west. The relatively dry soils of hilltops were once covered by longleaf pine forests that have been largely lost due to clearing, development, fire suppression, and conversion to plantations of other pines. Where not converted to pine plantations, the relatively moist ravines contain beech-magnolia forests, with both evergreen and deciduous magnolias. These rugged cove hardwood habitats give visitors to this region an Appalachian Mountain "feel." The very steep ravines between the Conecuh and Alabama Rivers harbor the threatened Red Hills salamander, found nowhere else in the world.

A very rugged subsection of the Red Hills is the Buhrstone Mountains or Lime Hills. This formation was once an ancient ocean basin. Soft limestone outcrops along its rivers contain an abundance of marine fossils, including bones of ancient whales and sea shells, looking like they were just washed up on a beach.

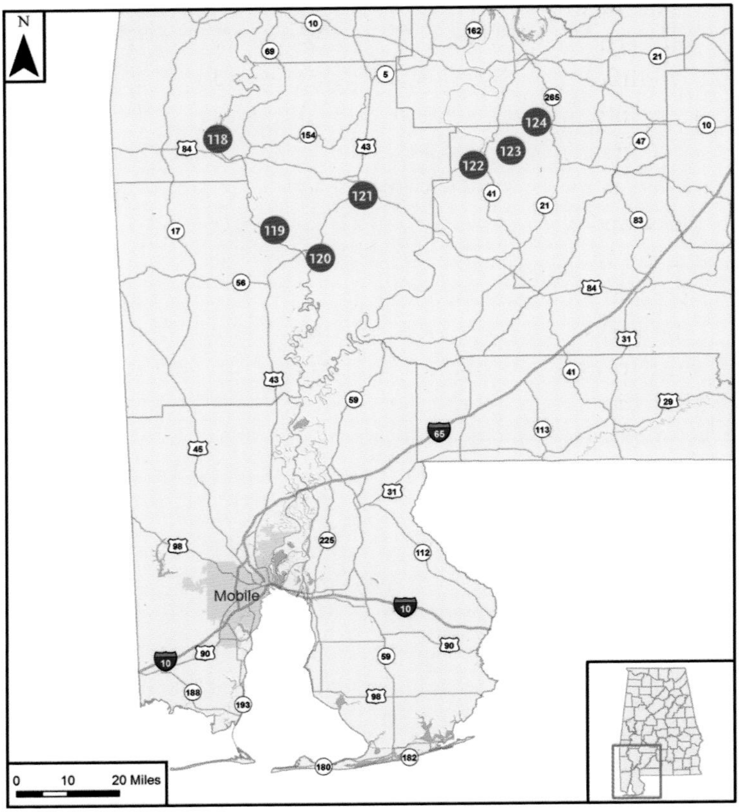

FORKS OF THE ALABAMA AND TOMBIGBEE RIVERS AREA

The area of southwest Alabama around the "V" formed by the confluence of the Alabama and Tombigbee Rivers is historically known as the Forks. The area contains a diversity of habitats including limestone outcrops, longleaf pine forests, bottomland hardwood forests, beech-magnolia forests, and a few prairies.

As the floodwaters of the Alabama and Tombigbee Rivers merge in southern Clarke County, the Mobile-Tensaw delta is born. Here the wildlife is very diverse and abundant: Red Hills salamanders burrow into the soft ravine soils, while swallow-tailed and Mississippi kites hunt the forest edges. Some conservation-minded landowners in the area were responsible for supporting deer, wild turkeys, and black bears while they were wiped out elsewhere in the state. In fact, deer and turkeys from this area were used to restock much of Alabama.

The Forks area is also rich in frontier history. This biologically diverse area was one of the Creek Indians' best hunting grounds during the colonial period, and European encroachment in the early 1800s created the animosity that eventually led to the Fort Mims Massacre and the Creek War of 1813. The Fort Mims site is located not very far south of the Forks in the upper Mobile-Tensaw delta area of Baldwin County.

Other historic spots are located in the Forks, such as salt wells and the vanished town of Suggsville. The Forks area features several history museums, and Monroe County has historic sites ranging from Rikard's Mill to the *To Kill a Mockingbird* literary locations of Monroeville. Natural and human history have long intertwined in this very rural, thickly forested land.

118 Choctaw NWR

31°46'07.44"N
88°11'08.15"W

The 4,218-acre Choctaw NWR is located on the floodplain of the Tombigbee River in Choctaw County. Here the river was impounded to form Lake Coffeeville, and this small reservoir backs up into some of the creeks and bottoms of the refuge, forming marshy habitats. The refuge contains bald cypress and a lot of bottomland hardwood, which is periodically harvested. The refuge is well known for its large heron rookeries, and it has an observation area where ibis, waterfowl, deer, and other wildlife can be seen.

Nearby is the 357-acre Bladon Springs State Park, which offers a pleasant picnic area surrounding some historic springs. Because of its supposed heath benefits, the water of Bladon Springs was once shipped to faraway places. In the past, the springs were a bit more artesian in nature, but nearby oil drilling has changed the hydrology. However, spring water can still be obtained using the site's old-fashioned hand pumps.

DIRECTIONS: From Coffeeville, take AL 84 west across the Tombigbee River. To reach Bladon Springs State Park, turn left onto Frankville Rd. Continue for approximately four miles, then turn left onto Co. Rd. 6. Travel less than one mile to the park entrance.

To reach Choctaw NWR, continue west on AL 84, then turn north on Co. Rd. 21. Continue north for four miles to Barrytown and turn east on Co. Rd. 14; follow Co. Rd. 14 to Womack Hill and turn right. Watch for NWR signs from AL 84 to the refuge entrance.

119 St. Stephens Historical Park

31°33'41.40"N
88°02'05.18"W

A little farther downstream on the Tombigbee River is St. Stephens Historical Park, which commemorates the first territorial capital of Alabama. The capital's site sits on top of a bluff composed of the relatively soft limestone underlying the Lime Hills subsection of the Red Hills. The lime rock was formed by the shells of dead marine microorganisms that settled in an ancient sea near its shore. The sea covered this area after most of Alabama (to the north) was dry land; whales swam over this area, and some of the best fossils of these huge creatures come from this part of Alabama.

The center of the property is an old quarry where the lime rock was mined. The rim of the quarry offers picnic facilities with great views out over the quarries, which are now filled with marshy lakes. Lime outcrops on the rim are extremely rich in fossils, especially shellfish.

Native Americans frequented this area and its white lime bluffs above the Tombigbee River. Later, Europeans discovered the shoals in the river that hindered navigation upstream from this point, creating a key spot for defense and trade. In the late 1700s Spain established a fort on top of nearby high bluffs that did not flood; the fort was later taken over by the Americans and became a border town along a boundary between Spanish Florida and the United States. The town, known as St. Stephens, served as Alabama's territorial capital.

When Alabama became a state, the capital was moved to Cahawba, and St. Stephens gradually faded away. People later came to the site to saw up its soft lime rock for use in building chimneys. During the 20th century, the top of the bluff was quarried for lime, but (fortunately) most of the old town was spared.

Visitors to the park can follow a trail through an upland hardwood forest to some of St. Stephens' remains, which are largely rocks and cellar holes. Down at the park's riverside boat launch you can see the old loading facilities, plus some of the area's low white lime bluffs.

Directions: From Jackson in Clarke County, take US 43 southwest over the Tombigbee River into Washington County, then take a left on Co. Rd. 34 heading into the modern town of St. Stephens. Follow the signs to the park.

120 Fred T. Stimpson Wildlife Sanctuary

31°30'23.04"N
87°53'42.22"W

The Fred T. Stimpson Wildlife Sanctuary is named after one of Alabama's leading early conservationists. The state owns all but 80 acres of this 5,800-acre preserve, so anyone interested in the natural history of Alabama can visit here.

Until recently, the area served as a sanctuary for deer and turkeys; the surplus animals were used to restock other areas of the state. Now that most of the state has been restocked, the sanctuary is open for hunting as well as other forms of outdoor recreation. This area contains a rare, very large example of what the upland forests of south Alabama looked like before the age of the pine plantation. As you enter the sanctuary from Co. Rd. 15, you will see a portion that has been heavily thinned to restore a more natural longleaf pine savanna. After a mile or so you will approach neat 1940s-looking staff housing and headquarters. From here on, you'd better have a good map because figuring out the road system can be tricky. Also, if it has been raining, the roads past the headquarters get really slick; on wet days it is best to park here and walk in as far as you can.

As you move west from the headquarters, heading downhill toward the Tombigbee River, you will pass through mixed pine and hardwood forest. These forests are lightly logged, but they retain good examples of shortleaf pine and various oaks. You will notice large grassy openings, which are super-sized food plots for deer and turkeys. The food plots also provide favorite burrow sites for the declining gopher tortoise.

As the roads start their steep descent to the river bottoms, expect to see good examples of magnolia-oak forest with spruce pine and flat lime rocks in the road beds. Once the bottoms are reached, you will enter bottomland hardwood with some huge swamp chestnuts and water oaks. Cypress swamps occur along sloughs and creeks. The refuge borders the free-flowing lower Tombigbee as well as a river channel that was cut off for navigation purposes, forming a future oxbow lake habitat.

Clarke County was the site of salt production during the Civil War, with water extracted from salt wells and evaporated to produce salt. The Stimpson refuge contains several such wells.

North of Jackson, the 1,920-acre Upper State Refuge offers similar habitats (minus the longleaf). This refuge has been set up for conservation education, with many stations built for that purpose. You must request permission in advance to visit this site.

If you want to camp in this general area, go to the Old Lock One Park a little north of the Upper State Refuge. This park is one of the few Corps parks that lies along a free-flowing river system. Here the Corps built and operated the first lock (heading upstream) on the Tombigbee–Black Warrior Waterway; later, after the bend and shoals were cut out of the river, the lock and dam became unnecessary for navigation. The old lock and the channel cutoff (future oxbow lake) can be seen next to the picnic/primitive camping area.

The park's facilities are set in a grove of pecan trees. Clarke County is helping the Corps to maintain the park's facilities, which include a boat launch. The boat launch provides access to the old river channel, the active channel, and the land in between, which make up the majority of this 620-acre site.

Directions: To reach the Fred T. Stimpson Wildlife Sanctuary, take US 43 west from Jackson and, just before crossing the Tombigbee

River, take a left onto AL 177, then a right onto Co. Rd. 2, then a right onto Co. Rd. 15, and head south. After several miles, you will see the entrance to the refuge on your right.

To reach the Upper State Refuge and Old Lock One Park, take US 43 west from Jackson and, just before crossing the Tombigbee River, take a right on AL 69 and head north. The turnoffs to both areas are on the left side of the highway and are marked with signs. The Upper State Refuge will be reached first.

121 Jackson Prairies (access is restricted)

The Lime Hills region supports a natural community associated with its alkaline rock outcrops known as Jackson Prairies. Such prairies can be found from central Mississippi to the Tombigbee-Alabama River Forks region of Alabama. These prairies support imperiled plants such as the Georgia rockcress and Alabama larkspur.

Currently, there are no Jackson Prairies accessible to the Alabama public. One such prairie is located on Marshall's Bluff downstream from Claiborne along the free-flowing Alabama River. This bluff can be seen by boat if you are on the river. If you want to get a taste of what a Jackson Prairie is like, you can visit a roadside site by taking Co. Rd. 1 south at Perdue Hill in Monroe County. As you drive south you will eventually see some lime rock formations in the road cut on the right or west side of the road. Park in a safe place on the road's shoulder before you view this formation. You will notice that the hill beyond the road cut is dominated by hardwood and red cedar with no pines, all reminiscent of the Black Belt. A good swath next to the road is completely treeless, with a cover of grasses and wildflowers. This area will give you a feel for the Jackson Prairie habitat—and will have to suffice, until one is protected and accessible to the public.

122 Haines Island Park

31°43'24.19"N
87°28'01.55"W

Haines Island Park is owned by the Corps, which does a good job of maintaining its limited facilities and its trails. The park's land covers a wide range of Red Hills habitats, and the adjacent Alabama River is part of the Lake Claiborne navigation impoundment. The river at Haines Island Park still looks natural, and it has an interesting car ferry that operates in the park. The park lands adjacent to the river include flood-prone bottomland hardwood as well as a large lake that looks like an old river channel.

The land along the river climbs up steep slopes and ravines to bluff tops. These bluff tops have an Appalachian feel about them because of the mixed pines and hardwoods, mountain laurel, and maple leaf viburnum. However, the Spanish moss tells us that we are in the Deep South. A playground at the park entrance has an overlook that has been allowed to grow up, but it still gives you a good view out over these south Alabama mountains.

The park's most special feature is the moist ravines and slopes between the relatively dry bluff tops and the wet bottomlands along the river. The park's slopes and ravines support some of the finest examples of beech-magnolia forest in the state. The park's trails "head" at the foot of the bluff; some lead into the bottoms while others take you deep into the forest. However, if you want a great beech-magnolia forest experience, follow the Bigleaf Magnolia Trail Loop. While its name serves to distinguish these forests from Appalachian cove hardwood, beech-magnolia forest is even richer in tree species. Signs along this trail identify many of the trees found in the beech-magnolia part of the park. American beech and the evergreen southern magnolia are abundantly present, but so are basswood, white ash, tulip poplar,

The cable ferry across the Alabama River at Haines Island Park

and many species reminiscent of Appalachian cove hardwood. As expected, bigleaf magnolia is abundant in the understory of the forest, making you feel like you are back up north in the coves of the Bankhead National Forest. The forest floor includes an assortment of herbs and wildflowers, including several types of ginger and wild geranium. Rocks are unusual in south Alabama, and the presence of moss-covered rocks and lush ferns further adds to the Appalachian feel of the place.

Haines Island Park is one of just a few protected and publicly accessible habitats of the threatened Red Hills salamander. This nocturnal, burrowing amphibian depends on the cool, moist beech-magnolia forest found on the slopes and ravines associated with the siltstone formations of this mountainous area.

Ragwort lines this floodplain road during early spring, Haines Island Park

DIRECTIONS: From Monroeville, take AL 41 north, and then take a left onto Co. Rd. 17. Follow this road until you see signs directing you to turn right into Haines Island Park.

123 Red Hills Complex

31°45'29.41"N
87°21'15.29"W

Recently (and thankfully), the Nature Conservancy and Forever Wild opened public access to two large tracts of the Red Hills salamander's habitat—a combined 4,376 acres. These tracts, near

Red dirt roads form the main hiking trails through the Red Hills Complex

Beatrice in northwestern Monroe County, consist of managed longleaf pine on the hilltops and southern magnolia-dominated bottoms. Old roadbeds allow for several miles of hiking.

Directions: Easy access to the Red Hills Complex is via River Ridge Rd., located directly east of the Co. Rd. 17 entrance to Haines Island Park, as described above.

124 Rikard's Mill

31°49'49.32"N
87°14'00.46"W

Rikard's Mill is a Monroe County Heritage Museum Park, and it is a good place for an afternoon family outing. This park features a unique style of grist mill, where water goes from the mill pond down through a hole in the bottom of a box to a turbine.

There has been a mill at this site on Flat Creek since 1845. The current mill was built around the time of the Civil War using local materials such as oak, heart pine, and bald cypress shingles. The park still grinds and sells meal. Other historic structures or replicas have been placed in the park to teach visitors about blacksmithing, cane syrup making, broom making, and bailing. The park has a covered bridge and gift shop full of local crafts, books, and music. The trees on the grounds include huge water oaks, hackberries, and sycamores.

The key natural attraction in the park is the 0.6-mile cypress swamp nature trail that runs along the terrace of Flat Creek. The forest contains a rich variety of trees including southern magnolia, tulip poplar, river birch, sweetgum, and large lobolly pines. The trees are labeled along the trail and in other areas of the park. Trilliums and other spring wildflowers grow along the nature trail and in the picnic areas.

DIRECTIONS: From Monroeville, take AL 21 north until you reach Beatrice. In Beatrice, take AL 265 north until you see a sign directing you to turn right into the mill site.

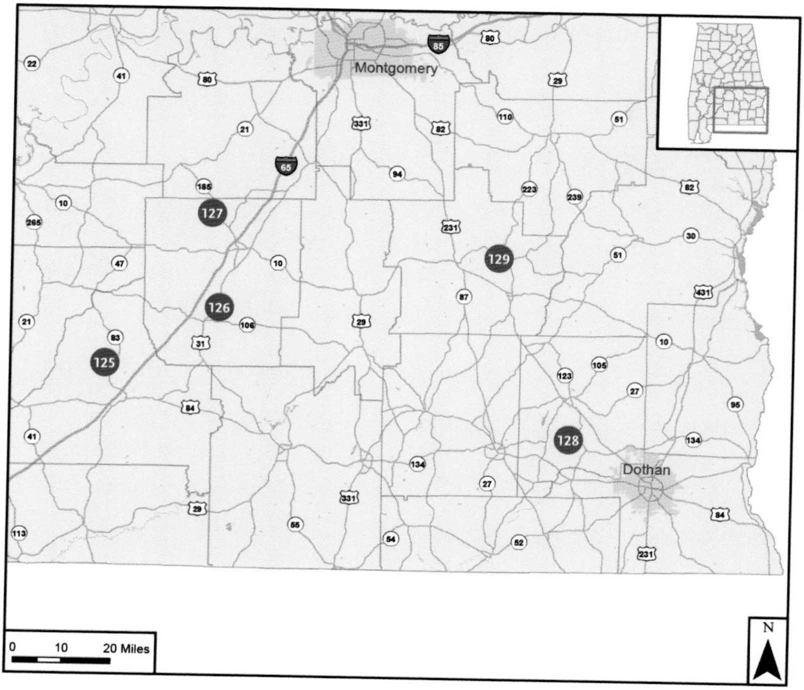

CENTRAL RED HILLS AREA

The central portion of the Red Hills offers a diversity of outdoor activities, including historical parks, several museums, and three major rivers, plus a large pocosin, one of the rarest habitats in Alabama.

125 Booker's Mill

31°31'36.74"N
87°01'55.95"W

Booker's Mill is a private site whose owners have generously decided to share it with the public. As far as we know, it is the only natural land in Conecuh County open to the public. This area is truly a jewel, offering everything from diverse natural habitat to historic structures.

Booker's Mill is gone, but a dam in its approximate location helps us remember how the site got its name. An old store building is on display, plus a cabin and sorghum mill. The site offers facilities for group functions and events, if arrangements are made ahead of time.

Behind the old store is the entrance sign to a nature trail. Before reaching the trail you will see a small but beautiful spring-fed pool that is full of the native, purple-blooming pickerel weed. After you enter this Lakeside Trail, you will pass by open water, a lily pad or spadderdock marsh, button bush swamp, and even some swamp tupelos on your left. To your right are hills covered by southern magnolia-oak forest. The slope and ravine forests contain some drier spots with mountain laurel, but much of it is covered in lush forest including southern magnolia, spruce pine, and white oak. One large magnolia has a crystal clear spring that runs out from under it.

Another good trail is the Swamp Trail, which lies above the small pond found to the right as you enter the site. This short trail passes through a tupelo-sweetbay magnolia shrub swamp before reaching a water quality education site on the pond. Past the pond, the trail leads to a quaint little church. You can loop around the pond back to your car from there.

Directions: From I-65 in the Evergreen area of Conecuh County, take exit 96 onto AL 83. Follow AL 83 north until you take a left onto Co. Rd. 21 going northwest. Follow Co. Rd. 21 until it reaches Co. Rd. 22. Take a left and go west until you see the dam and historic buildings of Booker's Mill on your right.

126 Chapman

31°40'15.90"N
86°42'43.96"W

Chapman is not far from Georgiana, the boyhood home of Hank Williams. Georgiana has a museum and festival to honor the singer, while Chapman contains landscapes that would have been more common when Hank was out hunting in the area back in the 1930s and 1940s.

As you approach Chapman while heading northeast on US 31, you will notice a change from the usual thick pine plantations of Alabama to open stands of mature pines, much like the forests of yesteryear. On the northeast side of Chapman, you will pass one such pine forest neatly bordered by white fences. Pull over to the side and stop, look and listen for birds, such as the declining Bachman's sparrow. Remember, though, that this is private land, so confine your observations to the roadside.

Directions: Take I-65 exit 114 in the Georgiana area of Butler County and follow AL 106 east to Georgiana. Take a left onto US 31 and follow it to Chapman.

127 Sherling Lake Park

31°55'11.59"N
86°41'27.44"W

Sherling Lake Park is a hilly, forested park bordering a couple of small man-made lakes; it is maintained by the city of Greenville. The park has surprising beauty, with mature loblolly pine and mixed pine-hardwood on the ridges, plus some hardwood ravines.

The site also contains a nice trail along the lakes, with bridges over its fingers. The beauty of this area is greatly enhanced by an abundance of Spanish moss hanging from hardwoods (especially the water oaks), pines, and even red cedars. Open spots within the forest show an abundance of asters and milkweeds, including the bright orange butterfly weed.

DIRECTIONS: Take I-65 exit 130 in the Greenville area of Butler County and follow AL 185 north. Turn left onto AL 263, which shortly passes by the park entrance on your left.

128 Rivers of the Red Hills

31°22'06.72"N
85°38'59.65"W

The Conecuh, Pea, and Choctawhatchee Rivers start in the Coastal Plain hills of east central Alabama and flow across the Red Hills and Lower Coastal Plain of Alabama and Florida to the Gulf of Mexico. These rivers have remained largely free-flowing for their entire lengths. The three rivers support species like the Gulf sturgeon, which migrates from the ocean to freshwater rivers to spawn. (These species have been lost from other river systems, such as the Mobile River drainage, due to the presence of dams.) In addition, the bald cypress–bottomland hardwood and low terrace beech-magnolia forests of the river corridors are mostly intact. These rivers can be visited by boat or canoe using bridge crossings and launches for access.

The Conecuh River flows from central Alabama to the south, growing progressively larger as it picks up tributaries like the Sepulga and Patsaliga Rivers. Big Escambia Creek joins up in north Florida, where the Conecuh becomes known as the Escambia River before it flows into its delta near Pensacola. The Pea

River flows south from east central Alabama to join the Choctawhatchee River at Geneva, Alabama.

The Choctawhatchee River is probably the most significant of all because it is one of the longest continuously free-flowing rivers in the nation. The Choctawhatchee starts in two headwater forks in east-central Alabama. The west fork flows past Blue Springs State Park, whose springs have been surrounded by a concrete structure to aid swimming. Despite the artificial surroundings, the ice cold, clear waters of the springs support easily seen fish and turtles. A spring run empties into the nearby river, and the banks of the river support a small amount of beech-magnolia forest.

Further downstream, the Choctawhatchee River flows by soapstone cliffs and over soapstone shoals. Such "white water" is unusual in the Coastal Plain of south Alabama. Some of the cliffs have crevices that can be canoed into, and they are often "seepy" and covered with ferns. The river passes beech-magnolia forests that contain tall spruce pines. The river also floods backwater cypress swamps and areas of bottomland hardwood with dwarf palmetto and needle palms.

Some tributaries of the Choctawhatchee flow out of Fort Rucker southwest of Ozark. This military base contains a large block of forest land and one of Alabama's few sustainable populations of gopher tortoises. Because AL 27 passes through the base going from Ozark to Enterprise, you can see some of the area's habitats from the road. The nearby Mabson Community Education Forest in Ozark has trails and interpretive stations relating to forest and soil conservation. Visitation here is by appointment only.

The Choctawhatchee flows out of the Red Hills and into the Lower Coastal Plain. Fowler Park contains a great view of the confluence as well as a boat launch. The town was founded during the age of river boats and, during times of low water, visitors can see the remains of an old boat on the right side of the confluence. If you are very lucky you might even see a giant gulf sturgeon,

Constitution Live Oak, Fowler Park, Geneva

since the Choctawhatchee is one of this fish's last strongholds. The rivers surrounding the park are lined with bald cypress, and a cypress pond is located in the park itself. The park has a shady picnic area including some dwarf palmetto palms and some of the northernmost live oaks in Alabama, including the giant Constitution Live Oak. This enormous tree has been growing here at least since the American Constitution was framed. It is marvelous to sit beneath its low, octopus-like limbs and listen to the tree frogs that call it home.

From its junction with the Pea River, the Choctawhatchee grows much larger as it flows south into Florida toward its delta in the Choctawhatchee WMA near Ebro, Florida. That WMA contains giant sturgeon and lots of old-growth bald cypress; and it has recently become famous for numerous reported sightings of the supposedly extinct ivory-billed woodpecker.

Directions: The Conecuh, Pea, and Choctawhatchee Rivers can be canoed between bridge crossings. Land access is limited, but there are a few places to enjoy the rivers from their banks.

The banks of the lower Conecuh River can be accessed from public boat launch parks at a few locations. Boat launch parks are located on Point A Lake (a small man-made impoundment) and below it on the free-flowing river near the town of River Falls, which lies on US 84 northeast of Andalusia in Covington County. The boat launch onto the free-flowing river is located at the US 84 crossing. Point A Lake can be reached by taking Co. Rd. 107 north off US 84 in River Falls and then taking a right onto Co. Rd. 59, which passes along the edge of the lake. Another such park is located south of Brewton in Escambia County where AL 41 crosses the river.

The banks of both the Pea and Choctawhatchee Rivers can be accessed in Geneva's Fowler Park, which sits in a peninsula between the two rivers and offers views of both. Fowler Park is reached by following AL 52 west to Geneva. Take a left at the first light, pass city hall, and take another left one block later. Follow this road into the park.

The banks of the west fork of the Choctawhachee River can be accessed at Blue Springs State Park. The park is reached by following US 231 southeast from Troy to Brundidge, then taking AL 10 past Clio to the state park.

129 Pocosin / Troy

31°48'31.02"N
85°58'12.89"W

Just east of Troy, Alabama, is a 190-acre Forever Wild property with an unusual natural community, known locally as the *pocosin*. The pocosin contains many broadleaf trees and shrubs that do not lose their leaves, which is unusual for a place so far north in Alabama.

This brushy, evergreen, upland hardwood community probably reminded early settlers of the evergreen pocosin shrub swamps found along the East Coast. Roland Harper, long-time botanist for the Geological Survey of Alabama, hypothesized that the formation of the pocosin was due to the fire protection provided by surrounding hardwood swamps combined with very sandy longleaf pine habitats, which had too sparse a ground cover to carry frequent fires into the pocosin.

The Alabama pocosin habitat was never common, and it has been mostly degraded by modern industrial forestry practices. The Forever Wild tract, along with the 18-acre Troy University-owned Pocosin Preserve, contains the last undisturbed examples of this natural community in Alabama. Unfortunately, the Forever Wild tract did not escape disturbance of its uplands, which were converted into sand pine plantations. A few openings within the pines provide glimpses of this dry, natural community that includes scrub oaks, reindeer lichens, British soldier lichens, and prickly pear cacti. A few portions of the property retain examples of the longleaf pine habitat that supports gopher tortoises.

To reach the pocosin, you should drop off the right side of the main road as you enter the tract, then follow a spiderweb of old road beds through pine plantations before reaching the edge of hardwood ravines, which contain the pocosin. It is a good idea to carry a compass or GPS and take a reading before you leave your car; if you get lost, the compass will lead you back to the main road, which bisects the tract.

The pocosin contains some hardwood stands with an evergreen canopy of laurel oak, which does not seem to drop its leaves in this area. However, most of the ravines have a largely deciduous canopy with a thick evergreen understory of American holly and sweetbay magnolia. Both deciduous beech and evergreen southern magnolia are present. The ravine bottoms contain branches fed by spring seeps, and the swampy land surrounding these branches supports large, evergreen, sweet bay magnolias, and swamp tupelos. In the past, the spring seeps of these secluded ravines or hollows must have attracted quite a bit of moonshine making, as evidenced by the remains of several stills.

Visiting the pocosin involves a bit of bushwhacking. If you want to follow easier trails through natural areas in the Troy area, check out the 75-acre Troy University Arboretum and the Pioneer Museum of Alabama.

DIRECTIONS: The pocosin can be reached by following US 231 south from Troy. After crossing a large, swampy creek, turn left onto a paved county road. This road ends at its intersection with Co. Rd. 26. Make a right onto Co. Rd. 26 and, soon after, another right onto an unmarked dirt road that passes through the Forever Wild tract. You will know that you have turned onto the correct road when you start seeing small yellow signs stating that this is state-owned land of the Forever Wild program.

The Troy University Arboretum is reached by taking George Wallace Dr. east from US 231 in the city of Troy. (Wallace Dr. is a few miles south of the US 29 and US 231 junction.) After going east on Wallace Dr. a short distance, take a left onto Pell Ave. Follow this road until you see the gate leading into the arboretum.

The Pioneer Museum of Alabama is located just north of Troy on US 231.

LOWER COASTAL PLAIN

The Lower Coastal Plain is the most recent subprovince of the Coastal Plain to be exposed above sea level. Its western portion is hilly, while its eastern portion is a flat plain covered with sand; the underlying limestone produces caves, springs, and sinkholes. Poorly drained sinkholes form natural lakes and cypress swamps, but some of these water bodies go dry, periodically, when their water finds an underground outlet. Many of these ponds are fishless, and this lack of predators provides critical breeding habitat for numerous species of amphibians.

Most of the Lower Coastal Plain's soils are poorly developed because they are not long removed from being ocean sand. Some areas are literally sand hills, which are extremely dry and support longleaf pine–scrub oak vegetation. This dry open habitat, with loose soil, is a favorite hangout for gopher tortoises. Their burrows provide sanctuary for nearly 400 species, including other threatened ones like the dusky gopher frog and Florida pine snake. The gopher tortoise has disappeared from most of its Upper Coastal Plain range, and in the Lower Coastal Plain its populations have become greatly fragmented. To "save" this one species would ensure the survival of untold others that use its burrows.

Some sandy soils of the Lower Coastal Plain have relatively

poor subsurface drainage and/or seasonal seepages. These habitats are wet for part of the year and dry at other times, making them both boggy and susceptible to frequent fires. Such areas contain wet longleaf pine savannas where the trees are broken up by pitcher plant bogs. These wet savannas support one of the highest diversities of plants in the world, including beautiful orchids and carnivorous pitcher plants, sundews, and butterworts. Like many ecosystems already mentioned in this book, wet pine savannas are dependent on frequent fires to kill back other woody species that both compete with the longleaf and shade out the herbs.

Fire suppression, land clearing, and conversion to pine plantations have drastically reduced all longleaf pine habitats, including longleaf-grass habitats of relatively moderate moisture. Extreme southeast Alabama is known as the Wiregrass Region because the original settlers found a flat landscape dominated by longleaf pine forests with a ground cover of wire grass. Before the Civil War, this lightly settled region was mainly used for cattle grazing. Toward the end of the 1800s, commercial logging came to the area and commercial fertilizers became available. Most of the longleaf timber was cut, and fertilizers made it possible to grow cotton on the poor but flat land with easily tillable soil. Ironically, longleaf pine and (especially) wire grass are now largely absent from the Wiregrass Region. However, many old farm fields are being planted back to longleaf pine and, hopefully, the wire grass and other aspects of the longleaf forest's rich herb layer will return as well.

Other habitats are found among the longleaf pine forests. Slash pine naturally occupies poorly drained habitats, which burn less frequently than longleaf forests. The previously mentioned sinkholes form natural lakes with edge marshes; as these lakes fill in, they form swamps dominated by pond cypress and swamp tupelo. Another fire-dependent wetland tree, Atlantic white cedar, grows along the edges of blackwater streams. Such streams have a unique beauty due to their dark, tea-colored water, which contrasts nicely with pure white sand bars. The water is "black" because the sandy terrain of the Lower Coastal Plain (in which these streams originate and through which they flow) produces little muddy sediment to mask other colors. The dark tannic acid produced by the wetlands of the river's corridor is thus free to dominate the water's color. (Ships sailing between the southeastern United States and Europe used to fill their casks with water from blackwater rivers because the tannic acid made the water last longer, taste-wise, at sea.)

Some Lower Coastal Plain habitats along river floodplains and their terrace slopes contain rich soils that support bottomland hardwood forests or diverse beech-magnolia forests. The beech-magnolia forests of the extreme lower Southeast contain the greatest diversity of trees, shrubs, and vines outside of the tropics.

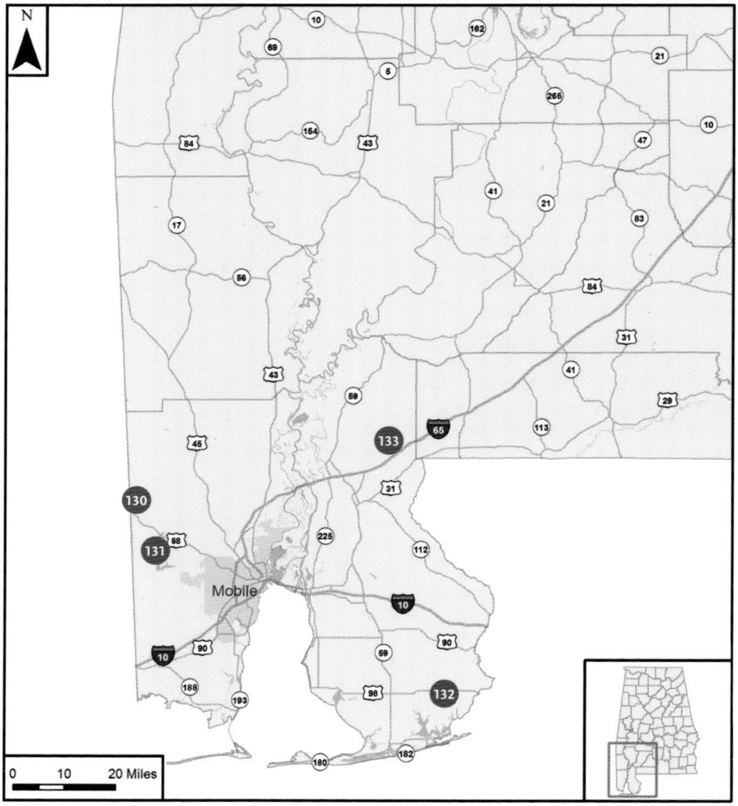

MOBILE AREA

Mobile offers many active and passive ways to examine the natural wonders of the Lower Coastal Plain. Opportunities to canoe, fish, and swim—or just stroll through a pitcher plant bog—are all close by.

130 Escatawpa River

30°51'35.23"N
88°24'46.38"W

The Escatawpa River is one of the finest blackwater rivers in the nation. It begins in Washington County, Alabama, and flows through western Mobile County and into Mississippi to join the Pascagoula River delta. The Escatawpa has huge white sand bars, which many people use for camping, and is the only Alabama stream where the razorback musk turtle lives. (This species is more common westward to Texas.) While motor boats can navigate the Escatawpa's tricky, ever-changing channels in times of high water, the river is best explored by canoe. Float trips can be launched from the various bridge crossings.

The Escatawpa is surrounded largely by upland forest, some of which sits upon short bluffs where the geologic layers of the Lower Coastal Plain are revealed. The forest surrounding the Escatawpa is a mixture of loblolly pine and various hardwoods including water oak, southern magnolia, and red maple. The shrub layer of the forest contains mountain laurel, which is normally associated with more northern environments, and the saw palmetto palm, which is only found in the warm southern fringe of Alabama. Some longleaf pines grow on the bluffs along the river; this habitat was probably much more common in the past. Unlike other blackwater rivers, the Escatawpa has only scattered bald cypress trees; its swift current and upland surroundings create an environment unfavorable for cypress along its banks.

The Escatawpa runs completely through private lands, so practically all access to the river corridor is by canoe or boat. The best place to experience the Escatawpa, with or without a boat or canoe, is Escatawpa Hollow Campground. This private campground

The Escatawpa River is best explored by boat

offers access to sandbar beaches, upland forests, and backwater tupelo swamps. The campsites along the river blend into the forest, which helps make it one of the most beautiful campgrounds in the South. In addition, the campground offers canoe rentals/ shuttles and boat launching.

Directions: The Escatawpa Hollow Campground can be reached by following US 98 west from Mobile. The campground is on the left just before you cross the Escatawpa River bridge near the Mississippi state Line.

131 Big Creek Lake / Gopher Tortoise Conservation

30°44'58.62"N
88°20'17.52"W

Big Creek Lake (officially, Converse Reservoir) is a 3,600-acre reservoir built to provide the Mobile area with water. The Mobile Area Water and Sewer System owns a significant amount of land around the lake, forming a critical buffer in this rapidly developing area. Big Creek Lake is surrounded by uplands, including some fire-suppressed pine forests, as well as patches of swamp forest and marsh along the lake's shore. Wildlife includes alligators and laughing gulls, which are normally found on the coast. However, the most significant wild inhabitants are in the area's 222-acre gopher tortoise conservation bank.

West of the Tombigbee River, the gopher tortoise is listed as a threatened species by the federal government. Although not federally protected east of the Tombigbee, gopher tortoises are afforded limited state protection throughout their range. The USFWS, the Mobile Water System, and several environmental groups worked together to develop the conservation bank at Big Creek Lake. If developers find gopher tortoises on their land, they can pay a fee to have them transported to the conservation bank on Water System land; the developers' fees are used to maintain and improve the tortoises' habitat through controlled burns and other means. The Water System has agreed to set the property aside from development and manage the land for tortoises on a permanent basis.

The conservation bank will support 125 gopher tortoises when at full population. Managing the land for the gopher tortoise will also help the longleaf pine natural community in the area. As mentioned previously, nearly 400 different species use gopher tortoise burrows and the associated longleaf pine habitat; thus, restoring this habitat helps other threatened and declining species, such as the black pine snake. Yes, the idea of relocating endangered species is controversial; but the conservation bank is succeeding in its attempt to create a sustainable tortoise population.

You can visit the banks of Big Creek Lake at access areas on

US 98 and at Fox Landing. However, you need a boat to see most of this large area. If you get out in a boat, *be extra careful* because high winds can turn this large, open lake into a "sea" of dangerous waves.

DIRECTIONS: The upper end of Big Creek Lake is accessed by taking US 98 west from Mobile. The highway crosses the upper end of the lake; side roads allow you to pull off and enjoy the lands along its banks. Fox Landing is reached by taking a left off of US 98 onto Howells Ferry Rd. several miles west of I-65. Follow Howells Ferry Rd. to the Fox Landing area.

132 Biophilia Nature Center

30°24'35.77"N
87°32'59.07"W

The Biophilia Nature Center is located on 20 acres near Elberta in Baldwin County. The center is an old farm that is being restored to a more natural condition. Its core natural habitat is a remnant tupelo swamp; pitcher plant bogs, with sundews and orchids, are being reestablished in open wet places on the property. The center also has an exhibit/bookstore building and a wide selection of native landscaping plants for sale, including pitcher plants, sundews, and orchids grown from seed.

The property has no nature trail system yet, but the owners will guide you around the site. The owners' knowledge and love of the land comes out on the tours. Visitors will see sensitive plants, native plums, lizard's tail, many ferns, and a possible wild ancestor of corn. However, the most unique thing about the tours is the butterflies. Outside, you will enjoy seeing caterpillars on their host plants and adult butterflies on their nectar plants. Inside, you will find various species of butterflies in display boxes with their favored plant foods, plus the amazing colors of their caterpillars and pupal cases as viewed under a microscope.

DIRECTIONS: Take US 98 east from Foley past the town of Elberta. Turn right onto Co. Rd. 95; the entrance to the center is on the right.

133 Splinter Hill Bog

31°01'30.49"N
87°41'07.15"W

Alabama's Lower Coastal Plain contains a scattering of conservation areas that are helping to protect lowland longleaf pine forest. One such area is the Splinter Hill Bog Preserve in northern Baldwin County, which has separate sections owned by the Nature Conservancy and the state's Forever Wild program. Some of the property is cut-over, but the property still contains some of the Gulf region's most intact seepage bog communities, along with longleaf pine savanna and interspersed sand hill habitats.

An interpretive trail on the Nature Conservancy section leads through pitcher plant bogs to some hardwoods along a drain. Numerous rare and declining species associated with seepage bogs, upland longleaf forests and coastal blackwater streams are found here. The preserve supports 12 species of carnivorous plants as well as one of the largest known populations of the imperiled panhandle lily. Some of the unique and rare plants known from the site include white-topped pitcher plant, Chapman's butterwort, Wherry's sweet pitcher plant, purple pitcher plant, parrot pitcher plant, yellow trumpets, sundews, spoonflower, pineland bogbutton, Drummond's yellow-eyed grass, and Chapman's yellow-eyed grass.

A similar trail has recently been opened through the Forever Wild section of the bog.

Splinter Hill Bog relies on prescribed burns to preserve its diverse array of carnivorous plants.

DIRECTIONS: Splinter Hill Bog can be reached by taking I-65 exit 45 (Co. Rd. 47) west for a few miles. A parking area and trailhead are located on the right (north) side of the road for the Forever Wild property; the same is true on the left (south) side of the road for the Nature Conservancy property.

Clockwise from upper left:
Summer azure butterfly captured by the sticky hairs of Tracy's sundew; little metalmark on inkberry; and yellow pitcher plant flower and pitchers, Splinter Hill Bog

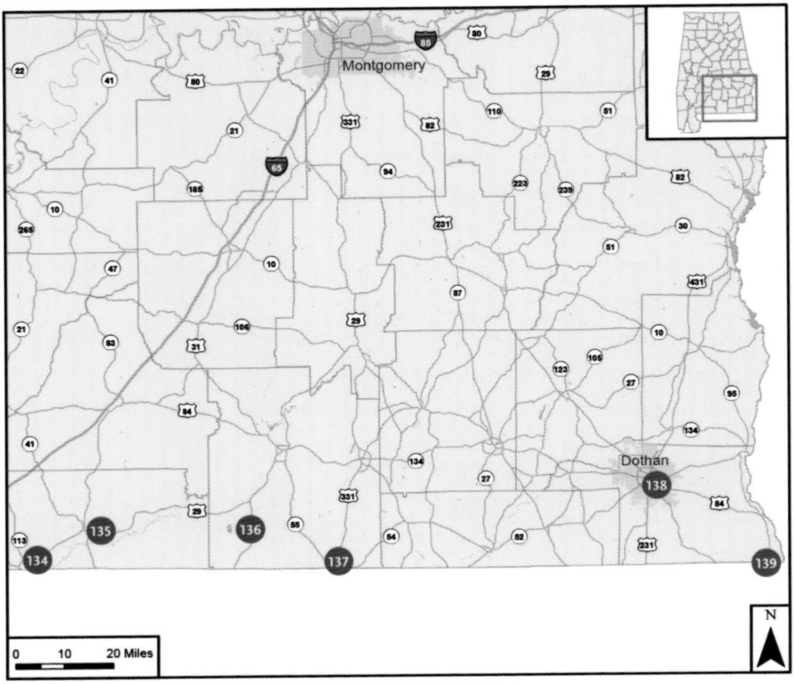

LONGLEAF PINE AREA

Opportunities to examine longleaf pine and associated habitats are mainly found in the southeastern corner of Alabama. These include national forests, state forests, state parks, community parks, and education centers.

134 Turtle Point Environmental Science Center

31°00'34.66"N
87°16'25.84"W

This 20-acre school-oriented environmental education center is located in a park within the city of Flomaton. The center has a museum housing several exhibits including the Alabama state fossil, an ancient whale. The grounds contain various gardens devoted to vegetables, herbs, geology, and butterflies. The center has a large bat house and nearby signs providing information on the beneficial, mosquito-eating habits of bats. The signs describe how (and why) bat species are declining, as well as how (and why) to help conserve them. While some trees are labeled along the old road behind the center, the main nature trail is its boardwalk through the wetlands of Big Escambia Creek.

The center is open weekdays during the school year.

DIRECTIONS: From the junction of US 29 and US 31 in Flomaton, take US 31 west; you will soon see the entrance to the education center.

135 Burnt Corn Creek Nature Park

31°06'18.79"N
87°04'19.36"W

Burnt Corn Creek Nature Park is a 26-acre city property along AL 41 in the downtown area of Brewton. Although the park has a manicured appearance, it is a great place to learn local native trees as well as some exotic species. Many of the trees and shrubs of the park are labeled: southern magnolia, beech, silverbell, hackberry, bald cypress, yaupon holly, and a fine specimen of sand live oak. The park also contains a fern display and provides both views of and access down to the sandbars of the park's namesake, Burt Corn Creek.

The Battle of Burnt Corn Creek started the Creek Indian War of 1813. The actual battle site is on another section of the creek that may soon be turned into a park.

Directions: Burnt Corn Creek Nature Park is located at the junctions of AL 41, US 29, and US 31 in downtown Brewton, Escambia County.

136 Conecuh National Forest

31°05'40.20"N
86°38'03.13"W

The 960-acre Little River State Forest, at the border of Baldwin and Monroe Counties, contains the cabins and other facilities of the former Claude D. Kelley State Park. These facilities surround a small impoundment set in a longleaf pine forest. The old park area and the rest of the forest have several trails through longleaf stands, which include some pitcher plant bogs.

The Geneva State Forest in western Geneva County conserves the easternmost significant area of lowland longleaf pine forest in Alabama. The forest contains characteristic longleaf pine habitat species such as fox squirrels and gopher tortoises. A section of the Alabama Trail is being built through this area, which will link the Appalachian Trail with the Florida Trail by way of the Pinhoti Trail in east-central Alabama.

The Escambia Experimental Forest is on 3,000 acres of T. R. Miller Mill Company land. This land, leased to the US Forest Service in 1940 for 100 years, has been a major player in improving our knowledge of how to cut, regenerate, and manage longleaf pine forest. Visitors will see well-managed, open mature stands of longleaf and younger, regenerating stands in experimental plots. The forest also contains other resources such as carnivorous sundews and a waterfall, which is very unusual for the Lower Coastal Plain.

Opposite: Winter scene at Open Pond, Conecuh National Forest

If you want to visit the interior of the forest you will need to call the Forest Service and make arrangements. If you want to do a quick roadside visit, you can see the experimental forest along AL 41 about seven miles south of Brewton. (Confine your observations to the roadside once you have found safe parking on the shoulder.) Three Notch Rd., which borders the southern boundary of the experimental forest and leads to its headquarters, allows you to see the forest at a slower, safer pace than does AL 41.

The largest concentration of lowland longleaf pine in Alabama is the Conecuh National Forest area. In fact, this area is the northern end of the largest remaining acreage of longleaf pine in the world, stretching south through Blackwater State Forest in Florida to the expansive longleaf habitats of Eglin Air Force base on Choctawhatchee Bay at the Gulf Coast.

The 83,861-acre Conecuh National Forest comprises large tracts of dry and wet longleaf pine forests, which contain the now uncommon wire grass and a variety of wildflowers, such as liatris, asters, and orchids. The pitcher plant bogs of the wet longleaf pine forests include unbelievable plant diversity, like insect-eating white-topped and yellow pitcher plants, sundews, butterworts, grass pink orchids, and white-topped sedges. Also, the rare pond pine is found in some of these areas.

An excellent pitcher plant bog can be viewed just outside the Escambia County Public Fishing Lake—if you are willing to walk through high grass and get your feet wet. Just avoid stepping on the rare plants. And watch out for eastern diamondback rattlers, which are known to live here as well.

The national forest provides habitat for declining longleaf dependent animals such as gopher tortoises, gopher frogs, and red-cockaded woodpeckers. Water-holding sinkholes foster various habitats depending on the water's depth and amount of peat formation. Deeper sinkholes form ponds while the more shallow ones are marshes. Many of these sinkhole habitats provide critical breeding sites for the dusky gopher frog and other amphibians because they do not contain fish, which would prey upon their youngsters. Sinkhole wetlands are generally populated with pond cypress trees, which have more narrow and upright needles than the common bald cypress; they also produce fewer knees and are more fire-tolerant. A good example of a pond cypress wetland is Mossy Pond along the Conecuh Trail west of AL 137. Other large natural sinkholes, such as Open Pond and Blue Pond, provide fishing, boating, and swimming opportunities for visitors. (The alligators are removed from these two ponds as soon as they show up.)

Shallow, poorly drained depressions contain thick, broadleaf evergreen shrub swamps made up of various bay tree species. The largest such depression is Bear Bay. While there is no longer a permanent bear population in the area, bears could someday move up from the Florida coast through the continuous longleaf pine forest; shrub swamps like Bear Bay would provide them with critical, secluded habitat.

The Yellow River forms the eastern boundary of the Conecuh National Forest. This gives the Yellow River one of the better protected stream corridors in Alabama, especially in the Coastal Plain. The national forest lands along the Yellow River include bald cypress and beech-magnolia forest with large spruce pines. These Forest Service lands even include a limestone cave with roosting habitat for the endangered gray bat. The cave was acquired with help from the Nature Conservancy.

The headwaters of the Yellow River lie just north of the national forest near Opp in a man-made reservoir on which the 2,050-acre Frank Jackson State Park is located. The state park has hiking trails in the forests surrounding the lake, including a walkway to one of the lake's islands.

Even though the headwaters of Florida's famous Blackwater River occur in the south-central portion of the Conecuh National Forest, there is little Forest Service land along this beautiful tea-colored river with contrasting white sand bars. Both the Yellow and Blackwater Rivers leave the Conecuh to flow south into Florida and eventually the Pensacola Bay area.

Many sites within the Conecuh National Forest can be explored by riding the roads and parking at interesting spots, but to really get back into the longleaf pine ecosystem you should do some hiking on the 20-mile-long Conecuh Trail system. These trails pass through most of the forest's habitat types and offer opportunities for short walks or overnight backpacking trips.

The 5,350-acre Solon Dixon Forestry Education Center lies within the boundaries of the Conecuh National Forest. It greatly complements the National Forest by providing an ample supply of habitats that are uncommon or absent in the national forest, such as sand hill communities, bottomlands, and upland hardwood forests. The forestry center is owned by Auburn University and was established by a local forest business owner, Solon Dixon. Years of well-planned management here have allowed the natural ecosystems to flourish while timber harvest and forestry experiments are carried out. Much of the property is left uncut for research purposes.

Surprisingly, the Conecuh National Forest does not have any land on the river of the same name, but the Solon Dixon Center has lots of acreage along that river. Habitats along the Conecuh River include beech-magnolia forest-covered slopes with limestone caves and old-growth limestone-associated bottomland hardwood, all with state champion trees. The property also has a large limestone sink, the Blue Hole, that periodically fills up and then suddenly drains dry into nearby springs, flooding the areas downstream.

Sand hill habitats occur on deep, dry sands. Called "deserts in the rain," they contain a scattering of longleaf pine, scrub oaks, and various herbs. Sand hills are among the preferred habitats of gopher tortoises—similar, in fact, to those used by tortoises of the southwestern United States. As expected, the sand hills at Solon Dixon contain an active gopher tortoise population. The center also features moist longleaf pine forests, and some of the experimental forestry areas are of conservation interest as well. The Solon Dixon Center has many roads and walking trails that allow access to the various natural habitats and experimental forest plots. To make the most of your visit, notify the center before you arrive or stop by the main office when you get there.

Directions: The Little River State Forest is reached by taking I-65 exit 57 near Atmore in Escambia County. Follow AL 21 north from the interstate for several miles; you will pass by the entrance to the forest's lake and trails area near the Little River bridge.

The Geneva State Forest is reached by traveling west on AL 52 out of Samson in Geneva County. Take a left onto AL 54 and then a right onto Co. Rd. 9, which leads through the state forest.

The Escambia Experimental Forest is located off AL 41 south of Brewton in Escambia County. To reach its headquarters, take a right onto Three Notch Rd.

The Conecuh National Forest and the Solon Dixon Forestry Education Center are located off US 29 south of Andalusia in Covington County. To reach the Forestry Center, continue on US 29 until you see a sign marking the entrance road, which is on your right shortly before crossing into Escambia County. Nature enthusiasts are welcome, but you need to call ahead or stop by the office before exploring the forest.

To see the major sites of the Conecuh National Forest, turn left off of US 29 S onto AL 137 well before reaching the Solon Dixon Forestry Center. Continue south on AL 137 and follow the signs to the Open Pond Recreation Area, where you can pick up the Conecuh Trail.

Open Pond lies near the junction of AL 137 and FS 305. To reach Bear Bay, follow FS 305 west; the northern edge of the bay swamp will be to your left just before you reach Co. Rd. 3. To see the west side of Bear Bay take a left onto Co. Rd. 3.

To enter the Yellow River drainage, go back to the FS 305-AL 137 junction and take Co. Rd. 24 east, which lies directly across from this junction. Follow Co. Rd. 24 until you take a right onto FS 337. Follow this road south through the national forest, passing by the Blue Springs and Five Runs Creek areas down to Co. Rd. 4. Take a right on Co. Rd. 4 and you will very soon reach the banks of the Yellow River, which has Forest Service land along its west bank.

To reach the southwest side of the national forest, go west on Co. Rd. 4 into Escambia County and pass over the Blackwater River; after several more miles, take a left onto Co. Rd. 11. Follow Co. Rd. 11 (Beaver Creek Rd.) south for 1.5 miles, then turn right on Parker Springs Rd. to Leon Brooks Hines Lake (Escambia County State Public Fishing Lake). A large pitcher plant bog lies in the uplands surrounding the lake, but it can be hard to find without on-site directions. Ask the lake's staff for more details regarding its location.

The non–longleaf pine habitats of Frank Jackson State Park can be reached by taking US 331 north out of Opp in Covington County.

137 Florala State Park

31°00'19.04"N
86°19'40.69"W

Despite its small size, 40-acre Florala State Park is well worth visiting. The park forms the northern shore of Alabama's largest natural lake, Lake Jackson (500 acres), an almost perfectly round sinkhole that holds water. The park forms a nice green space

A boardwalk allows easy access to Florala Wetlands Park

bordering the town of Florala, which takes its name from being located on the Florida-Alabama state line.

The large Spanish moss-draped pond cypress trees ringing the lake give it a wild, tropical quality. The south shore is outside the state park boundary and is largely private homes, while the north shore contains the state park's recreational facilities, such as paddle boats, picnic areas, and paved trails. The north shore also contains the lake's best mixture of pond cypress and edge marsh. Beneath the pond cypress are thick beds of marsh plants like pickerel weed—good places to fish for pickerels.

The city's Florala Wetlands Park is located next to the state park along the northwest side of the lake. It contains a handicapped-accessible boardwalk that passes through a pond cypress swamp before reaching the lake.

The lake itself is very clear and in its shallows you can admire the abundant aquatic vegetation. While the best way to see the lake is by canoe, canoeing should be done early in the morning before the jet skiers arrive.

DIRECTIONS: Florala State Park and Wetlands Park make up the south side of the town of Florala in Covington County. The day use facilities, walking trails, and campground are located on the north and east sides of the lake. The swamp boardwalk is on the west side.

138 Landmark Park

31°13'23.93"N
85°23'26.82"W

Landmark Park is a 100-acre park in the city of Dothan that provides opportunities to enjoy the area's natural and agricultural heritage. The park features a child-oriented interpretive center with an all-ages boardwalk/trail system that loops around a beaver pond. Beavers can be unnaturally destructive in small bottomland preserves, but in this case the beavers created a more significant habitat than was lost. The boardwalk dips down to the beaver wetland at two places and follows the surrounding slopes for most of its length.

The nature trail continues in a similar manner along the slopes and crosses a bridge near the beavers' dam. The slopes are largely covered by mixed hardwood forest with southern magnolia and spruce pine, plus lots of sweet bays in the understory. Many areas of the canopy are dominated by evergreen oaks. Some pine forest (including longleaf) occurs on a dry ridge above the lake. Future plans call for a longleaf–wire grass restoration area here.

Visitors can learn about animals found in various habitats by studying the display cases containing stuffed birds, mammals, and reptiles, which are located at various points along the trail; other interpretive exhibits are found near the beaver pond. The boardwalk at the upper end of the pond crosses a portion of the beaver wetland that has become a shrub swamp interspersed with various wetland herbs, such as golden club and swamp iris. The bridge crossing the lower end of the beaver pond offers views of the beavers' dams and some open water surrounding their lodge. Wildlife here includes herons, wintering ducks, and red-shouldered hawks.

Landmark Park is also a great place to experience a taste of our human past—the Alabama Agricultural Museum. This open air museum contains a collection of buildings and equipment from the 1890s. What makes this exhibit so authentic is the presence of live animals like mules, sheep, goats, chickens, and guineas. The most interesting animals are the rough pine woods cattle, which are adapted to foraging in the hot, buggy pine woods of the Deep South. Sugar cane and other crops are grown and processed on the grounds. Additional exhibits include an old church, school, and general store, where you can get honey made by bees at the park and a drink from an old-fashioned soda fountain.

Additional nature walks in Dothan are found on the trail system of the Troy University Dothan Campus and the 50-acre Dothan Area Botanical Garden.

Directions: Landmark Park lies on the west side of US 431 just north of central Dothan.

The Dothan Area Botanical Garden is located at 5130 Headland Ave. just off US Hwy. 431 N near Landmark Park.

The trail system of the Troy University Dothan Campus can be found behind the campus quad off of US 231 just north of central Dothan.

139 Chattahoochee Park

31°00'15.23"N
85°01'52.15"W

Chattahoochee Park, formerly known as Chattahoochee State Park, is now operated by Houston County. This park and Claude D. Kelley State Park (mentioned previously) were removed from the roll of state parks due to budget constraints. Fortunately, both areas are still publicly owned.

Despite its name, Chattahoochee Park does not lie on the Chattahoochee River, but it does surround a stream that flows into the upper portion of the impounded river (Lake Seminole) where Alabama, Georgia, and Florida meet. The spring-fed stream was dammed back in the 1930s by the CCC to create the lake that is the centerpiece of the park. The CCC built some beautiful rock walls here as well. The ruins of their old camp can be accessed by a nature trail.

The clean, clear lake is surrounded by marsh vegetation and some bald cypress trees. A resident population of Canada geese lives in the lake along with cooters and other wildlife. The park is one of the only known locations for the little grass frog in Alabama.

The park contains numerous old roads that have been turned into hiking trails. The Boy Scout Trail follows a gentle, moist slope above the lake through a diverse upland hardwood forest with southern magnolias, Florida maples, and spruce pines. (Spruce

A gopher tortoise burrow at Chattahoochee Park

pine is very similar to white pines in appearance and cone shape; unlike most pines, it is shade-tolerant and does well in mature hardwood forests.) The dry upland flats of the park were historically dominated by longleaf pine; now, these areas support loblolly pine with some upland hardwood stands. These areas are traversed by several trails where you have the possibility of seeing a gopher tortoise burrow and, possibly, the land turtle itself.

This park is part of the state lands set aside during early settlement times to "earn" money for schools. The area became a state park much later, while continuing to provide money for schools through timber sales. While timber sales are not always compatible with nature conservation, some timber cutting and other management in the pine forests of this park may help the gopher tortoise and other species. The state is working toward the goal of opening up the pine forest to restore its original character.

Hunting for those with handicaps is offered at the park during the deer season, and the park is frequently closed for that purpose.

In addition, Houston County maintains a park with a nature

trail and boat launch at Omussee Creek on the impounded Chattahoochee River.

DIRECTIONS: To reach Chatttahoochee Park, take US 84 east from Dothan nearly to the Chattahoochee River; before reaching the river, take a right onto AL 95. The park will be on your left just before crossing the Florida state line.

To reach Omussee Creek Public Use Area from Dothan, take AL 52 northeast toward Columbia. Just before reaching Columbia, take a right onto AL 95 and, soon after, turn left onto Omussee Creek Park Rd.

COASTAL ZONE

Alabama's Coastal Zone is the interface between the land and the Gulf of Mexico. This province's river deltas and beach dunes form the youngest exposed surfaces in the state. Because there is not much of a downhill gradient on this flat land near the ocean, much of it is poorly drained wetlands. Some areas, such as salt marshes, are inundated daily by tides.

The soils here run the gamut from almost pure ocean sand to the rich, muddy deposits of the Mobile-Tensaw delta. Because the province's climate is the warmest and wettest in the state, this subtropical ocean-land interface houses an incredible diversity of habitats and species. But because the Coastal Zone is developing rapidly, many of its special natural areas are among our most threatened.

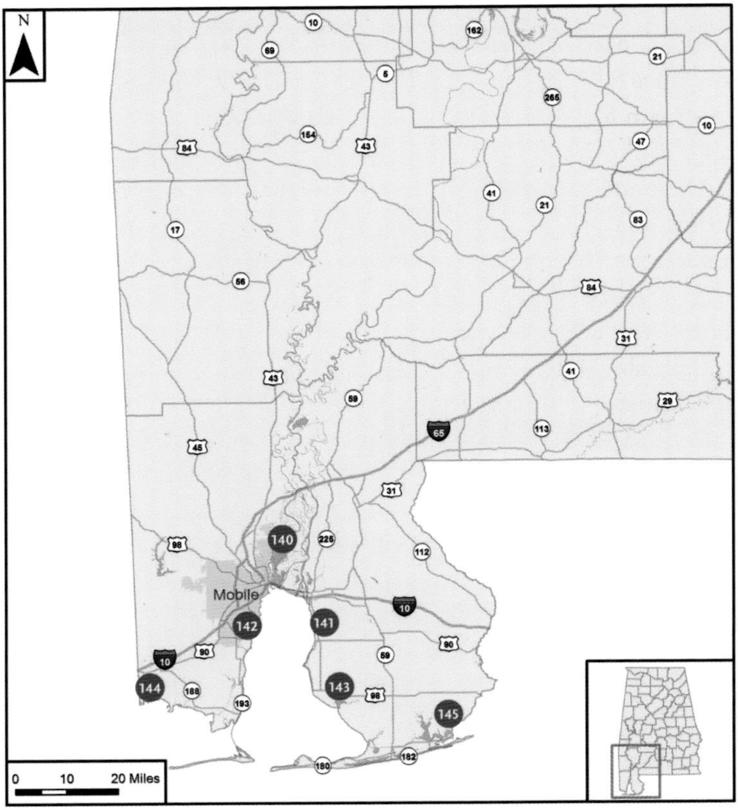

MOBILE BAY AND SOUND AREA

The natural communities of this province are best described by grouping them into the following habitat categories.

140 Mobile-Tensaw Delta

30°49'11.42"N
87°57'59.57"W

The 250,000-acre Mobile-Tensaw delta is our state's largest wetland and the nation's second-largest river delta. The delta stretches for 10 miles across the head of Mobile Bay and continues upstream for 40 miles to just beyond the junction of the Alabama and Tombigbee Rivers. It supports extensive bald cypress and bottomland hardwood forest in its northern half, shrub swamps in the quarter below that, and some of the nation's most diverse coastal marshes in its southern end. The area contains Alabama's largest alligator population and even provides habitat for black bears. The delta has more species of freshwater turtles than any comparably sized area in the world; this includes the endemic and threatened Alabama red-bellied turtle.

The delta was gradually built up as sediment from the above-mentioned rivers filled in the northern end of Mobile Bay with swampy land. At the head of the delta, near Mount Vernon, the Alabama and Tombigbee Rivers merge to form the Mobile River. This giant river soon splits into a channel to the west, which retains the Mobile River name, and a channel to the east called the Tensaw River. These two rivers split into even more channels as Mobile Bay proper is approached.

The delta drains most of the rivers in Alabama—the Coosa, Tallapoosa, Alabama, Cahaba, Black Warrior, and Tombigbee systems, collectively known as the Mobile Drainage. The massive amount of fresh water from this drainage flows through the delta and out into Mobile Bay, where it mixes with salt water to form estuaries. Such estuaries are the sea coast's most productive life zones, and most of the seafood caught on the Alabama Gulf Coast depends on the delta's marshes as a nursery. Thus, maintaining the health of these marshes is vital to maintaining the seafood catch along our coast.

Fortunately, the Nature Conservancy, Coastal Land Trust, the Corps, and the state of Alabama (including the Forever Wild program) have purchased large areas of the delta's marshes and forested wetlands for conservation and public recreation. Currently,

Above: The marshes near the Five Rivers Center mark the southern end of the Bartram Canoe Trail

Opposite: Middle reaches of the Mobile-Tensaw Delta

118,000 acres are protected, largely as part of the W. L. Holland/ Mobile-Tensaw Delta and Upper Delta WMAs. The greatest challenge to conserving the area is protecting the bluffs surrounding the delta, which serve as refuges for creatures during times of high water. These bluff lands are much more expensive to purchase than the wetlands, and they are in high demand in this rapidly developing area. Historic Blakeley State Park in Baldwin County, to be discussed later, protects a significant amount of bluff lands. Also, the recent purchase of bluff lands and swamps in the Bayou Sara–Jacinto Port area provides critical black bear habitat.

The 3,372-acre Bayou Sara–Jacinto Port area is worth additional mention because of its conservation significance and biological uniqueness. Bayou Sara flows out of the pine-covered hills of Mobile County to become one of the major waterways of the delta. The newly acquired lands include the transition zone from piney uplands to delta swamp. The uplands, which support some gopher tortoises, are being restored (through controlled burns) to fire-dependent longleaf habitat; they quickly drop down a few feet into tupelo-cypress swamp containing alligators. Combined, the uplands and swamps along Bayou Sara provide a critical corridor between the delta and one of the best remaining black bear breeding grounds, Hell Swamp. These linked, thick swamps make an ideal passageway for bears.

Most of the protected lands within the delta are included within the two previously mentioned WMAs, which stretch from the Alabama and Tombigbee Rivers south to Mobile Bay. Most of this area is accessible only by boat. There are tour boats available, including those starting from Dead Lake Marina on the west (Mobile County) side and the Five Rivers Center and Historic Blakeley State Park on the east (Baldwin County) side.

The delta is so huge that the most practical way to explore it is by personal motorboat; canoeing offers a quieter approach but with limited range. The Bartram Canoe Trail offers some great options and amenities including floating camping platforms. (The trail commemorates naturalist William Bartram's canoe trip across the Mobile-Tensaw delta around the time of the American Revolution.) One trail leads to the Bottle Creek Indian Mounds State Historic Site, nestled deep in the swamp. A waterway map and GPS unit are certainly “must haves” wherever you go in the delta, due to its many twists and turns.

Some of the most scenic spots in the upper delta (above I-65) are Mifflin Lake and the seemingly endless waterways found all along the Tensaw Lake system, which lead upstream to Stiggins Lake. The Tensaw Lake system can be accessed from private fishing camps as well as the Rice Creek Public Launch. Dead Lake Marina and public boat launch parks in Saraland and Satsuma offer scenic access points for exploring the Mobile County side of the upper and middle delta. The tide runs all the way up to Jackson, Alabama, so you may see the delta’s waters running backwards at times. This tidal influence helps keep the delta’s waterways full and accessible year-round.

The delta’s lakes are old abandoned river channels that have been turned into sloughs by tidal influence. These lakes have more bald cypress than the main river channels, including some old hollow giants left behind by past loggers. In fact, the state champion bald cypress tree grows in the delta swamps near Stockton. Bottomland oaks and other hardwoods occur on higher portions of the floodplain. In summertime, the floor of the swamp hosts beautiful spider lilies and swamp lilies, while the lakes become spadderdock lily pad marshes. Wildlife is abundant on these lakes—herons, egrets, ibises, swallow-tailed kites, and (hopefully) shy alligators. Large paddlefish ease out of the water revealing their strange paddle-like noses, which may help them sense electric currents associated with their prey. Mullets jump everywhere, even into your boat.

The middle delta (below I-65) contains lakes and basins, such as Basin Negro and Chuckfee Bay, which are surrounded by shrub swamps composed of swamp tupelo and bay trees interspersed with bald cypress. (Cypresses dominated much more of this area before the area was first logged.) Compared to the upper delta, the middle delta has more marsh plants, with pickerel weed growing along the shores of the rivers and lakes. Signs of the sea, which seem unusual this far inland, include laughing gulls, terns, and brown pelicans; crabs and barnacles embrace the tree roots. Manatees live in the middle delta as well.

The lower delta is largely composed of marshes and giant bays with some bald cypress on higher ground, where nonsalty water is always present. However, the high tidal water and salt have stunted or dwarfed many of these trees. The marshes contain tall cord grass and water lotus beds along with a great diversity of other species. Alligators are more abundant and visible here than in upriver areas. Moorhens, red-winged blackbirds, and shorebirds, such as the American avocet, feed along the edges of the bays. As late winter and early spring floods subside, salt water moves deeper into the lower delta, but the remaining fresh water floats on top of the denser, intruding salt water. Consequently, during certain times of the year, both fresh and saltwater fish can be caught in the delta's estuaries.

For those without a boat, canoe or kayak, there are several options for exploring this region. The 1,100-acre Chickasabogue Park in Mobile County offers hiking trails along uplands and wetlands of the blackwater creek that gives the park its name; the park also offers canoe rentals and shuttles upstream. Chickasaw Bogue Creek (spelled differently, for some reason) has dark, tea-colored water surrounded by white sandbars and Atlantic white cedar. It eventually flows into muddy delta waters and swamps.

The USS *Alabama* Battleship Memorial Park offers a boardwalk into the marshes at Pinto Pass near Civil War defense sites. Other more developed areas of the park reveal interesting birds like the long-billed curlew. (The bird's bill looks as long as its body, and you wonder how it manages to get around.) Besides the park's battleship, famously "saved" by a children's penny campaign, the site has a great collection of other military boats and planes.

The 1,327-acre Meaher State Park features short boardwalks

into marshes on the eastern, Baldwin County side of the delta. Moorhens, alligators, and other wildlife can be viewed up close among the marsh vegetation. The new Five Rivers Center is located across the highway from the state park, and its visitor center offers trails, a canoe/kayak launch, boat dock, boat tours, and a museum/gift shop. The museum features informative exhibits on the problems of controlling exotic popcorn trees in the delta and the area's logging history, plus mounted specimens of bears, albino deer, a giant alligator snapping turtle, and various freshwater and saltwater fishes. (The museum has live animals, too.) One really neat exhibit discusses the various paving technologies that can be employed to reduce runoff from parking lots by making them more porous. The center's parking lot was constructed using these technologies, designed to help protect natural hydrology and water quality.

The center and its trails are located on a piece of former wetland that was filled in during the construction of I-10. Behind the buildings and to the east, the trails have good views of the marshes and patches of swamp forest; as the trails turn inland upon the fill, you will pass through vegetation not normally associated with the very wet delta, such as mature pine plantations and nice young stands of live oaks.

The best land-based experience of the Mobile delta can be found at the 3,800-acre Historic Blakeley State Park, which is well worth visiting even if you have boated all over the delta. The park was established to preserve historic resources involved in the Civil War's Battle of Blakeley, which was fought as part of the Union's effort to capture the port of Mobile. (Due to the slow communications of the time, the battle was fought *after* the South had surrendered at Appomattox.) The park preserves earthworks associated with this siege type of battle. These earthworks are located among conserved open longleaf pine forest, which has suffered great decline in this area.

The park also preserves the site of the failed port of Blakeley, a town that many people thought would surpass Mobile. The site contains magnificent live oaks, which predated the town and have since survived it. (One old live oak that recently died was called the Jury Oak because court was held under its spreading branches. If the case went really badly for the defendant, that person was led to the nearby Hanging Oak, which still lives and bears rope marks on one of its *low-hung* limbs!) The beauty of the oaks is enhanced by a tropical-like collection of epiphytes. Spanish moss drapes the trees, and vines and resurrection ferns cover their branches. In addition, the limbs of many of the live oaks contain large populations of the rare green fly orchid, which blooms in mid- to late summer.

The uplands and bluffs surrounding the town site support beech-magnolia forest, including lots of live oak. The bluffs grade down into bottomland hardwood with a thick dwarf palmetto palm understory. The place where the first steamboat was built in Alabama is located on a trail that leads from the town site down the narrow bluff to a boardwalk. This boardwalk passes through bottomland hardwood, cypress swamp, and edge marsh, while providing views of the delta's large waterways and vast wetlands.

The rest of the park contains 15 miles of trails that pass Indian mounds and other interesting features; the Gatra Wehle Nature Center is open on weekends. The park also offers horseback riding, camping, cabins, and delta boat tours. Boats can be launched just upstream from the park at Cloverleaf Landing and Byrnes Lake Public Boat Launch Park. *But be careful.* The waters of the middle and lower delta are wide open and can be rough in windy weather.

DIRECTIONS: The lower delta can be accessed by water from several private boat launches on US 98 from Mobile east to Spanish Fort, as well as at Meaher State Park. The Five Rivers Center also has a canoe/kayak launch. (Meaher State Park and the Five Rivers Center lie across from one another on US 98 just west of Spanish Fort.) The USS *Alabama* is located on US 98 just east of Mobile.

Chickasabogue Park is located west of I-65 in Mobile. Take US 45 west and turn right on AL 213, then right on Culvert St., then left on Aldock Rd. to reach the park entrance.

The Mobile County side of the middle delta can be accessed by water from private fishing camps and public launches in Saraland and Satsuma, two towns located on US 43 north of Mobile.

The Mobile County side of the middle to upper delta is best accessed from county-owned Dead Lake Marina. Take I-65 exit 22 and follow the signs to the marina at the end of Dead Lake Rd. Another public boat launch is located upriver in Mount Vernon. Head north on US 43 from Mobile and then take Co. Rd. 96 east to the launch.

The Baldwin County side of the middle delta is reached by water from private fishing camps (like Cloverleaf Landing) and public boat launch parks (like Byrnes Lake), which lie along AL 225 between Spanish Fort and I-65. The two launches mentioned above lie north of Historic Blakeley State Park, located a few miles north of Spanish Fort on the west side of AL 225.

The Baldwin County side of the upper delta can be accessed from private boat and fishing camps; public boat launches are at Rice Creek and Live Oak Landing. Almost all of these launches serve as entry points to the Bartram Canoe Trail system. (Maps and information on this canoe trail, which includes camping platforms, can be obtained by visiting the Department of Conservation website.) To reach them, take I-65 exit 31 and go north on AL 225 to the Stockton area, then continue north to the town of Tensaw. Turnoffs (to the left) are marked by signs.

The Upper Delta WMA is accessed via roads that can be driven in hunting season and walked at other times. Consult WMA maps and schedules to determine where and when the roads will be open.

141 Eastern Mobile Bay

30°35'44.51"N
87°59'15.84"W

The giant Mobile Bay can be easily observed from parks on its eastern, Baldwin County side. One of these is the 54-acre Village Point Park Preserve owned by the city of Daphne. Village Point contains a variety of habitats and includes the Jackson Oak and other old-growth and champion-sized trees. The preserve's trails feature a bluff looking down upon the bay; in fact, this general area has the highest land along the sea coast between New England and Mexico. The high and dry land, combined with constant breezes from the west, made it an ideal summer retreat for European colonists trying to escape the hot, swampy, malarial environment of Mobile.

Near the beginning of Village Point's trail system resides the mighty Jackson Live Oak. This tree was even noted as being unusually large when Spanish land grants were surveyed here in the late 1700s. The story goes that Andrew Jackson climbed up in this oak during the War of 1812 to speak to his troops and keep them from deserting the American fight against the British. A boardwalk allows close inspection of the tree without damaging it. Visual and audio interpretation signs and boxes here and elsewhere in the park tell many such stories. Village Point was part of a colonial plantation from the period when Spain controlled the area, and an old family cemetery is located on the property. The state champion bluff oak and an ancient Indian mound reside near the cemetery as well.

The trails continue down the bluff and into a forested wetland containing bottomland hardwoods, slash pine, and bald cypress. A boardwalk leads out through marshy habitats to a sandbar in

A boardwalk traverses the swamps of Village Point Park Preserve

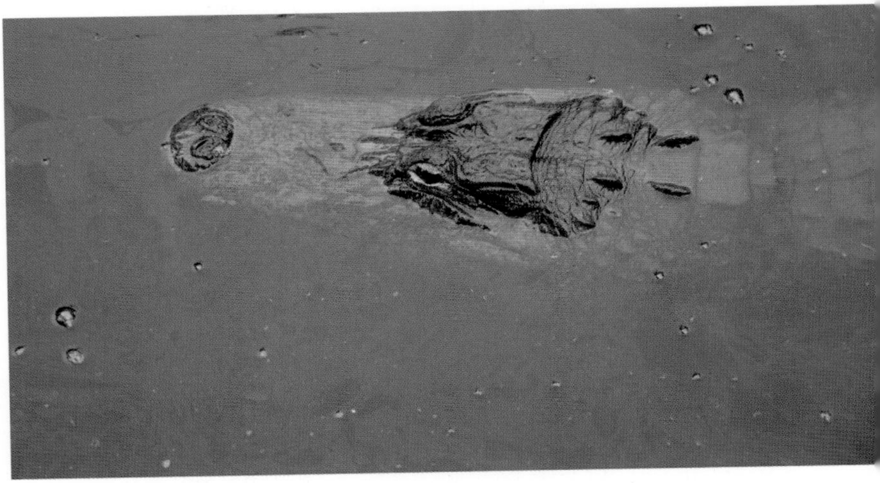

An alligator patiently awaits its next meal, Village Point Park Preserve

A wood duck house at the swamp margin, Village Point Park Preserve

Two lovers enjoy the sunset at Daphne Bayfront Park

the bay. Visitors here will see turtles, herons, waterfowl, and even alligators. This brackish water habitat forms a transition zone from the largely freshwater zones of the Mobile delta to the more saline ones of the bay.

The boardwalk continues to the north through the swamp to Daphne Bayfront Park, and the contrast between the developed park and the undeveloped preserve is quite striking. Village Point Nature Preserve thus gives us a glimpse of what the lands around Mobile Bay looked like before they were "civilized."

The city of Fairhope offers large areas of developed parkland along the bay, including portions of the walking paths that make up the Eastern Shore Trail. The trail leads down to Point Clear and the beautiful ornamental plantings, live oaks, and other native vegetation of the Grand Hotel Resort.

DIRECTIONS: Village Point Park Preserve and Daphne Bayfront Park are reached by taking I-10 exit 35. Follow US 98 south into Daphne; turn right onto Main St., which shortly passes the entrances of Bay Front Park and Village Point Park Preserve on the right.

The Eastern Shore Trail can be accessed in Fairhope by following Alt US 98 past the city's bayfront parklands.

142 Western Mobile Bay

30°42'00.13"N
88°09'15.42.81"W

Across the bay on the western shore is a great bird watching spot, Mobile County's Bay Front Park. The park features places to picnic, windsurf, and bird watch, plus access into a wetland habitat. Also, the 100-acre Mobile Botanical Garden offers green space near the bay, including a longleaf pine forest maintained by undercutting and burning. As its name implies, the 500-acre

Mobile County Environmental Studies Center has numerous environmental education facilities, including a planetarium. Natural habitats here are pine forests, pitcher plant bogs, and bay forests; the area may still provide habitat for the threatened black pine snake, which is declining due to habitat loss and fragmentation. Since this is a school-run facility, you should contact the center before visiting.

Mobile Bay has several islands that are important to wildlife. Gaillard Island is a man-made area built by deposition of dredge spoil from the Mobile Ship Channel. This unimpressive island, like other (increasingly rare) isolated places, provides sea birds with critical, undisturbed nesting grounds. Conservationists monitor and manage the bird populations on this island to help ensure successful nestings (and nestlings). One sign of success is that we now have more brown pelicans on the Alabama Gulf Coast than we have had in 50 years. Banning DDT and offering the birds protection has brought about this wonderful recovery. Gaillard Island and its birds should be observed only from a distance and only by boat, unless you are working on an authorized bird survey.

A unique phenomenon occurs in Mobile Bay and only a few other places in the world—the much anticipated Jubilee. During the summer months, there are periods when low oxygen water from the bottom of the bay is pushed upward by wind and water currents. Many creatures, including crabs, are forced toward the shore to escape this oxygen-poor water. During these times, local people (and wildlife) happily gather the abundant seafood. Some people say that an early sign of a Jubilee is the appearance of large numbers of hunting dolphins along the shore. Jubilee or not, such pods of dolphins are one of the most impressive sights on Mobile Bay.

Directions: Mobile County Bay Front Park is located in Alabama Port about one mile north of the Dauphin Island Bridge on AL 193.

The Mobile Botanical Garden can be reached by taking I-65 exit 5A west on Springhill Ave. Turn left on Pfc John New Dr., which dead-ends into Museum Dr. Turn right and look for the garden entrance on the left.

The Mobile County Environmental Studies Center is located at 6101 Girby Rd. in south Mobile.

143 Weeks Bay National Estuarine Research Reserve

30°25'09.89"N
87°49'51.65"W

Weeks Bay National Estuarine Research Reserve was established to protect and study a small, relatively pristine subsection of the Mobile Bay Estuary. The reserve covers 6,016 acres—1,600 acres of land and the rest water. The reserve is located in the northern half of Weeks Bay where the Fish River spills into it. It includes a nature center and boardwalks out into cypress-tupelo swamps and marshes; it also provides one of the best opportunities *anywhere* to observe a pitcher plant bog.

The pitcher plant bog has a boardwalk that allows visitors to see the bog without impacting it or getting their feet wet. The bog contains white-topped, yellow, and frog britches pitcher plants, various sundews, and other wildflowers like white-topped sedges. The bog—previously choked with thick brush—is being restored to its original condition through controlled burns. The bog's boardwalk continues out through shrub swamps to the Fish River, which is bordered by bald cypress and edge marsh.

DIRECTIONS: To reach the Weeks Bay area, take US 98 west from Foley. Shortly after passing through the town of Magnolia Springs, turn right onto Co. Rd. 17; you will soon reach the Weeks Bay

A grass-pink orchid adorns the bog at Weeks Bay Reserve

Reserve pitcher plant bog (on the right side of the road) and boardwalk (on the left). To reach the reserve's visitor center, continue west on US 98 to the bridge over the Fish River and the upper end of Weeks Bay. The visitor center is located on the left.

144 Grand Bay Savanna and Mississippi Sound

30°25'17.35"N
88°23'13.25"W

Grand Bay Savanna lies on the mainland of Mississippi Sound at the southern end of Mobile County and the adjacent area of Mississippi. The Grand Bay area contains the largest relatively undisturbed coastal pine savanna in the world. Such savannas are composed of low-lying pitcher plant bogs with a scattering of longleaf pine and pond cypress. These savannas contain an extremely diverse herbaceous layer as well as a great concentration of carnivorous plants.

The Nature Conservancy, which recognizes Grand Bay Savanna as one of our nation's Last Great Places, is working with the USFWS, Alabama's Forever Wild program, and private landowners to protect this area. These conservation efforts are partially directed toward providing additional habitat for the endangered Mississippi sandhill crane. This crane subspecies is currently restricted to an area around its namesake refuge in Mississippi, but hopefully the endangered bird can become established in Grand Bay as well.

The 14,000-acre Grand Bay NWR straddles the Alabama and Mississippi line, with its bulk lying in Mississippi. While the majority of the refuge is not very accessible from Alabama, Forever Wild's 3,500-acre Grand Bay Savanna Preserve is much more so. Marine Laboratory Rd., out of the quaint shrimp fleet town of Bayou LaBatre, leads west to the pitcher plant bog–pine savanna habitats of this preserve. In addition, Henderson Camp Rd., coming south from the town of Grand Bay, heads toward the waterways of the area's salt marshes and offers good canoeing opportunities. From Henderson Rd., visitors can access an old road/trail

Pine stand at Grand Bay Savanna

going east along the north boundary of the Forever Wild preserve, which passes through pond cypress swamp, patches of longleaf and wire grass habitat, and more pitcher plant bogs.

In addition, Bellingrath Gardens offers boat tours along the Fowl River and Mon Louis Island through the area's salt marshes. The state owns marshy Isle aux Herbes (Coffee Island) in nearby Mississippi Sound thanks to a gift from the Nature Conservancy. Islands like this and nearby Cat Island provide critical, undisturbed nesting habitat for water birds like the rare reddish egret.

Directions: Currently, access to the Grand Bay NWR is not easy from its Alabama side. Forever Wild's Grand Bay tract can be accessed by taking University Rd. west from Bayou LaBatre. Pitcher plant savannas lie to the north of this road after you are well into the tract. To view the marshes and narrow waterways of this area, take Henderson Camp Rd. south from the city of Grand Bay. If you park

Flower of white-topped pitcher plant, Grand Bay Savanna

at the tract's boundary and follow the road along the property line to the east, you will pass through shrub swamps, pond cypress stands, pine forest with wire grass, and large pitcher plant bogs.

Bellingrath Gardens is located on Co. Rd. 59 south of Theodore. Since Theodore lies southwest of Mobile, you can make a loop through the whole Grand Bay country by continuing south from Bellingrath Gardens to AL 188, then west to Bayou LaBatre and Grand Bay.

145 Perdido / Wolf Bay System

30°20'39.74"N
87°31'23.93"W

The Perdido River and its bay form the border between Baldwin County, Alabama, and Florida. The Perdido River is a blackwater system that is influenced by coastal tides. The upper river has tea-colored water and white sandy banks covered in pine, Atlantic white cedar, and pond cypress. Due to tidally influenced higher water levels, the lower river shows tidal sloughs rather than exposed sand bars.

Both the Styx River and Blackwater River join the lower Perdido River from the west. The Styx's tidal portions are becoming heavily developed with waterfront homes. However, as the Perdido flows south past the Blackwater toward Perdido Bay, it is surrounded by an increasing amount of pristine wetlands.

Lillian Swamp, located along Perdido Bay north of the town of Lillian, is one of the largest wetlands in the Alabama portion of the Perdido River drainage. While the bay is edged by salt marsh in places, much of the swamp is made up of a wet pine savanna complete with pitcher plants and other carnivores. Land purchases by ALDOT's wetland mitigation program and Forever Wild, plus conservation management of preexisting state school lands, have combined to conserve this area.

The Forever Wild lands are the most publicly accessible portions, and a visit to these properties will highlight the land trust's restoration efforts. A thick understory is being burned out of the slash and longleaf pine stands to restore the open bog habitats favored by sundews and other carnivorous plants.

After the Perdido River empties into its namesake bay, the bay continues to increase in size, and the Alabama side includes a subsection (Wolf Bay) that has significant wetlands. Perdido Bay then breaks up into smaller bays, known as bayous, which are separated by peninsulas and bay islands like Ono Island. Ono Island is highly developed, but the Nature Conservancy owns nearby Rabbit Island. Rabbit Island contains a small area of pine trees and salt marsh that is home to the declining marsh rabbit, and it supports good examples of marine grass beds, which are now uncommon. Due to the sensitive nature of the island's nesting birds (and rabbits), you must make prior arrangements to visit the island.

The Wolf Bay branch of the Perdido Bay system can be accessed from a series of canoe launches located on various side streets on the north side of AL 180 in Orange Beach. Observe the wind conditions before making a canoe trip; the bay can become quite rough in a strong wind.

The area around Orange Beach on the south side of the bay is largely developed, but the north side retains much natural habitat. The city of Foley is currently establishing the 400-acre Graham Creek Nature Preserve, which includes lands adjoining the Wolf Bay system. These lands support pitcher plant bogs with purple pitcher plants, the rare Barbara's buttons, and white spoonflowers. Trails and a canoe launch already exist, and the preserve will soon have an interpretive center.

Directions: The Perdido and Styx Rivers area can be accessed from a fishing camp on the Florida side of the US 90 bridge at the border of Baldwin County and Florida.

The Lillian Swamp area is best accessed by taking US 98 east from Foley to Lillian. Just before crossing Perdido Bay, take a left and follow Boykin Blvd. to near its terminus. Azalea Rd. (to your left) will lead you into the Forever Wild tract.

The Graham Creek Nature Preserve is on Stan Mahoney Ln. running off Wolf Bay Dr., which intersects with Co. Rd. 12 east of the Foley Beach Express.

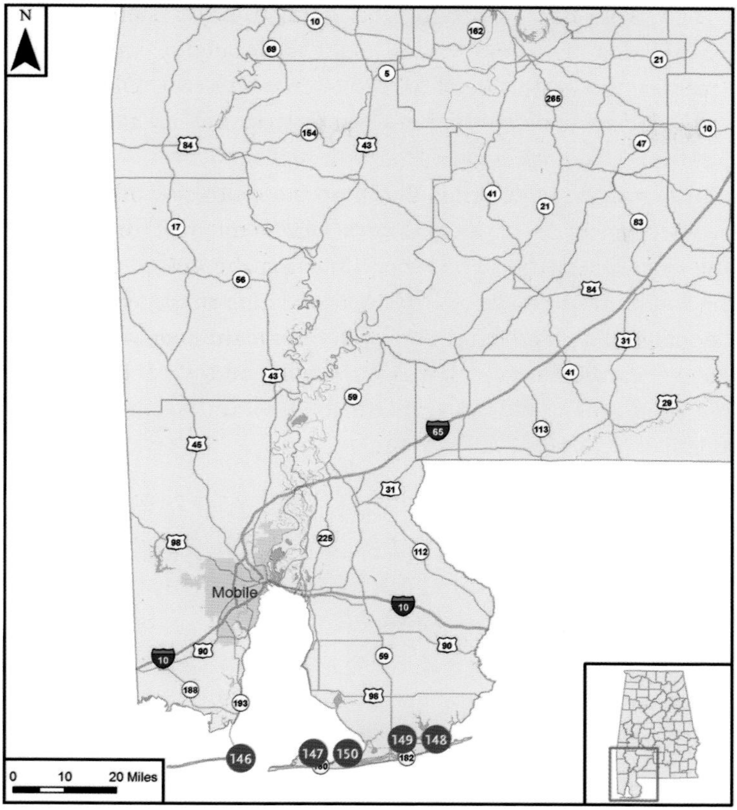

BEACH AND BARRIER ISLAND AREA

The lands along the Gulf of Mexico face the full fury of the ocean's waves and winds, and these forces have greatly shaped them. The gulf constantly pounds the shore with waves, which will either erode or build up beaches, depending on their force and sand load.

The Gulf Coast from Baldwin County, Alabama, to Apalachicola, Florida, is famous for its sugar-white sands. Composed of quartzite that was eroded from distant Appalachian Mountains and upland provinces, the sand particles wash down rivers to the ocean and later are redeposited as beach sand. Sand then blows around the beach until it is stabilized just above the surf zone by vegetation, such as sea oats. Depressions or swales between dunes are sometimes wet and filled with moisture-loving plants, including salt marsh vegetation. These ocean front dunes provide a critical, hurricane-absorbing barrier for more inland areas. When these front dunes are destroyed by human activities, the storms' effects on inland areas are greatly magnified. In this section we will refer to this vital narrow strip as the Coastal Barrier Zone.

Sea levels have risen and fallen over time, and they are currently rising unnaturally fast. As local sea levels fell in the past, they left dune systems inland of the active beach. These dunes and swales have gone through various stages of vegetational succession as their soils developed and their locations became more "inland" in character. While dunes and swales closest to the coast are covered in sea oats and marsh vegetation, those a little farther inland support oak and sand pine scrub. Saltwater, brackish, or freshwater lakes with edge marshes fill many of the dune swales. Even further inland, old flattened dune swales support wet slash pine forests, marshes, pond cypress swamps, and pitcher plant bogs. The oldest, flattest, and most inland dunes—especially those that have avoided frequent fires—are now maritime forests of live oak, southern magnolia, and other evergreen hardwoods.

While the Coastal Barrier Zone contains some of our state's greatest diversities of habitats, its special natural areas are among the most threatened by development. Heavy development in this zone led to the endangerment of several species, including sea turtles, the Alabama beach mouse, and the Perdido Key beach mouse. We are very fortunate that some critical lands on our coastal barriers have been protected. These areas are described below.

146 Dauphin Island

30°15'21.35"N
88°06'35.58"W

IMPORTANT BIRD AREA

Dauphin Island forms the western side of a pass where the estuarine waters of Mobile Bay meet the salty Gulf of Mexico. Dauphin Island is part of a series of protective barrier islands reaching west along the Mississippi Gulf Coast to Louisiana. While the Mississippi islands have been largely protected as part of the Gulf Islands National Seashore, Dauphin Island—located close to the city of Mobile and the mainland shore—was slated for development. A bridge and causeway were built, destroyed by Hurricane Frederick, and rebuilt at great taxpayer expense. Even so, Dauphin Island's developers did set aside some significant amounts of land for parks. There is a public beach beside the restored Civil War–era Fort Gaines on the east end of the island, and another, larger public beach in the center of the island.

View of the causeway from the north side of Dauphin Island

Left: White beach spider, Dauphin Island

Below: Sandwich tern, Dauphin Island

Local Audubon Society members worked with the island's parks board to establish the 155-acre Dauphin Island Audubon Sanctuary, which contains stands of live oak and magnolia, slash pine forests, a fresh-water pond, freshwater swamp forest, and some undeveloped gulf beaches. The sanctuary and nearby Shell Mounds Park are two of the most critical migratory songbird habitats in the nation. Songbirds, such as warblers and tanagers,

Spadefoot toad, Dauphin Island

spend their winters in Mexico and other countries of Latin America; they use these preserves as a rest area before making the unbelievable flight south over the Gulf of Mexico in the fall. But these preserves are even more critical in the spring, when returning birds—exhausted from their ocean crossing—are in desperate need of a safe place to land. In years when the returning birds have faced a strong head wind, the trees of the Dauphin Island preserves look like Christmas decorations, full of red-colored tanagers and yellow-colored warblers too worn-out to move. Needless to say, these preserves offer great birding opportunities.

The Dauphin Island Sea Lab's Estuarium is located near the Audubon Sanctuary, and its salt marsh, aquaria, and other exhibits offer opportunities to learn about the ecology of Alabama's coast and the importance of its estuaries.

The 11-acre Shell Mounds Park is on the grounds of the Alabama Department of Conservation Marine Resources Office.

Inner dune vegetation, Dauphin Island

Ospreys on their stick nest, Dauphin Island

Sea oats hold the dunes in place, Dauphin Island

These shell mounds were formed, long ago, while serving as a garbage dump for Native Americans, who discarded the shells of harvested oysters there; the site took on a regional ceremonial significance for following generations. The Shell Mounds are now covered with large live oaks, including trees that may be 800 years old. The mounds offer some of the best birding in Alabama, especially during times of migration—when the woods are crawling with birds and bird watchers. Bird watchers put out food for the painted buntings, orioles, and other colorful migrants, while a water feature offers tired migrants a drink. The park is great for finding birds accidently out of their normal ranges, like the black-whiskered vireo.

The grounds of the Marine Resources facilities next to the park contain additional shell mounds and offer an excellent view of the nearby sparse pine woods and marshes of Little Dauphin Island, which is a bay island protected as part of the Bon Secour NWR.

Dauphin Island's airport was built in a salt marsh before the value of wetlands was fully recognized. However, significant marsh habitat still surrounds the airport and provides good opportunities to see clapper rails and other marsh birds.

A local land trust bought up undeveloped island lots to protect them for migrating birds and people's enjoyment. One such tract, the Goat Tree, features a magnificent old live oak with low-hanging limbs festooned with Spanish moss. It's a great place to search for tiny golden prothonotary warblers.

The seven miles that form the extreme western end of Dauphin Island are currently undeveloped due to the federal government's decision not to subsidize insurance for private development in this very storm-prone area. Hurricane Katrina sliced off most of the west end of the main island, creating a separate island—at least for the time being. The island's government has recently established the West End Public Beach Park, which includes the two sides of the separation zone. A rock berm connects the two, giving visitors access to a beach area that had been closed for years. The tidal pools on the west island's bay side offer an excellent opportunity to see many species of shorebirds, such as piping plovers, marbled godwits, and short-billed dowitchers.

Hopefully, one day the entire west end of Dauphin Island will be protected and opened to the public, perhaps as the first Alabama section of the Gulf Islands National Seashore. Established in the early 1970s to conserve the barrier islands of the central Gulf Coast, the group has important natural and historic holdings in Florida and Mississippi but none yet in Alabama.

Currently, the greatest problem on Dauphin Island is high levels of erosion. Beaches naturally erode, and this causes most barrier islands on the Gulf Coast to look like a chicken's drumstick, with the broad east end tapering down to a narrow spit at the western end. This directional shape is due to the east-to-west longshore current that flows along the coast. Sand is eroded from beaches on the east end of the islands and redeposited by the current and waves on beaches further west. Barrier islands are dynamic places, migrating over time and brutalized by storms.

DIRECTIONS: Dauphin Island is reached by taking AL 193 south from Mobile; a bridge and causeway lead to the island center. Turn left to reach the Shell Mounds, Goat Tree, Audubon Sanctuary, Sea Lab, Estuarium, and Fort Gaines. Turn right to reach the airport marsh and public beaches at the middle and west end of the island.

147 Fort Morgan State Historic Site

30°13'42.07"N
88°01'18.84"W

Fort Morgan State Historic Site includes the Civil War–era fort, later Spanish–American war concrete fortifications, and various natural habitats. This site guards the pass into Mobile Bay, and it was originally the location of the wood and earth Fort Boyer. Later, brick-covered Fort Morgan was built, along with Fort Gaines on Dauphin Island, to better guard the bay. The two forts were taken over by the Confederacy at the start of the Civil War and became the sites of fierce fighting during the Battle of Mobile Bay, as the Union sought to close the last Gulf Coast port available to Confederate blockade runners. Fort Morgan continued to serve the reunited nation's coastal defense, with improvements made from the time of the Spanish–American war all the way to World War II. The Alabama Historical Commission subsequently acquired the site and developed it as a historic park.

Atlantic bottlenose dolphin, bay side of Fort Morgan

While touring Fort Morgan, visitors should climb up on its walls to take in a view of the coastline. From there you will see Fort Gaines on Dauphin Island three miles across the bay pass, and you will also likely see ocean-going ships sailing to or from Mobile. The remains of the original Sand Island lie out in the gulf in front of Fort Morgan; the island has largely washed away, but it still serves as an unstable base for Alabama's only lighthouse. (The rest of Sand Island has drifted along the gulf side

Brown pelican, bay side of Fort Morgan

of Dauphin Island.) The island provides an important feeding and resting area for shorebirds, which have lost much of their on-shore habitat.

The Fort Morgan site has both undeveloped gulf and bay beaches that can be explored. Many bird species, including the multicolored painted bunting, can be found in the park's scrub forest. During the autumn, visitors will see hundreds of sharp-shinned and Cooper's hawks, as well as other birds of prey, migrating along the coast down toward Latin America. Also, during the fall, monarch butterflies bunch up on this coast in preparation for flying to their winter home in the Mexican mountains. Large numbers of monarchs hang from any available tree, shrub, or tall herb.

Directions: From the Gulf Shores area, take AL 180 west to its terminus at the fort.

148 Gulf State Park

30°16'45.49"N
87°36'07.78"W

The 6,150-acre Gulf State Park is Alabama's oldest coastal conservation area. The park offers a few miles of undeveloped gulf front beach, plus three large natural freshwater lakes within sight of the gulf, which is very unusual. Scrub and slash pine habitats are also abundant in the park, and there is an extensive trail system that encourages exploration of the park's interior.

The eastern end of the park contains a large block of largely untouched land that can be explored from an old road that leads out of the campground. The road passes by one of the park's lakes that most visitors do not see.

The city of Orange Beach worked with the state park and other landowners to develop a great trail behind its sports complex. The

Above: Close-up of Spanish moss in bloom along an Orange Beach trail

Opposite: Spanish moss abounds along an Orange Beach trail

Clockwise from upper left:
Rose-mallow grows abundantly in Gulf State Park; buttonbush, Gulf State Park; and fragrant water lily at Cotton Bayou

trail passes through maritime live oak forest, rare sand pine forest, and low wet pine savannas.

Between the city of Gulf Shores and the state park is the Wade Ward Nature Park. Owned and operated by the city of Gulf Shores, the park has boardwalks going through coastal salt marshes that provide habitat for bitterns and rails.

Directions: As you enter Gulf Shores heading south on AL 59, you will soon see the Wade Ward Nature Park on your left. To reach Gulf State Park from the city of Gulf Shores, go east on AL 182. This road passes through the main unit of the park, and its side roads lead to the various facilities. Continue east on AL 182 to reach the very small park units that serve as public beach access points around Orange Beach.

The trail behind the Orange Beach sports complex can be accessed by visiting the Sportsplex, which is located on William Silvers Parkway, just off AL 180 (Canal Rd.) in Orange Beach, about one mile from the Foley Beach Express exit on Canal Rd.

149 Florida Point

30°16'31.36"N
87°33'01.84"W

The small Florida Point tract is a unit of Gulf State Park on the western end of Perdido Key, which straddles the Alabama-Florida state line. As Perdido Key was developed, the Perdido Key beach mouse, which is found only on that island, became restricted to the few undeveloped lands around Florida Point. Efforts to "save" these lands were largely unsuccessful, and continued development further limited the habitat of the endangered mouse.

Today, visitors to Florida Point can enjoy natural beaches, dunes and sea oats as well as views of the pass from the Perdido Bay system to the gulf. However, this small site is now totally surrounded by development, serving as a prime example of habitat fragmentation leading to the endangerment of a species.

Directions: From the city of Gulf Shores, go east on AL 182 and cross the bridge over the mouth of Perdido Bay. The access road to Florida Point lies immediately to your right.

150 Bon Secour NWR

30°14'27.91"N
87°49'28.05"W

The 7,000-acre Bon Secour refuge is located in four units along the Fort Morgan Peninsula as well as on Little Dauphin Island in Mobile Bay. The peninsular units include natural gulf beaches, scrub forest, lakes, maritime hardwood forests, longleaf and slash pine forests, pitcher plant bogs, and bayside salt marshes. The refuge provides important habitat for gopher tortoises, migratory songbirds, and waterfowl. The threatened loggerhead sea turtle uses the refuge's beaches for nesting. Most notably, the refuge protects most of the remaining habitat of the threatened Alabama beach mouse, which has been driven toward extinction by development.

The refuge has two trails, including the Friend Trail that loops around Little Lagoon. However, the best way to see the area's diversity is by hiking the two-mile (one way) Pine Beach Trail, for which an interpretive guide brochure is available. In addition to things pointed out in the guide, visitors will see the full succession of coastal dune habitats from bare beach to maritime hardwood forest.

The parking lot for the Pine Beach Trail is located under some large live oaks that are growing on the peninsula's most inland and sheltered lands. These oaks are rooted on old and worn, flat dune-swale systems, which have escaped frequent fire. The oaks are also part of the maritime forest that includes other broadleaf evergreen trees, such as southern magnolia. These forests have a tropical feel, with the epiphytic Spanish moss, hanging vines, and a ground layer made up of saw palmetto palm. In addition, there are flowers blooming 365 days a year in Bon Secour Refuge.

The Pine Beach Trail continues toward the ocean past slightly less-worn dunes and swales with slash pine forests on higher

Dunes and sea oats, Bon Secour National Wildlife Refuge

ground; marshes containing sawgrass occupy lower areas. Turpentine was harvested from these pine forests during the past century, and some of the sapping cuts ("cat faces") can still be seen on tree trunks. The trail then reaches the edge of Little Lagoon, a brackish water habitat between the older land of the peninsula and the younger, higher dune systems closer to the gulf. Visitors can see fossil shells left over from a time when the area was an oyster bed, and you might be lucky enough to see an alligator lying in the brackish water. Across a narrow spit of land

False rosemary at Bon Secour National Wildlife Refuge

from Little Lagoon lies the freshwater Gator Lake. This lake has a tall marsh around it, and there is a flat-bottomed boat available for poling around in this body of water.

The trail continues into easily recognizable higher dunes and swales covered in oak and sand pine scrub. (Natural sand pine is rare in Alabama, because its home range is largely central Florida.) The sand pine is mixed with dwarf live oak, prickly pear cactus, saw palmetto, and various herbs. These open sandy areas provide good habitat for gopher tortoises. The trail then progresses to the youngest dunes and swale systems, which are being colonized by sea oats and weedy vegetation such as morning glories. Finally, after a two-mile walk, the beach along the Gulf of Mexico is reached, one of the largest remaining wild beaches in Alabama. Visitors here will see typical seashore life in a natural setting, including ghost crabs, gulls, terns, pelicans, and sandpipers.

Directions: From the Gulf Shores area, take AL 180 west. After several miles you will reach the western end of Little Lagoon; the refuge headquarters is on the right. The Friend Trail is on the left, and a little farther west on AL 180 is the Pine Beach Trail (again, on your left). Just after that is the access road to the beach.

REFERENCES AND WEBSITES

Alabama Birding Trails. www.alabamabirdingtrails.com. (Currently, eight trails have been designated, each with 20–50 sites.)

Alabama Plant Atlas. www.floraofalabama.org. (The best source for updated information on the plants of Alabama.)

Alabama State Parks. www.alapark.com.

Bartram, William. *Travels through North & South Carolina, Georgia, East & West Florida, the Cherokee Country, the Extensive Territories of the Muscogulges, or Creek Confederacy, and the Country of the Chactaws.* Philadelphia: James & Johnson, 1791. (Many reprints are available; Francis Harper's 1958 Naturalist's Edition is highly recommended.)

Best, Troy L., and Julian L. Dusi. *Mammals of Alabama.* Tuscaloosa: University of Alabama Press, 2014.

Boschung, Herbert T., Jr., and Richard L. Mayden. *Fishes of Alabama.* Washington, DC: Smithsonian Books, 2004.

Bright, Sara, and Paulette H. Ogard. *Butterflies of Alabama: Glimpses into Their Lives.* Tuscaloosa: University of Alabama Press, 2010.

Dean, Blanche E., Amy Mason, and Joab L. Thomas. *Wildflowers of Alabama and Adjoining States.* Tuscaloosa: University of Alabama Press, 1973.

Duncan, R. Scot. *Southern Wonder: Alabama's Surprising Biodiversity.* Tuscaloosa: University of Alabama Press, 2013.

Exploring Wild Alabama. www.exploringwildalabama.info.

Forever Wild Acquisitions. www.outdooralabama.com.

Foscue, Virginia O. *Place Names in Alabama.* Tuscaloosa: University of Alabama Press, 1989.

Foshee, John H. *Alabama Canoe Rides and Float Trips.* Tuscaloosa: University of Alabama Press, 1975.

Gibbons, Whit, Robert R. Haynes, and Joab L. Thomas. *Poisonous Plants and Venomous Animals of Alabama and Adjoining States*. Tuscaloosa: University of Alabama Press, 1990.

Guyer, Craig, Mark A. Bailey, and Robert H. Mount. *Turtles of Alabama*. Tuscaloosa: University of Alabama Press, 2015.

Helms, Russell. *60 Hikes within 60 Miles; Birmingham*, 2nd ed. Birmingham: Menasha Ridge Press, 2008.

Howell, W. Mike, and Vitaly Charny. *Butterflies of Alabama*. Boston: Pearson Learning Solutions, 2010.

Imhof, Thomas A. *Alabama Birds*, 2nd ed. Tuscaloosa: University of Alabama Press, 1976.

Jackson, Harvey H., III. *Rivers of History: Life on the Coosa, Tallapoosa, Cahaba, and Alabama*. Tuscaloosa: University of Alabama Press, 1995.

Kral, Robert, Alvin R. Diamond Jr., Steven L. Ginzbarg, Curtis J. Hansen, Robert R. Haynes, Brian R. Keener, Michel G. Lelong, Daniel D. Spaulding, and Michael Woods. *Annotated Checklist of the Vascular Plants of Alabama*. Fort Worth: Botanical Research Institute of Texas Press, 2011.

Lacefield, Jim. *Lost Worlds in Alabama Rocks: A Guide to the State's Ancient Life and Landscapes*, 2nd ed. Tuscaloosa: Alabama Museum of Natural History, 2013.

Mettee, Maurice F., Patrick E. O'Neil, and J. Malcolm Pierson. *Fishes of Alabama and the Mobile Basin*. Birmingham: Oxmoor House, 1996.

Mirarchi, Ralph E., ed. *Alabama Wildlife Vol. 1, A Checklist of Vertebrates and Selected Invertebrates; Aquatic Mollusks, Fishes, Amphibians, Reptiles, Birds, and Mammals*. Tuscaloosa: University of Alabama Press, 2004.

Mirarchi, Ralph E., Mark A. Bailey, Jeffrey T. Garner, Thomas M. Haggerty, Troy L. Best, Maurice F. Mettee, and Patrick E. O'Neil, eds. *Alabama Wildlife Vol. 4, Conservation and Management Recommendations for Imperiled Wildlife*. Tuscaloosa: University of Alabama Press, 2004.

Mirarchi, Ralph E., Mark A. Bailey, Thomas M. Haggerty, and Troy L. Best, eds. *Alabama Wildlife Vol. 3, Imperiled Amphibians, Reptiles, Birds, and Mammals*. Tuscaloosa: University of Alabama Press, 2004.

Mirarchi, Ralph E., Jeffrey T. Garner, Maurice F. Mettee, and Patrick E. O'Neil, eds. *Alabama Wildlife Vol. 2, Imperiled Aquatic Mollusks and Fishes*. Tuscaloosa: University of Alabama Press, 2004.

Mount, Robert H. *The Reptiles and Amphibians of Alabama*. Tuscaloosa: University of Alabama Press, 1975.

The Nature Conservancy of Alabama. www.nature.org.

Porter, John F., Jr., ed. *A Birder's Guide to Alabama*. Tuscaloosa: University of Alabama Press, 2001.

Randolph, John N. *The Battle for Alabama's Wilderness: Saving the Great Gymnasiums of Nature*. Tuscaloosa: University of Alabama Press, 2005.

Sharpe, Patricia S. *Alabama Trails*. Tuscaloosa: University of Alabama Press, 1993.

Short, John W., and Daniel D. Spaulding. *Ferns of Alabama*. Tuscaloosa: University of Alabama Press, 2012.

Southeastern Cave Conservancy. www.scci.org.

Spencer, Thomas. *Five Star Trails, Birmingham: Your Guide to the Area's Most Beautiful Hikes*. Birmingham: Menasha Ridge Press, 2014.

Spornick, Charles D., Alan R. Cattier, and Robert J. Greene. *An Outdoor Guide to Bartram's Travels*. Athens: University of Georgia Press, 2003.

State Lands Division (Alabama). www.outdooralabama.com.

Thurmond, John T., and Douglas E. Jones. *Fossil Vertebrates of Alabama*. Tuscaloosa: University of Alabama Press, 1981.

Wildlife Management Areas. www.outdooralabama.com.

Williams, James D., Arthur E. Bogan, and Jeffrey T. Garner. *Freshwater Mussels of Alabama and the Mobile Basin in Georgia, Mississippi and Tennessee*. Tuscaloosa: University of Alabama Press, 2008.

Young, Beth M., and John C. Hall. *Headwaters: A Journey on Alabama Rivers*. Tuscaloosa: University of Alabama Press, 2009.

ILLUSTRATION CREDITS

Mark A. Bailey: 3

Vitaly Charny: 209

Alan Cressler: 19, 20, 21, 23, 24, 34, 48, 51(2), 52, 54, 57, 70, 86, 114, 151, 152(2), 153, 155(3), 164, 165, 166, 354

Larry Davenport: 11, 12, 13, 14, 15, 26, 27, 39, 40, 49, 80, 81, 82, 83(2), 85, 87, 88(top), 89, 92, 106, 107, 131, 132, 133, 143, 192, 193, 196, 202, 213, 214, 215, 227, 228, 236, 274, 275, 276, 300, 307, 325(2), 326, 327, 339, 342(top)

David Frings: 37(2), 42(2), 139, 140, 142(2), 144, 342(bottom)

Mike Howell: 65, 123, 128, 138(3), 211, 283, 297(3), 331, 334, 340(2), 341, 346, 347, 348, 349, 350(3)

Ken Wills: 88(bottom), 134, 135, 170, 176, 182, 185(2), 221, 243, 246, 251, 263, 264, 292, 296, 311, 316, 317, 333, 343, 353

INDEX